北京大学"翻译实务与语言服务"系列丛书
王继辉　主编

译本比较与正误

Version Comparison & Error Detection in Translation

陈小全　编著

北京大学出版社
PEKING UNIVERSITY PRESS

图书在版编目（CIP）数据

译本比较与正误/陈小全编著. —北京：北京大学出版社，2011.3
（北京大学"翻译实务与语言服务"系列丛书）
ISBN 978-7-301-18599-5

Ⅰ.①译… Ⅱ.①陈… Ⅲ.①翻译 Ⅳ.① H059-39

中国版本图书馆 CIP 数据核字（2011）第 028414 号

书　　　名：译本比较与正误
著作责任者：陈小全　编著
责 任 编 辑：孙　莹
标 准 书 号：ISBN 978-7-301-18599-5/H·2767
出 版 发 行：北京大学出版社
地　　　址：北京市海淀区成府路 205 号　100871
网　　　址：http://www.pup.cn
电　　　话：邮购部 62752015　发行部 62750672　编辑部 62754382
　　　　　　出版部 62754962
电 子 邮 箱：zbing@pup.pku.edu.cn
印 刷 者：北京大学印刷厂
经 销 者：新华书店
　　　　　　650 毫米 ×980 毫米　16 开本　9.75 印张　287 千字
　　　　　　2011 年 3 月第 1 版　2011 年 3 月第 1 次印刷
定　　　价：24.00 元

未经许可，不得以任何方式复制或抄袭本书之部分或全部内容。
版权所有，侵权必究　举报电话：010-62752024
　　　　　　　　　　电子邮箱：fd@pup.pku.edu.cn

北京大学 MTI 教育中心
北京大学"翻译实务与语言服务"系列丛书编委会

顾问委员会（按首字音序排列）

程晓堂　程朝翔　冯志伟　孔　岩　李　兵　李　未　林国夫　林戊荪
Mark Lancaster　　王立非　　王明舟　　向明友　　叶子南　　俞士汶

主　编

王继辉

副主编（按首字音序排列）

陈小全　崔启亮　林庆新　俞敬松　张　冰

编委会成员（按首字音序排列）

陈小全　崔启亮　丁林棚　胡一鸣　林怀谦　林庆新　蔺　熠
刘　璐　刘　微　王华树　王华伟　王继辉　王　巍　王维东
熊　伟　杨颖波　俞敬松　张　冰　张南军　朱宪超

总序

随着社会的发展，我国走向全球一体化的步伐正在逐年加快，社会对具有宽广国际视野、精湛翻译技能与技术、丰富行业经验的高级译者与语言服务业管理人才的需求也在与日俱增，在这一大格局下，我国根据教育部的统一部署，适时地开展了翻译硕士专业学位（MTI）教育。

作为 MTI 教育的十五个试点单位之一，北京大学 MTI 教育中心经过认真的思考与摸索，以外国语学院和软件与微电子学院强强联合的姿态，于 2007 年率先提出了"MTI+CAT[①]"翻译硕士培养模式。在此模式中，"MTI"强调人文学术基本素养、翻译技能与行业经验；"CAT"强调翻译技术对于翻译活动的支撑。几年来，朋友们正是在这一模式下，秉承北京大学优良学风，努力探索着培养集人文素养、翻译技能、语言服务技术和行业经验于一身的、符合当今业界发展需要的、高素质复合型翻译从业者与语言服务行业管理人才的道路。由北京大学出版社鼎力支持出版的这套"翻译实务与语言服务"丛书，即是学界和业界的朋友们在近三年的辛勤耕耘中所获得的部分劳动果实。

北京大学"翻译实务与语言服务"丛书计划分 10 册于今明两年陆续出版，其目标读者包括英语、翻译专业本科生和研究生、英语、翻译专业教育者和培训专家、翻译和本地化公司从业人员、翻译爱好者及翻译界自由职业者。出于上述群体对翻译技能训练与语言技术培训的特殊要求，这套丛书的编辑委员会刻意邀请了有翻译教学经验和语言服务企业从业经验的学者专家直接参与编纂工作，并请前辈学者和业界知名专家严格把关，以借助他们的学识与阅历，有效地传达我们产学结合的基本理念，推广与普及现代化翻译技能、语言服务和翻译技术的培训方法与实际应用，从而为我国翻译教育与翻译产业的发展再做一点有益的工作。

本套丛书的所有编纂者均对翻译教育与翻译产业抱有强烈的使命感和浓厚的参与热情，但由于水平的局限和时间的压力，各部小书都难免存有亟待澄清和进一步探讨的问题，甚至谬误，我愿借此机会代表参加这次编辑与写作工作的朋友们，真诚地向各界学者行家们寻求指教，以便尽可能完整地做好后续编纂与出版此套丛书的艰巨工作。

---

① MTI，即 Master of Translation and Interpreting（翻译硕士）；CAT，即 Computer Aided Translation（计算机辅助翻译）。2007 年，北京大学在国内率先开设了计算机辅助翻译硕士培养方向。

本丛书编辑委员会在筹划并实施这套丛书的出版计划过程中，有幸得到了很多业内行家以及北京航空航天大学、北京师范大学、对外经济贸易大学、南开大学、中国人民大学等单位相关领导和教授们的热情鼓励与无私支持，我们在此向帮助过我们的朋友们一并表示感谢。

王继辉

北京大学智学苑寓所

2010年9月22日

序言

长期以来，北大外语学院是以培养高水平人文学科外语人才著名的。三年前北大设立了 MTI 教育中心，利用多学科的优势，提出了"MTI+CAT"的培养模式，这应该说是翻译教学中难能可贵的创新。

现在中心积累了教学经验，出版一套集语言基本素养、翻译技能和翻译技术于一身的丛书，说明教授们在不断探索、勇于开拓，为我国的翻译教学读物另辟新径。

我们知道，在全球化、信息化以及生活和工作节奏大大加快的今天，社会对翻译的要求具有全新的特点，不仅涉及内容庞杂，而且质量与数量并重，有时，速度甚至成为优先的考虑。尤其是在日常经济生活中，诸如科技（如，工程项目）、法律（如协议、合同）等领域，要求将大量的资料在最短的时间内高质量地翻译出来。这里，借助于辅助翻译系统或工具就成了顺利完成任务的关键。

目前，我国翻译教学在结合翻译技能和翻译技术方面，还处于初创阶段，我认为，北大的这套丛书的价值正在于介绍这一领域的各类最新进展。相信我国的青年翻译工作者阅读和学习它会有所收获。

林戊荪
2010 年 11 月 10 日

前言

国内翻译市场最缺乏的是什么？答案是合格的翻译从业人员。怎样培养应对市场的翻译人才？答案是从翻译实战的语料入手。如何用真实的语料培养翻译人才？这就是本教材要解决的问题。本教材以语料库语言学理论为指导，从文学与非文学翻译对比入手，以翻译市场真实语料为主要素材，探讨了词语的意义、英汉互译句法结构转换、翻译中的文化与修辞以及翻译中的专业知识等问题。本教材以译本比较与正误分析为主要方法，以真实语料实战练习为辅助手段，旨在培养学习者获得应对翻译市场的能力。

目前社会上对翻译质量的批评越来越多，言辞也越来越激烈，如火如荼的翻译理论研究异彩纷呈，但鲜有为非文学翻译提供的理论支撑。鉴于此，本教材在编写理念上进行了大胆的尝试，主要体现在如下几个方面：

一、以语料库语言学理论为指导。语料库语言学认为自然语言是社会约定俗成的产物，尽管语言内部存在着规则系统，但规则对于人们学习掌握语言并不起决定性作用，人们对语言的掌握主要依赖于具体的语言经验。语料库对人们的最大启发是，人们使用的语言大多均具有约定俗成及可预见性的特点，换句话说，人们总是在有意识或无意识地重复着语言中业已存在的表达方式。因此，外语学习最好的方法似乎是回归传统，把大量接触语言实际作为最重要的学习手段，以使学习者大脑中储存足够的预制语块，在此基础上才能做好翻译工作。如今大谈特谈翻译理论和技巧的书籍甚为流行，殊不知翻译能力主要来自于译者对原语和译入语的良好掌握。因此，翻译课也应立足于促进两种语言水平的提高，而语言水平的提高反过来又可促进翻译质量的提高。一些翻译理论固然揭示了翻译现象中的某种真相，但这些真相的揭示无法替代译者运用两种语言的能力，而恰恰是这种对语言的运用能力，才决定着译者的水平和翻译质量的高低。

二、从文学语篇翻译入手。翻译能力的培养以简易文学作品作为开始最为合适，在此基础上方可逐渐过渡到非文学翻译领域。文学翻译与非文学翻译对译者的要求存在诸多差异，一个理想的文学译者应具有作家的文学修养和表现力，在把握原作精神实质的基础上，把内容与形式浑然一体地传达出来。一个理想的非文学译者需要具备广博的知识以及特定领域内的专业知识，但一定的文学翻译功底则是做好非文学翻译的必要前提。人们有时把文学翻译和非文学翻译对立起来，却忽视了它们对译者的一些共同要求。诸如两种语言的运用能力、缜密的逻辑思维、严谨的工作态度、深刻洞察语篇细节的能力、创造性解决问题的能力等等，无论对于文学译者还是非文学译者都是必需的。

三、熟悉自己所翻译的内容。非文学翻译涉及的内容非常广泛，很难想象一个不了解所译内容的译者能够顺利完成翻译任务。例如，国际商务合同的译者必须对国际贸易实务及国际商法有一定的了解，从事法律翻译的译者如果没有一定的法学知识也很难承担此任。掌握一门语言同具备专业知识完全是两码事，在我国精通外语者不懂专业、懂专业者外语不精的现象比比皆是，这两种人均不是专业翻译领域内的理想译者，但均有可能成为某一专业领域内的合格译者。语料库语言学对人们的启示是：一定要通过专业语篇掌握专业语言。学习本教材你会发现，语料库在这方面提供了一些切实可行的解决方案。

本教材编写过程中得到了北京大学 MTI 教育中心主任、北京大学英语系教授王继辉先生的大力支持，北京大学"翻译实务与语言服务"丛书编委会各位专家对本书提出了许多宝贵的建议，笔者在此向他们表示衷心感谢！笔者要特别感谢北京悦尔翻译公司总经理蒙永业先生，他为本书提供了大量的翻译市场真实语料，同时为本书若干章节提供了知识要点分析，本书的编写思路和章节安排也参考了他的若干意见。最后笔者还要感谢北京元培世纪翻译公司蒋小林总裁和陈文君女士，他们根据自己公司的翻译实践，向笔者提出了许多颇有价值的参考意见，同时也提供了不少来自翻译市场的双语语料。总之，这是一本理论与实践紧密结合的教材，相信学习者将受益于它的与众不同。

陈小全

2010 年 8 月

目录

第一章　文学与非文学翻译 1

第一节　文学与非文学语言的特点 2
一、文学语言的特点 2
二、非文学语言的特点 3

第二节　文学与非文学翻译对译者的要求 5
一、文学翻译对译者的要求 5
二、非文学翻译对译者的要求 5

第三节　文学与非文学翻译对"忠实"的解读 6

第四节　文学翻译的难点 7
一、文学翻译的意境传达 7
二、文学翻译的风格再现 8
三、文学翻译中的修辞格 11

第五节　非文学翻译的难点 12
一、非文学语篇中的知识 12
二、非文学翻译中的术语翻译 13
三、程式化语言的翻译 13
本章主要参考文献 14
翻译练习一 14

第二章　语料库与翻译 16

第一节　语料库的定义及其类型 17
一、什么是语料库 17
二、语料库的类型 17

第二节　语料库揭示了语言的本质 18

第三节　语料库对翻译的验证功能 19

第四节　翻译中的平行语料库运用 22

第五节　翻译中的可比语料库运用 23
本章主要参考文献 26
翻译练习二 26

第三章　词语意义与翻译对等 28

第一节　意义理论与分类 29

第二节　意义理论对翻译的启示 30
一、对外部世界的认知 30
二、了解原语文本信息 31

第三节　概念意义的重要性 32

第四节　翻译中的对等 34

第五节　译文对比分析 35
本章主要参考文献 39
翻译练习三 39

第四章 英汉句法结构差异与翻译 41
第一节 英汉句法结构的特点 42
一、"形合"与"意合" 42
二、英语中的句法结构 43
三、汉语中的句法结构 43
四、英汉句式中的施事与受事 43
第二节 英汉句法结构对比 44
一、文学语篇结构对比 44
二、非文学语篇结构对比 47
第三节 汉英句法结构转换 49
本章主要参考文献 51
翻译练习四 52

第五章 翻译中的文化与修辞 53
第一节 文化与翻译 54
一、词语中的文化信息 54
二、修辞的翻译 55
第二节 文化翻译策略 57
一、熟悉约定俗成的译法 57
二、文化中比喻修辞的翻译 58
三、翻译中的"假朋友" 59
第三节 翻译中的文化失真 60
第四节 文化与修辞翻译实例 62
本章主要参考文献 64
翻译练习五 65

第六章 翻译中的数字表达 66
第一节 英汉出版物数字用法规定 67
一、英语出版物数字用法规定 67
二、汉语出版物上数字用法的规定 68
第二节 确数的表达 71
第三节 概数的表达 73
一、表示大约数目 73
二、表示"少于"的数目 73
三、表示"差不多"的数目 73
四、表示"多于"的数目 74
五、表示"介于"的数目 74
六、表示"相邻"的数目 74
七、表示"数十"等数目 74
八、数字的虚指义 75
第四节 数字增减程度的表达 75
一、表示增加、上升等 75

二、表示维持在某种水平或程度 76
　　三、表示减少和下降 76
　　四、同比/环比的表达 77
　第五节 数量单位的表达 78
　　一、英语表达中一般不使用量词 78
　　二、英语表达中使用量词的情况 78
　第六节 数字相关翻译 79
　　一、容易望文生义的数字表述 79
　　二、英汉数字词汇空缺现象 79
　　三、习语中数词的修辞特点 80
　　本章主要参考文献 81
　　翻译练习六 81

第七章　专业知识与文本翻译 82
　第一节 冶金行业中的专业知识 83
　第二节 建筑工程行业的专业知识 87
　第三节 医药行业的专业知识 89
　第四节 经管文章中的专业知识 92
　　翻译练习七 94

第八章　法律与合同文本翻译 96
　第一节 法律文本翻译的难点 98
　　一、法律体系制约属性 98
　　二、对等词语的翻译 100
　　三、同义和近义词的翻译 102
　　四、法律翻译的风格把握 103
　第二节 法律文本的句子翻译 105
　　一、类属后置 105
　　二、同类排除 106
　　三、语境定义 107
　　四、常识判断 107
　第三节 合同文本翻译 108
　　一、合同文本翻译基本要求 108
　　二、合同文本翻译步骤 108
　　三、合同翻译实例 108
　　本章主要参考文献 112
　　翻译练习八 113

第九章　翻译实战 115
实战一：IT文章中译英 116
　【原文】 116
　【参考译文】 117
实战二：机电文章中译英 118
　【原文】 118

【参考译文】	118
实战三：电视解说词中译英	119
【原文】	119
【参考译文】	120
实战四：工程文章英译中	122
【原文】	122
【参考译文】	122
实战五：食品文章英译中	123
【原文】	123
【参考译文】	124
实战六：招标文件英译中	124
【原文】	124
【参考译文】	127
实战七：协议书英译中	130
【原文】	130
【参考译文】	131

翻译练习参考译文 133

翻译练习一 134
参考译文1 134
参考译文2 134

翻译练习二 135
参考译文1 135
参考译文2 135

翻译练习三 136
参考译文1 136
参考译文2 136

翻译练习四 137
参考译文1 137
参考译文2 137

翻译练习五 138
参考译文1 138
参考译文2 138

翻译练习六 139
参考译文1 139
参考译文2 139
参考译文3 139

翻译练习七 139
参考译文1 139

翻译练习八 140
参考译文1 140
参考译文2 140
参考译文3 141

第一章

文学与非文学翻译

第一节 文学与非文学语言的特点

文学通过塑造艺术形象反映社会生活,反映作者的思想感情和审美观念;文学是语言的艺术,文学作品通过语言的叙事、言情及画物去感染人和教育人,因此文学语言具有生动性、形象性和艺术感染力。小说、诗歌、散文、戏剧、影视等都属于文学的范畴。非文学范畴非常广泛,包括所有文学作品以外的各种文体,如商务、法律、金融、理论著作、学术著作、政论文章、公文合同等等。非文学文本的功能主要是传递信息,实用目的明确,非文学语言风格虽因文本类型不同而各异,但总体而论均具有内容准确、形式完整、语言规范和风格统一的特点。

一、文学语言的特点

生活的丰富多彩、作家的个体差异及文艺的多功能性,决定了文学作品的多样性和题材的广泛性,这些因素也造就了文学语言与其他语言的不同。文学语言大致有如下特点:

(一)文学语言具有形象性。例如小说创作主要是通过形象思维来完成,栩栩如生的细节描写可以营造某种氛围,渲染某种情绪,使读者有身临其境之感。在情节的描写中,作家崇尚具体形象的刻画,因而尽量避免抽象的演绎。

(二)文学人物的语言具有个性化特征。作家为了再现人物的不同个性,常常以符合人物身份、地位、教养及性格的口吻说话,其结果是,作家笔下的语言时而温文尔雅,时而粗俗不堪,时而使用方言土语,时而又咬文嚼字,而这些均为作家塑造人物形象的手段。

(三)文学语言中多用修辞格。文学语言是语言的艺术,作家为了描绘出引人入胜的情节、逼真的场景及栩栩如生的人物,常常大量使用修辞格,诸如拟人、比喻、讽刺、夸张、双关等手法常常被采用。总之,与其他任何类型语篇相比,文学语篇中使用的修辞格是最多的。

(四)文学语言中的句式复杂多变。作家为了使文字生动活泼,常在句子结构上做文章,如将长句和短句结合使用,将圆周句和松散句选用等等。这些多变的句式使得文学语言呈现出跌宕起伏、色彩斑斓的特点。

下面是威廉·莎士比亚(William Shakespeare)最著名的十四行诗第 18 首及其解释,该诗之所以有名原因是多方面的,其中多种修辞手段的运用无疑是个重要因素。这首诗包含了明喻、暗喻、拟人、头韵法和平行结构等多种手法,为该诗的意境营造增添了色彩。提供的两种译文亦出自名家之手,读者可从中领略到他们的创造力和独特个性。

Shall I compare thee to a summers day Sonnet 18 by William Shakespeare	Explanation of Shakespeare's Sonnet 18
Shall I compare thee to a summer's day? Thou art more lovely and more temperate: (temperate: calm, not overly emotional.)	Here, Shakespeare writes that his beloved is lovelier and more constant than a summer day. The word "than" is implied, even though it does not appear in the poem, so this is a simile.
Rough winds do shake the darling buds of May, (rough: stormy, or unpleasantly turbulent as a result of stormy conditions.)	Shakespeare personifies the wind by saying it "shakes" the May flowers. The verb "shake" implies deliberate action, which is a human quality that Shakespeare gives to the wind in this image.
And summer's lease hath all too short a date: (lease: the amount of time allowed for something, literally a contract giving temporary ownership of something.)	When Shakespeare writes "And summer's lease hath all too short a date," he means that summer goes by too quickly.
Sometime too hot the eye of heaven shines,	Shakespeare calls the sun the "eye of heaven," in order to convey its power. He says it sometimes shines too brightly.
And often is his gold complexion dimm'd; (complexion — the coloring of a person's face)	Shakespeare personifies the sun by using the masculine pronoun, "his," and saying the sun has a golden face. The poet writes that clouds and haze often weaken the sun's brilliance.

And every fair from fair sometime declines, (Alliteration — a figure of speech in which the same sound appears at the beginning of two or more words.)	The phrase "fair from fair" creates an alliterative effect with the repetition of the "f" sound. In this line, the poet observes that all beautiful things eventually lose their beauty.
By chance or nature's changing course untrimm'd; (untrimm'd — without decoration, with beauty having been taken away. "Trim" is another word for decoration. The word "untrimmed," therefore, means without decoration. Shakespeare drops the "e" when he writes this word.)	Shakespeare again uses alliteration with the words "chance" and "changing," as he repeats the "ch" sound. This line expands on the line before (which also contains alliteration), by saying luck or natural decline are the reasons things lose their beauty.
But thy eternal summer shall not fade,	Shakespeare compares the beloved's youthfulness to an "eternal summer," to convey his belief that his beloved will always remain young in appearance and character.
Nor lose possession of that fair thou owest;	Here, Shakespeare describes beauty as a thing that can be owned, in order to say the beauty his beloved possesses will never diminish.
Nor shall Death brag thou wander'st in his shade, (brag: show off, talk with too much pride: to talk with excessive pride about an achievement or possession.)	The poet personifies death by using the male pronoun "his" and giving death the human quality of speech (or bragging). Shakespeare says death will not take his beloved.
When in eternal lines to time thou growest:	This line can be considered metaphorical because the poet writes that his beloved will live forever in this poem. He therefore describes the poem as if it were a place where his beloved could live.
So long as men can breathe or eyes can see, (Parallel structure: repetition of a pattern of words within a sentence or passage.)	The poet repeats a similar pattern of words with the phrases "men can breathe" and "eyes can see," in order to create rhythm and describe the continuing cycle of life.
So long lives this and this gives life to thee.	The repetition of the word patterns in the phrases "So long as" and "So long lives" makes it clear to the reader that these last two lines (a couplet) go together, not just in their rhyme, but in their meaning. （http://udleditions.cast.org/CONTENT,sonnet_18,1.html）

梁实秋译本	辜正坤译本
我可能把你和夏天相比拟？ 你比夏天更可爱更温和： 狂风会把五月的花苞吹落地， 夏天也嫌太短促，匆匆而过： 有时太阳照得太热， 常常又遮暗他的金色的脸； 美的事物总免不要凋落， 偶然的，或是随自然变化而流转。 但是你的永恒之夏不会褪色； 你不会失去你的俊美的仪容； 死神不能夸说你在他的阴影里面走着， 如果你在这不朽的诗句里获得了永生； 只要人们能呼吸，眼睛能看东西， 此诗就会不朽，使你永久生存下去。	或许我可用夏日将你作比方， 但你比夏日更可爱也更温良。 夏风狂作常会摧落五月的娇蕊， 夏季的期限也未免还不太长。 有时候天眼如炬人间酷热难当， 但转瞬又金面如晦常惹云遮雾障。 每一种美都终究会凋残零落， 或见弃于机缘，或受挫于天道无常。 然而你永恒的夏季却不会终止， 你优美的形象也永远不会消亡。 死神难可口说你在它的罗网中游荡， 只因你借我的诗行便可长寿无疆。 只要人口能呼吸，人眼看得清， 我这诗就长存，使你万世流芳。

对照提供的注释你会发现，两译文似乎都有不够准确的地方，如梁实秋译本中"死神不能夸说你在他的阴影里面走着，<u>如果你在这不朽的诗句里获得了永生</u>"；以及辜正坤译本中"每一种美都终究会凋残零落，或见弃于机缘，<u>或受挫于天道无常</u>。"但文学翻译、特别是诗歌翻译，最重要的是看意境的传达，是看诗中韵味的再现，是看译文读者能否像原文读者那样从诗中得到同等的愉悦。两译文在众多译文中之所以能够成为佼佼者，就是因为它们读起来像"诗"，如辜正坤译本中的尾韵极富音乐性和流动感，极大地丰富了听觉感受。

二、非文学语言的特点

与文学语言形成鲜明对照的是，非文学语言是客观真实的反映，具有明确的实用目的，常以简洁明了的方式传递信息。非文学语言主要包括如下特点：

（一）内容准确、形式完整、语言规范和风格统一。例如，法律文本、商务合同、理论著作、学术著作等除了内容准确之外，都要遵循一定的格式，都要规范使用词汇和遵守句法规则，其他非文学语言或许呈现诸多其他特点，但这些均为非文学语言的一般性特征。

（二）非文学语言涉及多种学科知识。诸如国际贸易、国际金融、合同条约、法律法规等均具有较强的专业性，其语言的使用服务于知识信息的传递，语言的使用离不开相关的知识，而没有相关的知识也无从谈及语言的使用。

（三）非文学语言包括众多术语和专门用语。非文学语言涉及多种学科知识本身就决定了术语和专门用语的大量使用。术语和专门语都是规范化的，不能任意创造，需要遵循约定俗成的原则。

（四）非文学语言属于程式化语言，不用或少用修饰性形容词与副词，这一特点主要体现在法律、法规、条约、协定、合同、章程等之中。我们通过下面的两个实例，来探讨英汉非文学语言的特点。

【例1】

【原文】So what is behind this massive rally? Certainly it has been helped by a wave of liquidity from near-zero interest rates and quantitative easing. But a more important factor fuelling this <u>asset bubble</u> is the weakness of the US dollar, driven by <u>the mother of all carry trades</u>. The US dollar has become the major funding currency of carry trades as the Fed has kept interest rates on hold and is expected to do so for a long time. Investors who are shorting the US dollar to buy on a highly leveraged basis <u>higher-yielding assets</u> and other global assets are not just borrowing at zero interest rates in dollar terms; they are borrowing at very negative interest rates—as low as negative 10 or 20 per cent annualised–as the fall in the US dollar leads to massive capital gains on <u>short dollar positions</u>. (Nouriel Roubini: Mother of all Carry Trades Faces an Inevitable Bust, *Financial Times*, Nov.1, 2009)

【译文】那么资产价格大幅上涨的原因是什么呢？当然，这受益于由近零利率和定量宽松政策带来的一波流动性。但助长这轮资产泡沫的一个更重要的因素，是由所有<u>利差交易</u>之源动力造成的美元疲软。美元已成为利差交易的主要融资货币，因为美联储(Fed)一直维持利率不变，并预计将长期不作调整。那些做空美元、以很高的杠杆买入<u>高收益资产</u>和其他全球性资产的投资者，岂止是在以零利率借入美元；他们简直是在以负利率（年化利率为 −10% 或 −20%）借入美元，因为美元汇率的下跌会使美元<u>空头头寸</u>产生巨额资本收益。（梁艳裳译）

原文和译文中划线部分为一般译者不太熟悉的术语，译者如缺乏相关知识且不知术语在两种语言中的对等说法，则根本谈不上正确的翻译。翻译中对术语和相关知识了解的重要是不言而喻的。

【例2】

【原文】本次平面设计主要单体为水泵生产联合厂房，长 106.30 米，宽 82.3 米，一期设置在基地的中间靠西部位，生产车间二期贴邻一期东侧接建。办公和生活服务设施与联合厂房贴邻设计，布置在厂房北侧。变配电室在基地的东南角位置，基地南侧靠中间位置设计有单层仓库并预留二期发展，基地的西南角布置有危险品库。在变配电室的北侧布置有废料库棚。基地东北角布置有污水处理站、消防水泵房。（翻译公司材料）

【译文】This plan is mainly designed for the pump production complex, 106.30m in length and 82.3m in width. The first-phase facilities are located on the middle to the west of the Base, and the second-phase production facilities are built to the east of the first-phase facilities. The office and domestic service facilities are connected to and laid out in the north of production facilities. The power distribution house is located on the southeastern part of the Base, and the single-floor warehouse is designed on the middle of the southern part of the Base, and proper land is reserved for the extension of the second-phase facilities. The hazardous material warehouse is arranged on the southwestern part of the Base. The scrap material shed is arranged to the north of the power distribution room, and the wastewater treatment plant and fire pump house are designed in the northeastern part of the Base.（翻译公司译文）

原文语言准确严谨，几乎没有多余的词语，如果删除任何一个词语，都会影响到读者对平面设计的理解，从而找不准具体位置。英译文也须使用准确严谨的语言，不允许有任何文学性发挥，以达到译文准确的目的。

第二节 文学与非文学翻译对译者的要求

鉴于文学语言与非文学语言之间存在着诸多差异，文学翻译与非文学翻译对译者的要求也有所不同。由于文学本身所具有的形象性、艺术性以及作家独特的语言风格，理想的译者应具有"作家的文学修养和表现力，以便在深刻理解原作，把握原作精神实质的基础上，把内容与形式浑然一体的原作的艺术意境传达出来。"（郑海凌："文学翻译的本质特征"，《中国翻译》，1998（2））对非文学译者的要求其实也毫不逊色，一个理想的译者首先要有一定的文学翻译功底，否则也无法做好非文学翻译工作，翻译能力的培养以简易文学作品作为开始最为合适，在此基础上方可逐渐过渡到非文学翻译领域。一个理想的非文学译者还需具备广博的知识和具体领域内的专业知识。例如，国际商务合同的译者必须对国际贸易及国际商法有较深入的了解，而法律翻译人员如没有一定的比较法学知识，则无法想象其能够从事此项工作。除此之外，缜密的逻辑思维、严谨的工作态度、深刻洞察语篇细节的能力，以及创造性解决问题的能力，无论对于文学译者还是非文学译者也都是必须的。

一、文学翻译对译者的要求

对于文学作品而言，译者既是原作的读者又是译作的读者。作为原作的读者，译者应努力了解原作的方方面面，特别是原作的文化背景和思想内涵。然后考虑如何翻译，包括形式、内容、内涵、译入语读者接受度等问题。下面从翻译目的、翻译理解与翻译表达三个方面，简述文学翻译对译者的要求。

（一）文学翻译的目的

译者从事翻译活动都具有目的性，而一切翻译策略的选择都取决于翻译行为所要达到的目的。文学翻译的目的就是全面再现原文的审美意义，使译文具有与原创作品一样的文学功能，使译文读者能够与原文读者一样获得阅读享受。这样的目的决定了译者在翻译时必须具有创造能力，创造出具有与原文相同功能的文学作品是译者的中心任务。

（二）文学翻译的理解

译者对文学原作的理解，受制于译者的知识结构与审美能力。要翻译好一部文学作品，译者必须具备阅读与阐释的能力。在文学翻译中，译者对原作不仅要进行语言和逻辑层面的分析，更要对作品进行思想内涵和艺术特点的分析，从而挖掘出语言背后的社会意义。译者的经历、文化背景、思维方式、审美情趣、情感因素对于理解原作都很重要。

（三）文学翻译的表达

翻译表达与译者对原作的理解有关，也与译者对译入语的把握有关。译者一方面要对异域文化保持开放的态度，另一方面又要考虑如何将异域文化植入本土文化。理性的译者常会采用自己擅长的语言形式进行翻译。如对莎士比亚戏剧的翻译就有许多不同形式，包括散文体、诗体、章回体小说等形式。而语言的表达形式更是多种多样，这从《哈姆雷特》"To be or not to be, that is the question." 一句的翻译中可窥一斑，从卞之琳的"活下去还是不活"，朱生豪的"生存还是毁灭"，梁实秋的"死后还是存在，还是不存在"到方平的"活着好还是死了好"以及孙大雨的"是存在还是消亡"；凡此种种，不一而足。

二、非文学翻译对译者的要求

非文学翻译涉及内容十分广泛，仅学科知识一项就给译者带来巨大挑战。除此之外，译者的双语能力、对两种文化的了解、对不同语篇风格的把握等都是译者所应具备的。非文学翻译人员一般应满足如下基本要求：

（一）具备一定的文学翻译基础

非文学文本包含各类专业知识较多，文化、艺术信息较少，这是客观事实。但这并不意味着非文学翻译可以远离文化。事实上，一些新闻稿件、演讲、年度报告等都与语言中的文化密切相关。译者具有一定文学翻译基础，是从事非文学翻译的前提条件。语言中的文化无所不在，文化渗透在语言中的方方面面，非文学语篇中由于文化差异构成的翻译障碍也随处可见。另一方面，一定的文学翻译实践可以让译者获得基本的翻译能力，在此基础上才能顺利过渡到非文学翻译领域。

（二）掌握背景和专业知识

非文学翻译的首要标准是准确。合同翻译中的错误可能引起诉讼和金钱损失；条约、协议翻译中的错误会导致误解和行为混乱；医药文本翻译错误可能关系人的生命健康。要做到准确，译者必须了解相关的背景和必要的知识。译者对于自己不熟悉的内容，切不可不负责任地主观猜测，必须借助于网络、语料库、各类词典和工具书把问题搞清楚，否则就会带来严重的后果。对于非文学译者而言，有计划、有系统地学习一些专业知识是绝对必要的，只有坚持不懈地努力才能成为某一方面的行家里手。

（三）把握好译文的风格

文学翻译需要译者具有一定的创造能力，译者的个人风格往往渗透在译文之中。而非文学翻译对文体风格有着具体的要求。如商务信函风格就包括七个方面：正确、全面、具体、清楚、简洁、礼貌和体谅。法律文本的翻译则要求译文措辞严谨、行文规范、使用程式化语言以及避免歧义的特定表达方式，其风格具有庄重、保守的特点，所有这些均需译者在长期的翻译实践中逐步掌握。非文学翻译中风格的把握是翻译质量的组成部分，如果说文学翻译中呈现某种风格是译者的才华展示，那么在非文学翻译中则被视为翻译质量有问题。

第三节 文学与非文学翻译对"忠实"的解读

文学翻译与非文学翻译都以忠实于原文作为追求目标，但两者追求的"忠实"却有所不同。如果译者想要重现文学作品中的全部意义，充其量也只能做到最佳近似。这是因为文学作品中措辞和内容同等重要，译者必须考虑文学表述中的内涵及其外延，通常文学翻译中的意义缺损是不可避免的。而非文学翻译追求的是客观事实，因此有可能在准确方面达到很高的程度。文学翻译重在表达作者的言外之意，而非文学翻译则关注客观事实的表述。

下面是三个学生就罗伯特·弗罗斯特"Stopping by Woods on a Snowy Evening"一诗给出的三种译文，我们借他们的译文探讨一下文学翻译对"忠实"的解读。

Stopping by Woods on a Snowy Evening —Robert Frost	（一） 雪夜林中小驻 ——罗伯特·弗罗斯特	（二） 雪夜林边驻足 ——罗伯特·弗罗斯特	（三） 雪夜滞宿林边 ——罗伯特·弗罗斯特
Whose woods these are I think I know. His house is in the village though; He will not see me stopping here To watch his woods fill up with snow.	我知道这林地归属谁家， 邻村里有庄宅在他名下， 他不会见到我停留此地， 注视着这片林布满雪花。	老友村落将近眼， 不访故人驻林边。 四周寂寥无人顾， 放眼山林雪满天。	陋舍深野锁， 柴木雪中栖。 未闻客所至， 但凭银素裹。
My little horse must think it queer To stop without a farmhouse near Between the woods and frozen lake The darkest evening of the year.	此情景困惑住我的小马， 因何故走荒野远离农家？ 驻足在冰之湖林间寒雪， 一年中最暗淡黑夜无涯。	小马不解主人意， 缘何歇停荒野前。 冰天雪地封湖面， 经年最暗雪夜间。	浮云心惊疑， 农家何处是？ 丛林冰湖间， 经年最暗时。
He gives his harness bells a shake To ask if there is some mistake. The only other sound's the sweep Of easy wind and downy flake.	摇一摇身上鞍铃声初炸， 这小马试问我究竟为啥？ 有微风拂落片孤声低语， 无垠夜万物眠无一作答。	小马摇身铃铛响， 促我趁早往家撵。 呜呜风啸过山林， 绒绒雪花飘满天。	摇曳马驼铃， 试问歧路否？ 唯唯应耳声， 落瓣惹清风。
The woods are lovely, dark and deep, But I have promises to keep, And miles to go before I sleep, And miles to go before I sleep.	漆黑夜林深邃美有加， 可是我早已把诺言下达， 几里路不走完不去返家， 几里路不走完不去睡下。	暮色降临山朦胧， 积雪难掩青松情。 承诺在胸说不尽， 再行数里雪夜间。	幽林虽柔谧， 箴言诺在前， 待到千里遥， 睡意共炕边。

上面三种译文各有特色，为了行文优美或照顾韵脚等因素，都存在着不同程度的增译、减译、漏

译和改译现象。如译文（一）中的"因何故走荒野远离农家？"以及"这小马试问我究竟为啥"；译文（二）中的"暮色降临山朦胧，积雪难掩青松倩"等。译文（三）采用了五言诗的形式，如果不说是译文，读者一定会认为那是一首中文诗。文中借柴木代林木，借浮云称谓作者之马，一语双关（一语马，二语漂泊之人）。译者的文采不容置疑，但留给了读者太多的中国文化联想，同时译文与原文意义上也有差距。上面三译文并非出自名家之手，同样反映了诗歌翻译中译文迥异的现实。其实名家的译作也常常风格迥异，也或多或少存在着增译、减译、漏译和改译的现象。人们在评判诗歌翻译时，往往更多关注意境的传达，而对个别词句的忠实程度，则采取一定的容忍态度。

非文学翻译追求的是客观事实，在准确方面要求极高，译文必须是原文的准确表述。虽然表述方式允许差别的存在，但不能有翻译缺失、增译、漏译及改译等现象。我们看下面的例子：

【例1】

【原文】Article 34　Disclaimer on Effectiveness of Documents

A bank assumes no liability or responsibility for the form, sufficiency, accuracy, genuineness, falsification or legal effect of any document, or for the general or particular conditions stipulated in a document or superimposed thereon; nor does it assume any liability or responsibility for the description, quantity, weight, quality, condition, packing, delivery, value or existence of the goods, services or other performance represented by any document, or for the good faith or acts or omissions, solvency, performance or standing of the consignor, the carrier, the forwarder, the consignee or the insurer of the goods or any other person.（UPC600）

【译文】第三十四条　关于单据有效性的免责

银行对任何单据的形式、充分性、准确性、内容真实性、虚假性或法律效力，或对单据中规定或添加的一般或特殊条件，概不负责；银行对任何单据所代表的货物、服务或其他履约行为的描述、数量、重量、品质、状况、包装、交付、价值或其存在与否，或对发货人、承运人、货运代理人、收货人、货物的保险人或其他任何人的诚信与否，作为或不作为、清偿能力、履约或资信状况，也概不负责。（《跟单信用证统一惯例》，国际商会第600号出版物）（官方译文）

【例2】

【原文】在双方约定以信用证为付款方式时，在合同规定的最晚装运日前30天，由买方通知开户银行开出以卖方为受益人的不可撤销的信用证，凭第5项单据条款规定的单据电汇付款。信用证的内容应与合同规定相符。信用证的到期日为最晚装运日后的第21天。（外贸公司材料）

【译文】In the event that the parties hereto agree to make payment by letter of credit, the Buyer shall cause the opening bank to issue an irrevocable letter of credit in favor of the Seller within 30 days prior to the latest shipment date provided by the Contract, and the payment shall be made by wire on the basis of the documents provided in Article 5-Documents. The content of the letter of credit shall be consistent with the terms and conditions of the Contract. And the expiry date of the letter of credit shall be the 21st day after the latest shipment date.（外贸公司译文）

上面例子中不仅两种文字的意义相同，而且许多表达方式也很固定，且不说"发货人、承运人、货运代理人、信用证、开户行"等必须与英文中的说法一一对应，而且诸如 in favor of（以……为受益人）等说法也不能随便翻译，否则就是贻笑大方的外行话。由此可见，文学翻译与非文学翻译对译者的要求在许多方面截然不同。

第四节　文学翻译的难点

一、文学翻译的意境传达

文学作品尤其是诗歌，往往讲求音韵美和意象美，这就是文学作品的意境。意境的传达受到多种因素的影响，如译者的审美能力、文学再创造能力、对语言差异和文化差异的把握以及必要的灵感和才气。下面是罗伯特·弗罗斯特（Robert Frost）（1874—1963）《修墙》（"Mending Wall"）的全文，以及其中部分诗行的两种译文。

Mending Wall

Something there is that doesn't love a wall,
That sends the frozen-ground-swell under it
And spills the upper boulders in the sun,
And makes gaps even two can pass abreast.
The work of hunters is another thing:
I have come after them and made repair
Where they have left not one stone on a stone,
But they would have the rabbit out of hiding,
To please the yelping dogs. The gaps I mean,
No one has seen them made or heard them made,
But at spring mending-time we find them there.
I let my neighbor know beyond the hill;
And on a day we meet to walk the line
And set the wall between us once again.
We keep the wall between us as we go.
To each the boulders that have fallen to each.
And some are loaves and some so nearly balls
We have to use a spell to make them balance:
"Stay where you are until our backs are turned!"
We wear our fingers rough with handling them.
Oh, just another kind of outdoor game,
One on a side. It comes to little more:
There where it is we do not need the wall:
He is all pine and I am apple orchard.
My apple trees will never get across
And eat the cones under his pines, I tell him.
He only says, "Good fences make good neighbors."
Spring is the mischief in me, and I wonder
If I could put a notion in his head:
"Why do they make good neighbors? Isn't it
Where there are cows? But here there are no cows.
Before I built a wall I'd ask to know
What I was walling in or walling out,
And to whom I was like to give offense.
Something there is that doesn't love a wall,
That wants it down. I could say "Elves" to him,
But it's not elves exactly, and I'd rather
He said it for himself. I see him there,
Bringing a stone grasped firmly by the top
In each hand, like an old-stone savage armed.
He moves in darkness as it seems to me,
Not of woods only and the shade of trees.
He will not go behind his father's saying,
And he likes having thought of it so well
He says again, "Good fences make good neighbors."

（一）补墙

有一些东西，大概是不喜欢墙的，
它使冻土地在墙角下隆起，
使墙头石块在阳光下洒落满地，
足可容两个人并肩而过。
猎手行猎时干的是另一码事：
他们使墙上的石块纷纷跌落，
我跟着他们后面去修补，
但是他们要把兔子赶出藏身洞，
让狂吠的猎犬高兴。
我要说的是那些缺口，
怎么会产生，
谁也没见过，也没有听说过，
但到春季补墙时，
却发现它们就在那里。
（《英语世界》1994 年第 5 期）

（二）修墙

一定有不爱界墙的某种力量，
它使墙下冻土隆鼓胀，
它使墙中卵石脱落普见阳光，
缺口大得两人并行也无妨。
猎人的作为则另是一样，
春天，对我简直是嬉闹一场。
我要他想一想，
"为什么修好界墙，睦邻不伤？"
难道是因为，
他有成群的牛羊，
我这里却是空荡荡。
在修墙前我该想想，
到底我要把什么圈在墙内，
又把什么隔在一旁，
这样做会把什么人冲撞。
（冯伟年：《美国十二名人传略》，西安交通大学出版社，1985 年 3 月）

中国自古就有"诗无达诂"之说，即人们对诗歌的理解和鉴赏存在着差异性。罗伯特·弗罗斯特的这首诗具有多层次内涵，虽然表面上谈论的是修补界墙，但却隐含着深刻的哲理，给读者留下了想象的空间。例如，有人认为此诗表达了邻里之间修补界墙的观念冲突，也有人认为反映了人们潜意识中根深蒂固的隔膜，甚至有人从国际关系的视角出发，认为国与国之间只有修好界墙，才能保持良好的关系。然而诗歌的译者似乎更关心技巧的再现及意境的传达，而对诗歌内涵的解读完全可以留给读者去完成。

对比两个译文不难看出，前者非常贴近原文，后者似乎有"不忠"之嫌。但如果研究一下两译文的完整版本，就会发现【译文二】对原作的理解更加深刻，译者在对原诗进行大胆改造的同时，又充分发挥了汉语的声律优势，使得整个译文读来清新流畅，富有音乐美感。【译文二】的胜出在于，译者把握住了原作的精神实质，因而较好地传达出了原作的艺术意境。（两译文详尽对比参阅冯伟年：《新编实用英汉翻译实例评析》，清华大学出版社，2006，第 293—299 页。）

二、文学翻译的风格再现

在讨论翻译风格之前，先看选自《黑种如我》（1961）（"Black Like Me"）中的几段，作者是美国记者约翰·霍华德·格里芬（John Howard Griffin），他化装成黑人到美国南方各州旅行，亲身体验了黑人所遭受的不平等待遇。

【原文】In the bus station lobby, I looked for signs indicating a colored waiting room, but saw none. I walked up to the ticket counter. When the lady ticket seller saw me, her otherwise attractive face turned sour, violently so. This look was so unexpected and so unprovoked I was taken aback.

"What do you want?" she snapped.

Taking care to pitch my voice to politeness, I asked about the next bus to Hattiesburg.

She answered rudely and glared at me with such loathing I knew I was receiving what the Negroes call "the hate stare." It was my first experience with it. It is far more than the look of disapproval one occasionally gets. This was so exaggeratedly hateful I would have been amused if I had not been so surprised.

【译文一】在长途汽车站大厅里，我找来找去就是不见黑人候车室的牌子。我走到柜台前。<u>当那位女售票员看见我的时候，她在其他情况下很动人的面孔变了，显出愠怒，强烈的愠怒。这种脸色是那样出乎意外，而且是那样无缘无故，使我大吃一惊。</u>

"你要什么？"她厉声喝问。

我特别注意礼貌，以谦和的口气询问开往哈蒂斯堡的下一班车是怎么个情况。

<u>她粗鲁地回答，并以那样的厌恶向我瞪眼，我知道我正受到黑人们叫做"仇恨的凝视"的那种东西。初次领教，这是那样夸张地可恨，我本来会觉得有趣，如果我不是那样惊讶的话。</u>

【译文二】在长途汽车站大厅里，我找来找去就是不见黑人候车室的牌子。我走到柜台前。那位女售票员看见我，原来颇为动人的芳容勃然变色。本无冒犯，因何发火？我为之愕然。

"你有什么事？"她厉声喝问。

我特别注意礼貌，以谦和的口吻询问开往哈蒂斯堡下一班车的情况。

她回答时出言粗鲁，怒目而视，嫌恶之情尽在脸上；我知道这就是黑人常说的"仇恨的白眼"。我从未有过如此经历，它比人们偶尔遭受的白眼不知恶劣多少。要不是我一时吃惊的话，那超乎寻常的凶相一定会使我发笑。（译文一和译文二均选自翁显良：《意态由来画不成？》，北京：中国对外翻译出版公司，1983。此处引用略有改动。）

对照原文稍加分析即可看出，【译文一】中下划线部分受原文束缚过重，使得译文读起来不够自然，因而违背了原文清晰流畅的风格。【译文二】充分考虑到了汉语的表达习惯，因此在风格上更加贴近原作。不过，注重汉语表达习惯也有个度的问题，否则同样会使译文风格远离原作。看下面的例子：

【原文】I wanted to go off to another town, but then everyone got busy matchmaking and they were after me so they nearly tore my coat tails off. They talked at me and talked until I got water on the ear. She was no chaste maiden, but they told me she was a virgin pure.

【译文一】　鄙人意欲远走他乡。然而，此时人人皆忙于为在下做媒，在下所到之处，红娘紧随其后，形影不离，几乎将在下之燕尾扯下。他们滔滔不绝，口若悬河，致使在下双耳嗡鸣。此女既非大家闺秀，亦非小家碧玉，本无贞操可言。然而，他们却称此女乃圣洁之贞女也。（周方珠：《翻译多元论》，北京：中国对外翻译出版公司，2004。）

【译文二】　我很想去另外一个城市，可大家都在忙着为我牵线搭桥，无论我身在何处他们都紧随其后，几乎把我外套的下摆扯了下来。他们缠住我说个不停，直到我的两耳嗡嗡作响。女方本不是个贞洁的姑娘，可他们却说她是个纯洁的处女。（学生译文）

原文出自1978年诺贝尔文学奖得主艾·巴·辛格（Isaac Bashevis Singer）的短篇小说《傻瓜吉姆佩尔》（Gimpel the Fool），上述引文出自小说主人公吉姆佩尔之口，他差不多就是个目不识丁的文盲，而【译文一】给人的印象似乎是，他是个满腹经纶的老夫子。译文风格远离原作其实也是对原作的"不忠"。除此之外，"此女既非大家闺秀，亦非小家碧玉，本无贞操可言"之说似乎是在暗示，除了大家闺秀和小家碧玉，别的女子皆无贞操可言，这既有悖于常理，又不符合原作的本意。相比之下，【译文二】从风格上更接近原作。

下面是一个汉译英的例子：

【原文】您自管酽酽沏一壶茉莉花茶，就着紫心萝卜芝麻糖，边吃边喝，翻一篇看一篇，当玩意儿。要是忽一拍脑门子，自以为悟到嘛，别胡乱说，说不定您脑袋走火，想岔了。

今儿，天津卫犯邪。

赶上这日子，谁也拦不住，所有平时见不到也听不到的邪乎事，都挤着往外冒。天一大早，还没亮，无风无雨，好好东南城角呼啦就塌下去一大块，赛给火炮轰的。

邪乎事可就一件接一件来了。（冯骥才：《三寸金莲》）

【译文】So just brew yourself a pot of strong jasmine tea, find some red-hearted turnip or sesame-seed candies, and sip and snack while you slowly flip through the story. Enjoy yourself. And if you should slap your forehead after some great insight, don't go spouting off. Your imagination has probably misfired and taken you some silly tangent.

Today Tianjin turned weird.

Nobody could stop them. It seemed like all the weird happenings you normally don't see and don't hear were just itching to gush forth. Early in the day, before dawn, there was a cannonlike boom, and a stretch of the city wall near the southeastern corner came tumbling down. And there wasn't a drop of rain or a breath of wind.

And the weird happenings continued one after another. (Translated by David Wakefield and Howard Goldblatt)

原文中充满了京津两地方言，如"当玩意儿"、"一拍脑门子"和"邪乎事"等等，语言中的这种地域特色翻译起来极其困难，常常使译文几乎无法保留原作风格。假如有人不看原文，把上段译文回译成汉语，相信其风格与原作风格大相径庭。对于此类风格传递问题，译者也只能在译文中适当运用一些相应的俗语。我国著名翻译家张谷若在国内外译界享有盛名，他翻译的《德伯家的苔丝》被称为"译作的楷模"，但随着翻译理论的不断发展，人们对他用山东方言来对译威塞克斯方言提出了质疑，一个让译者无法回答的问题是：难道德伯家的故事发生在山东？

文学翻译风格再现是个异常复杂的问题。《辞海》把风格定义为："作家、艺术家在创作中所表现出来的艺术特色和创作个性。作家、艺术家由于生活经历、立场观点、艺术素养、个性特征的不同在处理题材、驾驭体裁、描绘形象、表现手法和运用语言等方面都各有特色，这就形成了作品的风格。风格体现在文艺作品内容和形式的各要素中。"根据这个定义，我们可以得出风格是难于模仿的结论。如果我们承认不同作家的生活经历、立场观点、艺术素养和个性特征不可能一样，那么以此为基础形成的写作风格必然不同。如果这一观点成立，那么不同译者也自然有着各自不同的翻译风格，译作对原文风格的再现也不免带上译者的个人风格。看下面的原文和两个译文：

【原文】And I want beauty in my life. I have seen beauty in a sunset and in the spring woods and in the eyes of divers women, but now these happy accidents of light and color no longer thrill me. And I want beauty in my life itself, rather than in such chances as befall it. It seems to me that many actions of my life were beautiful, very long ago, when I was young in an evanished world of friendly girls, who were all more lovely than any girl is nowadays. For women now are merely more or less good-looking, and as I know, their looks when at their best have been painstakingly enhanced and edited. But I would like this life which moves and yearns in me, to be able itself to attain to comeliness, though but in transitory performance. The life of a butterfly, for example, is just a graceful gesture: and yet, in that its loveliness is complete and perfectly rounded in itself, I envy this bright flicker through existence. And the nearest I can come to my ideal is punctiliously to pay my bills, be polite to my wife, and contribute to deserving charities: and the program does not seem, somehow, quite adequate. There are my books, I know; and there is beauty "embalmed and treasured up" in many pages of my books, and in the books of other persons, too, which I may read at will: but this desire inborn in me is not to be satiated by making marks upon paper, nor by deciphering them. In short, I am enamored of that flawless beauty of which all poets have perturbedly divined the existence somewhere, and which life as men know it simply does not afford nor anywhere foresee. (见"第二十一届韩素音青年翻译奖竞赛"，《中国翻译》，2009（6），第78页)

【译文一】我希望生活中有美。我曾在落日余晖、春日树林和女人的眼中看见过美，可如今与这些光彩邂逅已不再令我激动。我期盼的是生命本身之美，而非偶然降临的美的瞬间。我觉得很久以前我生活行为中也充溢着美，那时我尚年轻，置身于一群远比当今姑娘更为友善可爱的姑娘之中，置身于一个如今已消失的世界。时下女人不过是多少显得有几分姿色，而据我所知，她们最靓丽的容颜都经过煞费苦心的设色敷彩。但我希望这在我心中涌动并企盼的生命能绽放出自身之美，纵然其美丽会转瞬即逝。比如蝴蝶的一生不过翩然一瞬，但在这翩然一瞬间，其美丽得以完善，其生命得以完美。我羡慕一生中有这种美丽闪烁。可我最接近我理想生活的行为只是付账单一丝不苟，对妻子相敬如宾，捐善款恰宜至当，而这些无论如何也远远不够。当然，还有我那些书，在我自己撰写以及我可随意翻阅的他人所撰写的书中，都有美"封藏"于万千书页之间。但我与生俱来的这种欲望并不满足于在纸上写美或从书中读美。简而言之，我所迷恋的是那种无暇之美，那种天下诗人在志忑中发现存在于某处的美，那种世人所知的凡尘生活无法赐予也无法预见的美。（曹明伦 译）

【译文二】我渴望自己的生命之美。我领略过落日余晖的美景，春日林中绿色的风情，风姿各异女人的眼神。往日里光影斑斓的愉悦时刻，如今已不再令我怦然心动。我希冀生命的本色之美，而不再是与美的邂逅相遇。我生命中那久违的青春涌动才是美之绚烂，那时我依然年轻，置身于花季少女的国度，她们与我共享着纯真的友情。如今这国度早已不在，那时的女孩比现在的任何一个都更加可爱。如今的女人仅有着娇好的面容，据我所知，她们生命中最靓丽的容颜在煞费苦心中得以增色，留下了人工剪辑的痕迹。我愿充满激情与渴望的此生，凭借自身的力量攀援上升，抵达尽善尽美的境界，哪怕只有片刻的辉煌。看那蝴蝶的一生，虽只有瞬间的优雅闪现，但瞬间中的妩媚无与伦比、圆满一生。我妒嫉那个一生闪亮扑动双翅的精灵。而我的理想却远离完美，充其量不过是认认真真的付账、对妻子的善待与敬重，还有刻意筛选的慈善之举：我的人生规划似乎颇有些不合时宜。我当然知道自己还拥有作品，其中不乏"永留尘世瑰宝"之美，这种美也留香于我随意翻阅的他人作品。然而，我植根心底的欲望却远远超出了我在纸上的留痕，也绝非仅仅是对于书本的解读。一言以蔽之，我所痴情的是无瑕之美，是诗人的诚惶诚恐及奉若神明；是凡夫俗子的不可企及和无法预知。（本书中句子或段落的译文，包括英译汉和汉译英，除了已注明译者之外，均为本书编者所译，后文不再一一标注。）

两个译文对原文的理解个别地方虽略有出入，但它们之间的最大区别就是风格的不同。虽然译文的风格理论上应当贴近原作，但同一作品不同译本的风格总是存在着差异。鉴于译者很难去模仿他人的风格，因此，译者在翻译时应选择适合自己的作品。

三、文学翻译中的修辞格

英语中的修辞格有几十种，修辞手法的运用可以产生某种特殊效果：如生动活泼、幽默诙谐、意境深远、富于美感等。常见的修辞方法包括：比喻、夸张、双关、仿拟、排比、移就、拟人等等。由于不同民族的生活环境、风俗习惯、思维方式和审美情趣的差异，修辞格的翻译有时不能采取直译，而是要根据不同语境进行灵活处理，以达到修辞格翻译的准确、简明、连贯和得体。看下面的例子：

【原文】Down in the valley where the green grass grows, there sat Dee Dee as pretty as a rose. Antony sucked in his breath audibly — what a beauty! Tall and lissome, long legs and magnificent breasts, and a face to rival Helen's — lush red lips, skin as flawless as a rose petal, lustrous blue eyes between thick dark lashes, and absolutely straight flaxen hair that hung down her back like a sheet of hammered silver-gilt. (Cintra Wilson: Colors insulting to nature, New York, U.S.A: Fourth Estate, 2004)

【译文一】山谷下绿草如茵，迪迪就坐在那里，<u>美丽得像一朵玫瑰</u>。安东尼出声地吸了一口气，真是太美了！高挑柔美的身材，修长的双腿，挺拔的胸部，<u>一张可与海伦媲美的脸</u>－水嫩般的红唇，<u>肌肤如玫瑰花瓣完美无瑕</u>，浓黑的睫毛，蓝色的双眼炯炯有光，亚麻色的头发笔直地垂在后背，如同打造的一方镀金银片。

【译文二】山谷下绿草如茵，<u>如花似玉</u>的迪迪就坐在那里。安东尼惊呆了，真是太美了！高挑柔美的身材，修长的双腿，挺拔的胸部，秀美的脸庞无与伦比——水嫩般的红唇，<u>肌肤宛如美玉无瑕</u>，浓黑的睫毛，蓝色的双眼炯炯有光，亚麻色的头发笔直地垂向后背，如同打造的一方镀金银片。

在把英语中各种"比喻"翻译成汉语时，译者必须考虑原喻体是否保留或替换，也要考虑在多大程度上能够保留或替换原喻体。上面【译文一】中保留原喻体的情况多一些，【译文二】保留原喻体少一些。两译文中至少划线部分均有可能引起争议。关键的问题在于，译者能否吃透原文并把握好目的语读者的接受度。例如，"一张可与海伦媲美的脸"和"秀美的脸庞无与伦比"哪个更好？如果读者具备相关的背景知识，知道海伦（Helen）是希腊神话中斯巴达王的妻子，是世界上最美的女人，前者译文似乎更好一些，而后者译文对于不知海伦何许人的读者则更容易理解。

再看一个汉译英的例子：

【原文】父亲在墨水河里玩过水，<u>他的水性好像是天生的</u>，奶奶说他见了水比见了亲娘还急。父亲五岁时，<u>就像小鸭子一样潜水</u>，粉红的屁股眼儿朝着天，双脚高举。父亲知道，<u>墨水河底的淤泥乌黑发亮，柔软得像油脂一样</u>。河边潮湿的滩涂上，<u>丛生着灰绿色的芦苇和鹅绿色车前草</u>，还有贴地生的野葛蔓，支支直立的接骨草。滩涂的淤泥上，印满螃蟹纤细的爪迹。（莫言《红高粱》）

【译文】Father had gone swimming so often in the Black Water River that <u>he seemed born to it</u>. Grandma said that <u>the sight of the river excited him more than the sight of his own mother</u>. At the age of five, <u>he could dive like a duckling</u>, his little pink asshole bobbing above the surface, his feet sticking straight up. He knew that <u>the muddy riverbed was black and shiny, and as spongy as soft tallow</u>, and that the banks were covered with pale-green reeds and plantain the color of goose-down, coiling vines and stiff bone grass hugged the muddy ground, which was crisscrossed with the tracks of skittering crabs. (Translated by Howard Goldblatt)

葛浩文（Howard Goldblatt）是当今西方最杰出的汉英文学翻译家，他在处理这段翻译中的比喻时，完全采用直译的方法，只要不影响读者理解尽量保留了原文中的喻体。即使是文化负载词语的翻译，他也尽量采用直译。葛浩文的翻译策略反映了他对跨文化翻译的态度及驾驭能力。

第五节 非文学翻译的难点

一、非文学语篇中的知识

非文学翻译语篇往往涉及不同领域内的知识，译者缺乏相关知识则无法完成翻译任务。有些知识属于一般性的，只要有所了解即能理解语篇并翻译。看下面的例子：

【例1】

【原文】Once dominated by boutique players, the stakes have been raised in the provision of fund administration services for alternative investments. While alternative investments are becoming part of the mainstream, increasing interest in hybrid structures is introducing a greater degree of complexity into service provision. However, fund administration providers have it all to play for and the still healthy fees associated with the service mean that providers are readily upgrading their services. (选自 Fund Administratiion, FTSE Global Markets, May/June 2006)

【译文】另类投资曾经只属于少数玩家，如今也能通过基金管理服务筹措到大笔资金。随着另类投资的渐入主流，人们对混合结构产品的兴趣不断增加，基金管理服务也变得越来越复杂，基金管理服务商将各种业务大包大揽，但资金运行依然良好，这意味着服务商正在提高自身的服务水平。

笔者曾就这段文字做过调查，发现那些对"另类投资"（alternative investment）概念不甚了解的同学，仿佛坠入云里雾里，不知道本段讲的是什么。不过只要对另类投资概念大致有所了解，并知道英语中的 alternative investment 就是汉语中的"另类投资"，即能够迅速理解并翻译。

【例2】

【原文】In order to support substantial deviation from business-as-usual emissions levels in forested developing countries, predictable and sustainable sources of public and market-linked financing for REDD will be required throughout Step 3. For the period 2013–2017, the vast majority of financing for REDD should come from public and market-linked sources, such as the auctioning of emission allowances. To the extent that parties decide to create a market mechanism to allow REDD credits to offset developed country emissions obligations, such credits should be in addition to domestic reductions of at least 30% in Annex I parties as a group and to reductions achieved through REDD as part of developing countries 20–35% deviation from business-as-usual and could only be brought into the compliance system in Phase 3, when a country has achieved MRV-able national-level emission reductions from REDD.（翻译公司材料）

【译文】为支持林木丰富的发展中国家大幅减少正常的排放量，在步骤3的实施过程中需要有用于 REDD 的可预见和可持续的公共资金和与市场挂钩的资金。2013—2017 年，用于 REDD 的绝大多数资金将来源于公众资金和与市场挂钩的资金，如拍卖排放津贴。当一个国家已经完成了 REDD 的 MRV-able 国家减排量时，若各方决定建立市场机制以准许用 REDD 额度抵消发展中国家的减排义务，这种额度应为除了完成附件 1 中各方作为一个群体规定的至少 30% 的国内减排量，和作为发展中国家的一部分通过 REDD 完成的排放量以外，与正常水平有 20–35% 的偏离，且要在阶段 3 被纳入到遵约体制中。（翻译公司译文）

本段翻译涉及两方面的问题：一是诸如 REDD 等缩略语的意义和表达的问题（REDD=Reducing Emissions from Deforestation and Forest Degradation in Developing Countries = 减少发展中国家由于伐林和林地退化产生的排放），二是相关背景知识的问题。我们很难想象，一个不了解文中所讲内容的译者能够完成翻译任务。由于译文目标读者是相关专业人士，故译者保留了原文中 REDD 和 MRV-able 的形式。

二、非文学翻译中的术语翻译

在非文学翻译当中，术语翻译起到非常关键的作用。在拥有良好双语知识的基础之上，熟知术语的译者才能够将专业领域的文章翻译好，能够让专业人士读懂。

【原文】The boom in alternative investment vehicles such as private-equity firms and hedge funds is wonderful for those who earn a fortune working for them. More debatable is whether it is good for the efficiency of the capital markets, and thus for the economy as a whole. Private-equity firms have been accused of wrecking companies since the 1980s, if not before. Hedge funds have come under heavy fire since George Soros forced sterling out of Europe's exchange-rate mechanism in 1992. (The Economist print edition, September 28, 2006)

【译文】另类投资工具的迅速发展，如私募股权公司和对冲基金的发展，对于那些获利颇丰的业内人士来说，无疑是件大好事。但此类发展是否对资本市场的效率乃至整个经济结构有利，人们众说纷纭。至少从上个世纪 80 年代开始，私募股权公司就常被指责为"打捞公司"，对冲基金则因 1992 年乔治·索罗斯迫使英镑退出欧洲货币汇率机制而臭名昭著。（学生译文）

应当说"对冲基金"（hedge fund）、"资本市场"（capital market）等术语如今已逐渐成为人们常识的一部分，而"另类投资"（alternative investment）、"私募股权"（private equity）等术语对于一部分译者来说，还需要进一步学习掌握。译者熟悉术语的基本概念，并掌握它们在译语中的对等表达是必须的，否则就无法完成翻译任务。

三、程式化语言的翻译

法律条文、合同条款等许多非文学翻译中的程式化语言俯拾皆是，对于译者来说唯一的、也是最好的办法就是花大力气把它们掌握好，特别是把程式化语言的句法特征进行分类整理。译者一旦做足功课就会发现，其实这类语言是有规律可循的，并非人们想象的那样难。看下面的例子：

【原文】Governing Law & Dispute resolution—The governing Law of this agreement shall be that of the People's Republic of China. The parties will attempt to resolve any disputes amicably. In the event of such amicable settlement not forthcoming within thirty days of the dispute, the Parties shall submit their disputes for arbitration before the China International Economic and Trade Arbitration Commission and the arbitration is final and binding to both parties.（翻译公司材料）

【译文一】政府的法律与争议解决——本协议政府的法律应为中华人民共和国法律。当事人将努力友好协商解决争议。如果争议发生后 30 天之内协商无法解决，双方应将争议上交给中国国际经济贸易仲裁委员会，并且仲裁是最终的，约束双方。

【译文二】适用法律与争端解决——本协议适用中华人民共和国法律。双方应友好解决任何争端。如争端在三十天内仍未友好解决，双方应将争端提交中国国际经济贸易仲裁委员会进行仲裁，仲裁是终局的，对双方均具有约束力。（翻译公司译文）

"将争端提交 XXXX 仲裁委员会进行仲裁，仲裁是终局的，对双方均具有约束力"是中文合同中的程式化语言，与英文具有严格的对应，不能单纯按照英文字面进行翻译。译文二中"终局的"是指本次仲裁判决就是最后一次仲裁判决，不像法律诉讼那样，在一审判决后，仍然可以上诉要求进行二审判决。

本章主要参考文献：

翁显良:《意态由来画不成？》，北京：中国对外翻译出版公司，1983。

严明，宋月霜:《大学英语翻译教学理论与实践》，吉林出版集团有限责任公司，2009。

郑海凌:"文学翻译的本质特征"，《中国翻译》，1998（2）。

Mary Snell-Hornby：*Translation Studies: An Integrated Approach.* Revised ed. Amsterdam: John Benjamins, 1995.

Peter Newmark: "Non-literary in the Light of Literary Translation".

http://www.jostrans.org/issue01/art_newmark.php

翻译练习一

1. 将下面诗歌译成汉语：

Creation Speaks
Sharon Du Preez, New Zealand

I see the mountains with peaks of white
The setting sun lighting them ablaze
A butterfly flutters from plant to plant
Beauty around me transfixing my gaze

I see tulips slowly opening their hearts
To the bustling bees going about their day
A cottonwool cloud floats slowly by
The breeze ripples the mirrorlike bay

I see a horse majestic and strong
Gallop across an emerald plain
The clouds push together in a black frenzy
The world explodes with the smells of rain

The world is filled with colours and smells
Flavours and sights, feelings and fears
With rainbows and wonder and thunderous sounds
And many more things which nobody hears

All was made by our awesome creator
For our enjoyment, to use and admire
And my soul is filled to overflowing
With love and worship—a consuming fire.

2. 将下面段落译成汉语：

Since translating is a skill, which requires considerable practice, most people assume that it can be taught, and to an extent this is true. But it is also true that really exceptional translators are born, not made. Potential translators must have a high level of aptitude for the creative use of language, or they are not likely to be outstanding in their profession. Perhaps the greatest benefit from instruction in translating is to become aware of one's own limitations, something which a translator of Steinbeck's *Of Mice and Men* into Chinese should have learned. Then he would not have translated English mule-skinner into a Chinese phrase meaning "a person who skins the hide off of mules".

For many people the need for human translators seems paradoxical in this age of computers. Since modern computers can be loaded with dictionaries and grammars, why not let computers do the work?

Computers can perform certain very simple interlingual tasks, providing there is sufficient pre-editing and post-editing. But neither advertising brochures nor lyric poetry can ever be reduced to the kind of logic required of computer programs. Computer printouts of translation can often be understood, if the persons involved already know what the text is supposed to say. But the results of machine translating are usually in an unnatural form of language and sometimes just plain weird. Furthermore, real improvements will not come from merely doctoring the program or adding rules. The human brain is not only digital and analogic, but it also has a built-in system of values, which gives it a componentially incalculable advantage over machines. Human translators will always be necessary for any text, which is stylistically appealing and semantically complex — which includes most of what is worth communicating in another language.

The most difficult texts to translate are not, however, highly literary productions, but rather those texts which say nothing, the type of language often used by politicians and delegates to international forums. In fact, a group of professional translators at the United Nations headquarters in New York City have insisted that the most difficult text to translate is one in which the speaker or writer has attempted to say nothing. The next most difficult type of text is one filled with irony and sarcasm, since in a written text the paralinguistic clues to the meaning are usually much more difficult to detect than when someone is speaking. And perhaps the third most difficult type of text is a book or article on translating in which the illustrative examples rarely match... （Eugene A. Nida: *Language, Culture, and Translating*, Shanghai Foreign Language Education Press, 1993.）

第二章

语料库与翻译

20世纪60年代中期，诺姆·乔姆斯基（Noam Chomsky）在其转换生成语法理论的基础上，提出了语言能力（competence）和语言行为（performance）的概念。乔姆斯基所说的"语言能力"是指抽象的语言能力，他所说的"语言行为"才是人们通常所理解的语言使用能力。乔姆斯基认为，语料不过是语言行为的取样，与人的语言能力完全是两回事。所以，分析真实语篇对解释语言的语法不可能起任何作用，更不用说形成一种普遍的语言学理论。语言学的任务是研究语言能力，而不是语言行为。受到乔姆斯基语言学理论的影响，20世纪语言研究的总体特征可以用"高度抽象"加以概括。

20世纪90年代以来，在计算语言学界刮起了一股"经验主义"的旋风。所谓经验主义方法就是一种基于语料库的方法、一种基于概率统计的方法。大批具有计算机专业背景的学者和研究人员开始进入这一领域，语言研究的高度抽象趋势也由此失去了主导地位。人们发现经验主义的研究方法依然有其合理成分，而理性主义的研究方法也存在缺陷。以自然语言处理研究为例，IBM语音研究小组基于理性主义的语音识别系统研究举步维艰，于是对乔氏理论产生了怀疑，该项目负责人弗雷德·贾里尼克（Fred Jelinek）试图把有关语言学家排除在项目之外，他不无讽刺地说道："每当我解雇一个语言学家，语音识别系统的性能就会改进一步。"（Every time I fire a linguist the performance of the recognizer improves.）（冯志伟："自然语言处理中的概率语法（修改稿）"，《当代语言学》，2005（2）。）贾里尼克的话相当偏激，但经验主义研究方法有其合理性却得到了证实。后来研究表明，语言的运用离不开具体的社会文化因素，光凭抽象的"语言能力"难以完成语言交际任务，正如著名学者戴维·沃克（David Walker）所言："人类对语言的领悟和创造依赖于以往具体的语言经验，而不是依赖于抽象的语法规则。"（转引自王建新：《计算机语料库的建设与应用》，北京：清华大学出版社，2005，第113页。）

现代语料库是基于当代信息技术的真实语言材料处理、存储和检索系统。近二十年来，基于语料库的语言研究取得了长足发展，与之相关的语言研究方法也得到了学界的广泛认同。基于语料库的语言研究克服了以往规范性研究中的个人主观性和局限性，可以充分地观察和发现更多的语言事实，从而充分地描写和解释。对于翻译而言，语料库可为翻译提供如下帮助：

1. 语料库提供的都是真实的语例，具有现实指导意义。因为凭空臆造的翻译文本很容易误导读者，或造成理解困难。
2. 语料库可以使译者认识自己的语言本领，清楚地看到自己平时没有留意但却是经常使用的语言形式。
3. 语料库可以提供词语使用的语境，通过条件检索，确定译文的通用性。
4. 语料库为语法提供语义基础。通常一个具有两种意思的词也意味着它有两种语法结构。
5. 语料库提供大量语言使用的变体以及新鲜而有创意的形式，体现出语言的最新发展和变化。

第一节 语料库的定义及其类型

一、什么是语料库

冯志伟在《语料库语言学与计算语言学研究丛书》序中把语料库定义为："为了一个或多个应用目标而专门收集的、有一定结构的、有代表性的、可被计算机程序检索的、具有一定规模的语料的集合。"

二、语料库的类型

1. 按语料选取的时间划分，可分为历时语料库（diachronic corpus）和共时语料库（synchronic corpus）。
2. 按语料的加工深度划分，可分为标注语料库（annotated corpus）和非标注语料库（non-annotated corpus）。
3. 按语料库的结构划分，可分为平衡结构语料库（balance structure corpus）和自然随机结构的语料库（random structure corpus）。

4. 按语料库的用途划分，可分为通用语料库（general corpus）和专用语料库（specialized corpus）。专用语料库又可以进一步根据使用的目的来划分，例如，又可以进一步分为语言学习者语料库（learner corpus）、语言教学语料库（pedagogical corpus）。

5. 按语料库的表达形式划分，可分为口语语料库（spoken corpus）和文本语料库。

6. 按语料库中语料的语种划分，语料库也可分为单语语料库（monolingual corpora），双语语料库（bilingual corpora）和多语语料库（multilingual corpora）。多语种语料库又可以再分为比较语料库（comparable corpora）和平行语料库（parallel corpora）。比较语料库的目的侧重于特定语言现象的对比，而平行语料库的目的侧重于获取对应的翻译实例。

7. 按语料库的动态更新程度划分，可分为参考语料库（reference corpus）和监控语料库（monitor corpus）。参考语料库原则上不作动态更新，而监控语料库则需要不断地进行动态更新。

第二节 语料库揭示了语言的本质

语料库的出现使人们原先无法凭直觉完成的工作有望得以完成，语料库不仅为人们提供了真实的语料，而且提供了相关的统计数据，人们可以据此验证现行理论是否正确以及构建新的理论。语料库对人们认识语言最大的启发是，人们使用的绝大部分语言均具有约定俗成和可预见的特点，换句话说，人们总是无意识地重复着语言中业已存在的表达方式。

约翰·辛克莱在《语料库、检索与搭配》一书中提出两个概念，一个是"熟语原则"(the idiom principle)，另一个是"开放选择原则"(the open-choice principle)。(John Sinclair: Corpus, Concordance, Collocation. Oxford: Oxford University Press, 1991.)所谓熟语原则是指母语使用者头脑中储存有大量"预制语块"（prefabricated chunks），在表达思想时首先选择使用这些语块，所谓开放选择原则是指母语使用者按照语法规则构造新的表达方式，通常在缺乏预制语块的情况下才去使用。由此可见，语块是语言中的最基本单位，每个语块均作为整体记忆，在使用时直接提取。辛克莱的发现可解释如下事实，即人们为什么在用母语表达思想时，其关注点并不在词汇和句式的选择上，而是在所表达内容的思考上。预制语块研究无论对外语学习还是翻译都具有重要意义，它强调了外语学习大量接触语言本身的重要，也揭示了译者（特别是译入语为非母语的译者）在翻译时出现诸多问题的根本原因。

有越来越多的证据表明，人们在使用语言进行交际时，在很大程度上依赖于头脑中存储的预制语块，使用外语进行交际时常出现的各种不适当，主要是因为缺乏足够的语块储存，而语法规则的掌握对于外语正确使用的作用非常有限。因此，在语料库语言学家看来，语言就是词语的用法，语言的语法存在于词汇当中，词汇和语法没有原则性的区别。为了说明问题，看下面的一些真实例子：

【例1】The price of the computer is too expensive.
正确的说法应该是 The computer is too expensive. 或者 The price of the computer is too high. 在英语中 price 和 expensive 不搭配。

【例2】A: How do you sell the fish?
B: If you give me the money, I'll give you the fish.
对话是笔者在英国一家鱼店听到的，其中 A 是中国人，B 是英国人。由于英语中没有 How do you sell... 的说法，B 将问话理解为以什么方式才能买他的鱼。更大的可能性是，他在嘲笑买鱼者错误的英语表达。

【例3】我出去的时候，平时用公共汽车。
在这一具体语境中，汉语说"坐公共汽车"，不说"用公共汽车"。

【例4】他们谈一谈了一下儿……，就开心地回家了。
中国人不可能写出"谈一谈了一下儿"这样的句子。

【例5】A: I think Peter drank a bit too much at the party yesterday.
B: Eh, tell me about it. He always drinks much.
A: When we arrived he drank beer. Then Mary brought him some vodka. Later he drank some wine. Oh,

too much.

　　B: Why are you telling me this? I was there.

　　A: Yes, but you told me to tell you about it.

英语中 tell me about it 是套话，相当于汉语里的"那还用说，就是嘛！"A 仅仅从字面上理解，没有结合语境理解这句话的真正内涵。

　　分析一下上面的例子可以看出，尽管语言内部存在着规则系统，但规则对于人们学习掌握语言并不起确定性作用，人们对语言的掌握主要依赖于具体的语言经验。因此，学好一门外语最好的办法是大量接触语言实际，以便在大脑中储存足够的语块。只要有了足够的语块作为基础，翻译也就变得容易起来。学好两种语言对于翻译的重要怎样强调也不过分，这一点一直以来人们强调得不够。翻译理论只在宏观层面揭示翻译中的某种真相，但它们不能代替译者的语言运用能力，而恰恰是这种语言运用能力，决定着译者的水平和翻译质量的高低。

第三节　语料库对翻译的验证功能

　　语料库是真实语料的集合，反映的是语言的自然现象。通过语料库人们可以确定词语搭配和习惯用法是否正确，也可以验证句法结构是否有问题。根据帕特里克·温德姆·汉克斯（Patrick Wyndham Hanks 1996）的观点，词语之间的搭配是有限的，而词语可使用的句式结构大多不超过六种，英语中大多数词的使用仅局限于一种句式。看下面的两个列表，它们反映的是两种极端情况。表 2.1 具有结构复杂（syntactically complex），语义直接（semantically straightforward）的特点，表 2.2 具有结构简单（syntactically complex），直接宾语丰富的特点。（Patrick Wyndham Hanks: "Contextual Dependency and Lexical Sets", *International Journal of Corpus Linguistics* 1 (1), John Benjamins, 1996.）

表 2.1：Bother 的各种句法模式

Lemma: bother, bothers, bothering, bothered
Pattern 1.1: [[Human]] [[Not]] bother to [[Do]]
Pattern 1.2: [[Human]] [[Not]] bother [[Do]]+ing
Examples: They did not bother to vote.	If you think I have no chance, I won't bother risking disappointment.
Pattern 2: [[Human]] [[Cannot]] be bothered to [Do]]
Example: The calculations are so tedious that theorists can't be bothered to do them.
Pattern 3.1: [[Human]] [[Not]] bother about [[Something or Someone]]
Pattern 3.2: [[Human]] [[Not]] bother with [[Something or Someone]]
Examples: He did not bother about the noise of the typewriter because Danny could not hear it above the noise of the tractor.	Don't bother about us.	The only rocks worth bothering with are 'hard' rocks.	Who bothers with such folk?
Pattern 4.1: [[Human]] [[Not]] be bothered about [[Something]]
Pattern 4.2 [[Human]] [[Not]] be bothered with [[Something]]
Examples: The only thing I'm bothered about is the well-being of the club.	I'm not particularly bothered about how I look.	Mrs Sprott didn't want to be bothered with such things.
Pattern 5.1: [[Human]] be bothered by [[Problem]]
Pattern 5.2: [[Human]] be bothered that [CLAUSE]
Pattern 5.3: [[Problem]] bother [[Human]]
Examples: Ava was bothered by my infidelity.	Poor Philip was particularly bothered by this symptom.	Neal Grossman is bothered that the press has dubbed this 'California cuisine'.	It is an issue which bothers journalists.	... all hot and bothered.
Pattern 6: [[Human $_i$]] [[Not]] bother [[Human $_j$]]

Examples: She decided not to bother him now with the Russian material. | I'm sorry to bother you at work. | I realize this has been a blow to you, Mr Pertwee: we won't bother you much longer.

Pattern 7: [[Fact]] [[Not]] bother [[Human]]

Example: Looks don't bother me; it's personality that counts.

表 2.2：abandon（只用作动词）的直接宾语

Lemma: abandon, abandons, abandoning, abandoned

Pattern: [[Human]] abandon [[Anything]] (to [[Abstract[Bad]]]] or [[Wild_Creature]])

Presupposition: The abandoner formerly had possession or control over the thing abandoned and found it useful or pleasing.

Implication: The abandoner has relinquished possession or control of it and gone away, leaving it to its fate, either a) because of force majeure, or b) because he/she no longer wants or values it, or c) because he/she can no longer look after it.

Types of direct object, with examples:

1.1 [[Human]] (one's wife, children, new-born baby, lover, client, ... a political party, the working classes) or [[Animal[[Pet]]]] (dog, cat, ...)

1.2 [[Vehicle]] (which is, of course, a kind of physical object, but the implications are more specific; car, van, lorry, bicycle, motorbike ...)

1.3 [[Physical Object]] (a gun, hammock, sofa, rhubarb tart, school clothes, piano, luggage, ...)

1.4 [[Location]] (a stronghold, a military position, the road, a house, home, Birmingham, Warsaw, a factory, one's country, a backwater, ...)

1.5 [[Abstract]] (one's principles, position, a belief, idea, policy, theory, plan, system; a pretence, certainty, hope, caution, commitment, control, ...)

1.6 [[Process]] (which is, of course, itself a kind of abstract thing: a debate, discussion, experiment, attempt, practice, a career, a way of life, the armed struggle, a race, an event, a match, a meeting, ...)

上面两表反映的是两种极端的情况，英语中大部分词语的句式结构和搭配复杂情况都介于两表之间。既然词语的句式结构和搭配都是有章可循的，都能在语料库中得到反映，我们就可以利用语料库对翻译的正确与否进行验证。看下面的各个例子：

【例1】

【原文】雨声渐渐的住了，窗帘后隐隐的透进清光来。推开窗户一看，呀！凉云散了，树叶的残滴，映著月儿，好似莹光千点，闪闪烁烁的动着。——真没想到苦雨孤灯之后，会有这么一幅清美的图画！（冰心《笑》）

【译文】As the rain gradually ceased to patter, a glimmer of light began to filter into the room through the window curtain. I opened the window and looked out. Ah, the rain clouds had vanished and the remaining raindrops on the tree leaves glistened tremulously under the moonlight like myriads of fireflies. To think that there should appear before my eyes such a beautiful sight after the miserable rain on a lonely evening! (Translated by Zhang Peiji)

如果想验证一下 the rain gradually ceased to patter 是否合适，可在英语单语库中输入关键词，找到下雨场景中 patter 一词的用法，下面是在美国语料库（americancorpus.org）中找到的例子：

● Rain began to patter against the roof.
● Behind him the rain began to patter harder and louder on the cement, like a train gathering steam.
● Rain began to patter against the sliding glass door, and I turned my head from the fan to watch the rain.
● A little light rain began to patter and strengthened as we made our way to a low, windowless building with an industrial look to it.

由于没有找到 gradually, cease 和 patter 三个词相关的搭配，再次利用语料库寻找 "雨渐渐的住了" 的说法，这次在美国语料库（americancorpus.org）和英国国家语料库 (corpus.byu.edu/bnc) 中找到了下面的例子：
- The rain died off at sunset.
- The wind and rain have died down.
- The rain has died down, leaving a general mist.
- Gradually, the rain petered out. A wind blew. All was silence, save for the dripping roof outside.(bnc)
- The rain will gradually die down from the west, to leave only a few showers in the south-east by the end of the day.(bnc)

在英国国家语料库 (corpus.byu.edu/bnc) 中还找到与原文场景类似的一段话：

As the rain gradually died away, birds began to fight and squabble like fractious children just allowed out after being cooped up indoors; but then they didn't have leaky roofs; neither did they have to climb up there as soon as it was light to inspect the damage; or have a meeting with Leo. （Richmond, Emma. Richmond, Surrey: A Stranger's Trust. Mills & Boon, 1991）

雨渐渐的住了，鸟儿开始玩耍争斗起来，就像关在屋子里调皮的孩子刚刚被放出来。然而，鸟儿们没有漏雨的屋顶，也不必爬到上面去……

通过语料库的调查，发现"雨渐渐的住了"在英语里有若干表达方式（to die away, to die down, to die off, to peter out）等，其中 rain + die down 的搭配最为普遍。其他的表达也有"渐渐停止"的意思。就"雨渐渐的住了"一句翻译而言，将其翻译为 As the rain gradually died away 似乎比较合适。

【例2】

【原文】树干高三十多米，在树干上钻一个直径5厘米的孔洞，二三小时内，就可流出一二十升金黄色的油状树液，成分十分接近柴油。

【初译】When drilling a 5 cm-diameter hole on its trunk, this over-30m-high tree may flow 10–20 liters of golden oily sap in 2–3 hours. The components of the sap are similar to those of diesel.

译文有个明显的错误，分句中 drilling 的逻辑主语不能是 tree，因此改译如下：

【二译】Once a 5cm-diameter hole is drilled on its trunk, this over-30m-high tree may flow 10–20 liters of golden oily sap in 2–3 hours. The components of the sap are similar to those of diesel.

查证词语搭配：golden oily sap 和 components of the sap。发现 components 常指机器的部件，树干中流出的液体成分可用 composition。

【三译】Once a 5cm-diameter hole is drilled on its trunk, this over-30m-high tree may flow 10–20 liters of golden oily sap in 2–3 hours. The composition of the sap is similar to that of diesel.

查证 on its trunk 用法是否正确，因为英语中一些类似的情况常常使用介词 in。发现 drill a hole 后面只跟介词 through 和 in，下面是（http://corpus.byu.edu/time/）中的几个例句：

- He drilled a hole right through his foot.
- Three men had drilled a hole in the road behind their car.
- They drilled a hole in the floor to the bank's data-processing center.
- Carefully the diggers drilled a hole in the side of the stone block.

综合考虑后给出最后译文：

【四译】Once a 5cm-diameter hole is drilled in its trunk, this over-30m-high tree will flow 10–20 liters of golden oily sap in 2–3 hours. The composition of the sap is similar to that of diesel.

【例3】

【原文】迄今为止，180个国家与国际组织已确认参加2010年上海世博会。

【译文一】So far, 180 countries and international organizations have confirmed to attend the 2010 Shanghai World Expo.

(http://en.beijing2008.cn/news/olympiccities/shanghai/n214198803.shtml)

【译文二】So far, 180 countries and international organizations have confirmed their presence at the 2010 Shanghai World Expo.

语料库中找不到 have confirmed to do something 的说法。前面我们曾提到过，英语词语的句式结构一般不超过六种。To confirm to do something 的表达形式一般被认为是不存在的，该词的主要结构有三种：to confirm + NP, to confirm having done something 以及 to confirm + that clause。英语中还有一些动词也不用不定式，如：enjoy, appreciate, excuse, miss, deny, avoid, escape, risk, mind, keep, postpone 等等。

第四节　翻译中的平行语料库运用

　　双语平行语料库建设在我国正处于起步阶段，已经建立起来的一些不是仅限于内部使用，就是收费颇高。目前中国在线翻译网提供免费的双语语料库（http://www.chinafanyi.com/juku.asp）语料有限，与单语大型语料库相比差别甚大。尽管如此，通过双语语料库协助翻译的发展趋势已经明朗。当前的网络搜索引擎可以提供范围最广的双语检索，涵盖双语语料库尚不能涵盖的语言现象。但需要注意的是，网络搜索引擎对所收录的语料没有进行人工筛分与质量评估，极有可能出现误导，因此还需要译者付出极大的努力，最终才能得到理想的译文。

　　双语平行语料库最大的优势是查询各类对等说法，如各类术语、固定表达方式、文化负载词语、引文之原文等等。假如你想知道"长期共存、互相监督、肝胆相照、荣辱与共"的英文说法，你最好到权威的双语文本中去找，因为这类说法大多已经约定俗成，查找似乎是译者的最佳选择。看下面一段双语材料：

　　【原文】坚持和完善<u>人民代表大会制度</u>，保证人民代表大会及其常委会依法履行职能，保证立法和决策更好地体现人民的意志。优化人大常委会组成人员的结构。坚持和完善<u>共产党领导的多党合作和政治协商制度</u>。坚持"<u>长期共存、互相监督、肝胆相照、荣辱与共</u>"的方针，加强同民主党派合作共事，更好地发挥我国社会主义政党制度的特点和优势。（十六大报告）

　　【译文】We should uphold and improve <u>the system of people's congresses</u> and ensure that the congresses and their standing committees exercise their functions according to law and that their legislation and policy decisions better embody the people's will. We should optimize the composition of the standing committees. We should uphold and improve <u>the system of multiparty cooperation and political consultation under the leadership of the Communist Party</u>. We should uphold the principle of "<u>long-term coexistence, mutual supervision, treating each other with all sincerity and sharing weal and woe</u>", step up our cooperation with the democratic parties and better display the features and advantages of the Chinese socialist system of political parties. （官方译文）

　　商务语篇中的许多专业术语和固定说法，在质量合格的双语文本帮助下，会节省译者许多的时间和精力。看下面的例子：

　　【原文】Starting in the United States <u>subprime mortgage market</u>, the financial crisis spread quickly, infecting the entire United States financial system and, almost simultaneously, the financial markets of other developed countries. No market was spared, from the stock markets and real estate markets of a large number of developed and <u>emerging-market economies</u>, to <u>currency markets</u> and <u>primary commodity markets</u>. The <u>credit crunch</u> following the collapse or near collapse of major financial institutions affected activity in the <u>real economy</u>, which accelerated the fall in private demand, causing the greatest recession since the Great Depression. The crisis has affected most strongly companies, incomes and employment in the financial sector itself, but also in the construction, <u>capital goods</u> and <u>durable consumer goods</u> industries where demand depends largely on credit. In the first quarter of 2009 <u>gross fixed capital formation</u> and manufacturing output in most of the world's major economies fell at double digit rates. Meanwhile problems with solvency in the non-financial sector in many countries fed back into the financial system.(Trade and Development Report, 2009, United Nations)

　　【译文】始于美国<u>次贷市场</u>的金融危机迅速蔓延，横扫整个美国金融体系，几乎同时席卷了其他发达国家的金融市场。从众多发达国家和<u>新兴市场经济体</u>的股票市场和<u>房地产市场</u>，到<u>货币市场</u>和<u>初级产品市场</u>，无一幸免。经历大型金融机构倒闭或摇摇欲坠之后，<u>信贷紧缩</u>接踵而至，影响到<u>实体经济</u>的活动，加速了私人需求的下滑，造成自大萧条以来的最大衰退。受危机影响最严重的是金融部门本身的公司、收入和就业，但也影响到建筑业、资本货物和耐用消费品这些需求严重依赖信贷的行业。2009 年第一季度，全世界主要经济体大部分固定资本形成总值和制造业产量以两位数速率下降。同时许多国家非金融部门的偿贷能力问题使金融系统雪上加霜。

问题是质量合格的双语文本并不好找，互联网上的许多内容良莠不齐，在这种情况下译者在参考别人双语材料的同时也要进行验证，否则也难免会出现问题。验证的方法可从英汉两种语言中查找有关对等说法的定义。下面我们以 capital goods 和"资本货物"以及 credit crunch 和"信贷紧缩"为例，查找一下它们各自的定义：

capital goods: goods used in production: goods that are used in the production of other goods, as opposed to being sold to consumers. （Encarta® World English Dictionary© & (P)2009 Microsoft Corporation.）

资本货物：企业用来生产产品的任何货品。此类货物不直接用于满足人类消费的需要，而是用来生产其他的货物。

credit crunch: a situation in which the amount of available credit in an economy is restricted and so slows down economic activity. （Encarta® World English Dictionary© & (P)2009 Microsoft Corporation.）

信贷紧缩：指因为信贷风险增加，银行、其他机构或个人不愿向企业贷款。简言之就是减少市场货币投放量，造成各经济主体资金紧张。

将两对英汉定义进行比较，结果发现，虽然解释用词和方式不同，但意义基本一致。由此我们可断定它们是对等词语。鉴于双语平行语料库不好找到，译者可以通过自建语料库完成翻译任务。例如，把一些权威性的双语文本放在一起，按照主题分门别类，需要时即可使用。

第五节 翻译中的可比语料库运用

先看一看可比语料库的定义：

A comparable corpus is one which selects similar texts in more than one language or variety. There is as yet no agreement on the nature of the similarity, because there are very few examples of comparable corpora." （The EAGLES–Expert Advisory Group on Language Engineering Standards Guidelines 1996）（http://www.ilc.pi.cnr.it/EAGLES96/browse.html）

我们这里所说的可比语料库与上面的定义略有不同，即使是上面的定义也谈到，"相似文本"有着不同的所指。这里所指的"相似文本"（similar texts）是就文本内容而言的，而且是英汉两种语言的"相似文本"。具体而言，如果我们准备翻译一篇关于金融危机方面的文章，不管是英译汉还是汉译英，首先收集一定数量关于金融危机的英语文本和汉语文本，这就是你的可比语料库。研读后你会发现，原先不懂的地方明白了许多，而且还可以找出两种语言之间的许多对等说法，此时你便可以开始翻译了。下面是 2009 年 09 月 15 日《中国证券报》上一篇文章的前三段，该文的标题是："金融危机给中国带来了什么？"翻译这篇文章时是为了给学生做练习，现拿来说明可比语料库在翻译当中的运用。

金融危机给中国带来了什么？
What Can the Financial Crisis Bring to China?

去年今日，华尔街大型投行雷曼兄弟公司宣布破产，以此为标志，百年一遇的金融危机迅速席卷全球。有赖于各国政府及时携手推出了一系列救市计划，一年后的今天，全球经济渐露复苏迹象。

One year ago today, Wall Street's major investment bank Lehman Brothers Holdings Inc. declared bankruptcy, which marked the beginning of this once-in-a-century financial turmoil that rapidly spread around the globe. All governments were urgently required to work together to unveil a series of bailout packages. One year after, the global economy is beginning to show early signs of recovery.

无论大小强弱，全球所有经济体在危机中得到的教训都是刻骨铭心的。中国作为全球最大的发展中国家，在金融危机中，沉着应对惊涛骇浪，金融危机给我们的教训和机遇显得更加珍贵。

All economies, regardless of their size and strength, have drawn lessons painfully wrought from the crisis. As the largest developing country in the world, China has remained calm and firm in response to the choppy seas of the financial turbulence, and gained lessons and opportunities of special value.

金融危机对中国最直接的影响是，自 2003 年以来中国 GDP 连续多年保持 10% 以上的高增长速度不得不放缓，国民财富遭受难以估量的损失。为了刺激经济，中央政府不得不背上 9500 亿元的财政赤字；全球资产价格的大幅缩水，使得中国的海外投资蒙受巨大的账面亏损；2 万亿美元的外汇储备面临美元贬值的威胁；全球股市下挫，无论是投资 A 股市场还是购买 QDII 产品的投资者，都饱尝市值蒸发的痛苦。

There are immediate contagious effects of the financial crisis on China: a moderate slowdown in GDP growth rate, which has remained at more than 10 per cent since 2003, and the incalculable loss of national wealth. The central government has to shoulder a burden of Rmb950bn fiscal deficit so as to stimulate national economy. China's overseas investment has suffered heavy paper losses due to the large-scale contraction in global assets. In addition, China's $2 trillion in foreign reserves are currently under the threat of the dollar depreciation. And investors in the A-share market and QDII products have suffered the emotional pain of the evaporation of market capitalization as a result of the downturn in global stock markets.

可比语料库对此篇汉英翻译的作用无须多说，只一句话就能说明问题：英译文中划线部分都是抄来的。

利用可比语料库还可以解决一些翻译中的特殊问题。目前，我国许多国家标准等效采用或修改采用 ISO、IEC、ASTM 等国际通用标准，在参考国际标准中文翻译版的基础上，按照中文的表述习惯及中国国家标准格式，制定出相关的中国国家标准。对于这些等效采用或修改采用国际标准的中国国家标准，许多英文版的翻译并没有将当初采用的英文原版纳入翻译当中，带了不必要的交流不便。在翻译这类稿件时，应该通过"相似文本"进行验证，下面，我们以国家标准《金属材料室温拉伸试验方法》(GB/T 228-2002) 的英文版翻译为例，探讨"相似文本"的验证作用。在这个国家标准的前言中就明确说明："本标准等效采用国际标准 ISO 6892:1998《金属材料室温拉伸试验》。在主要技术内容上与 ISO 6892:1998 相同，但部分技术内容较为详细和具体，编写结构不完全对应"。这给了译者非常明确的指令：要翻译好这个标准，需要找到 ISO 6892:1998 的"相似文本"。

【例 1】国际标准 ISO 6892 由 ISO/TC164 金属力学性能试验技术委员会 SC1 单轴试验分委员会制定。

本第二版取代第一版（ISO 6892:1984）。

附录 A~D 都是标准的附录。

附录 E~L 都是提示的附录。

（选自《ISO 前言》部分）

【译文一】The international standard ISO 6892 was established by ISO/TC164 Technical Committee for Metallic Mechanical Property Test - SC1 Sub-committee for Monaxial Test.

This second version substitutes the first version (ISO 6892:1984).

Appendix A-D is standard appendixes.

Appendix E-L is suggestive appendixes.

【译文二】International Standard ISO 6892 was prepared by Technical Committee ISO/TC164, Mechanical Testing of Metals, Sub-committee SC1, Uniaxial Testing.

This second version cancels and replaces the first version (ISO 6892:1984), which has been technically revised.

Annexes A to D form an integral part of this International Standard. Annexes E to L are for information only.

【译文一】是译者自己根据中文意思进行翻译的，而【译文二】就是 ISO 6892:1998 前言内容，意思原封不动，只是中文略微删节了部分内容。在这类翻译当中，直接使用英语原文即可。

【例2】1. 范围

本标准规定了金属材料拉伸试验方法的原理、定义、符合和说明、试样及其尺寸测量、试验设备、试验要求、性能测定、<u>测定结果数值修约</u>和试验报告。

本标准适用于金属材料室温拉伸性能的测定。但对于小横截面尺寸的金属产品，例如金属箔、超细丝和毛细管等的拉伸试验需要协议。

【译文一】This standard specifies the principle, definitions, symbols and descriptions, sample and dimension measurement, test equipment, test requirement, performance determination, <u>rounding off of numerical values of the test result</u> and test report of tensile testing method of metallic materials.

This standard <u>applies</u> to the determination of the tensile performance of metallic materials at ambient temperature. But an agreement <u>is needed</u> for the tensile test of metal product with small section dimension, such as metal foil, super-fine wire and capillary.

【译文二】This standard specifies the principle, definitions, symbols and descriptions, test piece and dimension measurement, test equipment, test requirement, performance determination, <u>rounding-off of the test result data</u> and test report of tensile testing method of metallic materials.

This standard is applicable to determine the tensile performance of metallic materials at ambient temperature. But an agreement must be made for the tensile test of little-cross-section metal products such as metal foil, super-fine wire and capillary.

原文中"测定结果数值修约"【译文一】表述为"rounding off of numerical values of the test result"，而"rounding off"是"四舍五入、修约"的意思，由短语转变为专有名词，这里应该使用连字符连接成为"rounding-off"，确保表述没有歧义。【译文一】将"适用于"翻译为"applies to"，没有考虑到英文当中施动与受动的关系，在这里应该采用"be +adj"形式。"需要"翻译为"is needed"是中文意思的表述。然而，我们必须区分清楚，在标准用词当中，"需要"相当于"必须"，应该翻译为"must"；类似的"应该"翻译为"shall"（不是 ought to），"宜"翻译为"should"，"可以"翻译为"may"（不是 can）等，这些在标准用词说明中都有所规定。

【例3】2. 引用标准

下列标准所包括的条文，通过在本标准中引用而构成本标准的条文。本标准出版时，所示版本均为有效。所有标准都会被修订，使用本标准的各方<u>应探讨使用下列标准最新版本的可能性</u>。

【译文一】2 Referenced Standards

The provisions contained in the following standards constitute the provisions of this standard through citation in this standard. All the showed versions are valid when this standard is published. All the standards will be revised; each party that uses this standard shall <u>search the possibility of using the latest version of the following standards</u>.

【译文二】2 Normative References

The following standards contain provisions which, through reference in this text, constitute provisions of this standard. At the time of publication, the editions indicated were valid. All standards are subject to revision, and parties to agreements based on this standard are encouraged <u>to investigate the possibility of applying the latest editions of the standards indicated below</u>.

这一节是典型的程式化语言，几乎所有国内外标准都采用与【译文二】同样的表述。【译文一】是根据中文表述进行的翻译，划线的地方还出现了词语搭配的错误。

通过上面的例子，我们可以认识到可比语料库中"相似文本"对于译文验证的重要性。对于这类程式化语言的翻译，与其辛辛苦苦翻译，不如找到"相似文本"。其中的好处不仅仅是省时省力，更重要的是能够使译文与国际通用表述保持一致。

本章主要参考文献：

冯志伟："自然语言处理中的概率语法（修改稿）"，《当代语言学》，2005（2）。

王建新：《计算机语料库的建设与应用》，北京：清华大学出版社，2005。

John Sinclair: *Corpus, Concordance, Collocation.* Oxford: Oxford University Press, 1991.

Patrick Wyndham Hanks: "Contextual Dependency and Lexical Sets," *International Journal of Corpus Linguistics* 1 (1), John Benjamins, 1996.

翻译练习二

1. 将下面段落译成汉语：

US Has Little to Teach China about Steady Economy
By Joseph Stiglitz

There is a second myth: that China would benefit from letting its exchange rate float freely, letting market forces set the price. No market economy has foresworn intervening in the exchange rate. More to the point, no market economy has foresworn macroeconomic interventions. Governments intervene regularly in financial markets, for instance, setting interest rates. Some market fundamentalists claim that governments should do none of this. But today, no country and few respectable economists subscribe to these views. The question, then, is what is the best set of interventions in the market? There is a high cost to exchange rate volatility, and countries where governments have intervened judiciously to stabilise their exchange rate have, by and large, done better than those that have not.

Exchange rate risks impose huge costs on companies; it is costly and often impossible to divest themselves of this risk, especially in developing countries. The question of exchange rate management brings up a broader issue: the role of the state in managing the economy. Today, almost everyone recognises that countries can suffer from too little government intervention just as they can suffer from too much. China has been rebalancing and, over the past two decades, markets have become more important, the government less so. But the government still plays a critical role. China's particular blend has served the Chinese well. It is not just that incomes have been rising at an amazing 9 percent annually, and that high rates have been sustained for more than two decades, but the fruits of that growth have been widely shared. From 1981 to 2001, 422m Chinese have moved out of poverty.

The US economy is growing at a third the pace of China's. Poverty is rising and median household incomes are, in real terms, declining. America's total net savings are much less than China's. China produces far more of the engineers and scientists that are necessary to compete in the global economy than the US, while America is cutting its expenditures on basic research as it increases military spending. Meanwhile, as America's debt continues to balloon, its president wants to make tax cuts for the richest people permanent. With all this in mind, China's leaders may not feel they need to seek advice from the US on how to manage either the exchange rate or the economy.

（http://news.ft.com/cms/s/79797f04-fe00-11d9-a289-00000e2511c8,dwp_uuid=2aaa1c16-afc8-11d9-ab98-00000e2511c8,ft_acl=_ftalert_ftarc_ftcol_ftfree_ftindsum_ftmywap_ftprem_ftspecial_ftsurvey_ftworldsub_ftym_ftymarc_ic_ipadm）

2. 将下面段落译成英语：

不过，中国在危机中获得的经验教训是无法用金钱衡量的。

一是中国深刻认识到，超过50%的外贸依存度减弱了中国实体经济抗击危机的能力。出口占国民经济的比重过高是经济结构不平衡的根源，而金融危机恰好为结构调整创造了良好的契机。

二是危机创造了促进全民消费的环境。当外需不值得期待的时候，扩大内需被寄予厚望。今年以来政府采取的完善社保体制、实施全面医改、国有股划转社保基金，以及正在酝酿的收入分配制度改革等都是旨在增加居民收入、拉动消费之举。

三是此次金融危机让中国外汇储备单一化的风险暴露无遗，也让中国清楚地认识到现有国际货币体系的不足之处。中国加速外汇储备资产的调整是必然之举，而中国倡导的超主权国际储备货币的建议，也有助于全球金融体系更健康。（社评："金融危机给中国带来了什么？"，《中国证券报》，2009年9月15日）

第三章

词语意义与翻译对等

第一节 意义理论与分类

关于意义的定义目前尚无定论,有关意义的理论也多种多样,如指称论(Reference Theory)、概念论(Ideational Theory 或 Conceptualism)、语境论(The Theory of Situation)等等。每一种意义理论都有其合理的成分,同时也都存在一些问题。新理论在修正旧理论的同时,也往往带来了新的问题。例如,指称论的代表人物柏拉图(Plato)、奥古斯汀(Augustinus)、维特根斯坦(Ludwig Wittgenstein)和罗素(Bertrand Russell)都认为,语言和现实之间存在着直接关系,语言形式与其代表的事物之间存在着一种直接的指称关系。而概念论则认为意义即概念,头脑中的概念是词语和事物相联系的中间环节。概念论修正了指称论的缺陷,即有意义的词语不一定都有指称,如英语中的"独角兽"(unicorn),汉语中的"美猴王"(monkey king)等等。但概念论也存在问题,因为概念本身是看不见摸不着的,因而该理论对意义的定义也是不明确的。

进入20世纪90年代,吉勒·福科尼耶(Gilles Fauconnier)等人从认知角度研究自然语言的意义,建立了心理空间理论。福科尼耶认为,句子的意义不具有逻辑表现形式,也不来源于高度形式化的句法结构。只有完整的话语加上特定的语境,才能真正地从生成的角度创造出意义。随着认知科学的发展,人们认识到意义具有认知的属性,语境也同样具有认知的属性,语境是人的大脑中逐渐形成的认识世界、理解世界的知识储备。我们只有通过认知语境才能制定意义,因为意义不是孤立的,它与人们对外部世界的认识有着千丝万缕的联系。

20世纪70年代中期,英国著名语言学家杰弗里·利奇(Geoffrey Leech)在其《语义学》(*Semantics*)一书中提出,"词义"可以分为七种主要类型,它们分别是:

Types of meaning	Definitions of types of meaning
1. Conceptual meaning	logical, cognitive, or denotative content
2. Connotative meaning	what is communicated by virtue of what language refers to
3. Social meaning	what is communicated of the social circumstances of language use
4. Affective meaning	what is communicated of the feelings and attitudes of the speaker or the writer
5. Reflected meaning	what is communicated through association with another sense of the same expression
6. Collocative meaning	what is communicated through association with words which tend to occur in the environment of another word
7. Thematic meaning	what is communicated by the way in which the message is organized in terms of order and emphasis

利奇所说的 conceptual meaning(概念意义)是指词的基本意义,是词典中词条所收录的意义,概念意义通常具有稳定性、明确性和有限性,人们对概念意义的理解也趋于一致,否则语言便失去了其交际功能。其他几类意义可统称为 associative meaning(联想意义),其中 connotative meaning(内涵意义)主要指词语在语境中所隐含的文化背景信息,由于相同概念意义词语可能具有不同内涵,译者在译文中必须表达出相同的内涵意义,而不是概念意义。social meaning(社会意义)是指社会环境中语言使用的意义;affective meaning(感情意义)是指人们表达感情或态度的意义;reflected meaning(反映意义)是指通过与同一个词语的另一意义的联想来传递的意义;collocative meaning(搭配意义)是指通过经常与之同时出现的词的联想来传递的意义;thematic meaning(主题意义)是指通过信息的组织方式(语序、强调手段)所传递的意义。应当指出,真实语句中往往交织着多种联想意义,诸多联想意义有时也很难区分。看下面两段:

1. Five teenagers were loitering on the corner. As their raucous laughter cut through the air, we noticed their sloppy black leather jackets and their greasy dyed hair. They slouched against a building with cigarettes dangling contemptuously from their mouths.

五个小青年懒散地站在街角,粗野的笑声刺破了空气中的宁静。我们注意到,他们身穿黑色皮夹克,看上去邋里邋遢,染色的头发油乎乎的。他们懒洋洋地斜靠着大楼,嘴里叼着烟卷,一副蔑视一切的样子。

2. Five youngsters stood on the corner. As the joy of their laughter filled the air, we noticed their

smooth loose-fitting jackets and the gleam of their colorful hair. They relaxed against a building smoking evenly on cigarettes that seemed almost natural in their serious young mouths.

　　五个年轻人站在街角，欢乐的笑声荡漾在空中。我们注意到，他们穿着光滑而宽松的皮夹克，发色各异，闪闪发亮。他们轻松地倚靠着大楼，不紧不慢地吸着烟，香烟衔在口中，显得悠然自得。

　　上面两段描写的是同一个场景，涉及到的联想意义可谓多种多样。第一段中的 loitering on the corner, raucous laughter 和 greasy dyed hair 等表述，表现了作者的厌恶之情；而第二段中 joy of their laughter, gleam of their colorful hair, evenly 及 serious 的使用，则表达出了作者的欣赏之意，这些无疑与"情感意义"有关。两个段落表达了对青少年吸烟的不同看法，这又与"社会意义"有关；第一段中 sloppy 一词具有 loose-fitting so as to be casual and comfortable 的意思，如 a big sloppy sweater 就指衣服的宽松肥大，丝毫没有任何贬义。但通过语境我们知道，sloppy 在文中不可能是这样的意思，它一定是 messy 以及 lacking order or tidiness 的意思，这似乎又与"反映意义"有关。当然，我们也可认为 sloppy 一词具有两个不同的意义。总之，语篇中的联想意义常常很难分清，对于译者来说，更重要的是把握好词语的概念意义，然后通过文本信息和背景知识的了解，努力揣摩好作者的意图，把握好原作的口吻，最终把原文意义用目的语恰当地表达出来。

第二节　意义理论对翻译的启示

　　人们对意义认识的不断深化为解释翻译现象提供了新视角，也为译者提高翻译水平提供了理论依据。过去人们曾认为，翻译就是原语和译语两种语言之间的转换，这种说法其实是不准确的，因为翻译就是翻译意义，就是把一种文字的意义用另一种文字表达出来。好的译文首先离不开对原文的正确理解，在理解原文的过程中，对词汇、句子、语篇的理解涉及到许多方面的问题。

一、对外部世界的认知

　　所谓对外部世界的认知就是译者对相关背景的了解。有这样一个例子，美国纽约 Times Square 长期以来被称为"时代广场"，此种译法以讹传讹，流传甚广。近期人们发现，我国媒体已将"时代广场"改为"纽约时报广场"。原来这是由于人们理解了 Times 一词的真正内涵。1904 年 4 月 8 日，位于当时朗埃克（Longacre）广场的《纽约时报》塔楼的钢筋结构刚刚建好，纽约市政委员会便通过了一项法令，将"朗埃克广场"更名为"时报广场"，这是《纽约时报》发行人阿道夫·奥克斯为宣传该报成功游说时任市长小乔治·B·麦克莱伦（George B. McClellan, Jr.）的结果。这个例子说明，词语的意义离不开人们对外部世界的认知。再看下面一段未必是真实的对话，但同样说明了译者对外部世界认知的重要。

　　Policeman: Why are you driving on the right side of the road?
　　Visitor: Do you want me to drive on the wrong side?
　　Policeman: You are driving on the wrong side.
　　Visitor: But you said I was driving on the right side.
　　Policeman: I meant to say that you were on the right side, and that was wrong.
　　Visitor: A strange country. If right is wrong, I'm right when I am on the wrong side. So why did you stop me?

　　理解这段对话的关键在于，读者必须知道在英国开车必须左行，当然也要知道 right 一词既有"右边"的意思，也有"正确"的意思。由于上文 right 两个义项汉语中只能用两个词语表达，因此，这段对话几乎无法翻译。

　　再看一个例子：
　　【原文】Being a soccer fan at World Cup time in America is <u>a little like being Jewish in December in a small town in the Midwest</u>. You sense that something big is going on around you, but you're not really a part of it. And the thing you're celebrating and enjoying is either ignored or misunderstood by your friends, peers, and neighbors. It can be a lonely time. But the World Cup is much bigger than Christmas. After all, only a couple of billion people in the world celebrate Christmas; the World Cup is likely to garner the attention of a much

larger audience. Yet in the world's largest and most important sports competition, the American team, and the American audience, is a marginal, bit player. And for those of us who love the game of soccer and the World Cup, and for the few of us who followed <u>the ups and downs of Landon Donovan's career</u>, these next couple of weeks are likely to be bittersweet. (Daniel Gross: *The Loneliness of the American Soccer Fan.* www.slate.com/id/2256618)

【译文】世界杯期间身在美国的球迷犹如 12 月份身在中西部某小城的犹太人，你能够感觉到身边进行着某项盛事，但你却没有真正参与其中。你所庆祝的或是陶醉的事可能被你的朋友、同事或邻居所忽视或误解，你会因此感觉到孤独。然而世界杯要比圣诞节更加盛大，毕竟世界上庆祝圣诞节的人只有一二十亿，而关注世界杯的人却多得多。在这个世界上最宏大、最重要的体育赛事中，美国队和美国观众只不过是个小角色。对于那些热爱足球、热爱世界杯的美国人来说，特别对于我们少数关注兰登·多诺万职业生涯起起落落的人来说，接下来的几周很有可能是亦喜亦悲。（丹尼尔·格洛斯："美国足球迷的寂寞"）（修改后学生译文）

作者为什么说世界杯期间美国的球迷就好像 being Jewish in December in a small town in the Midwest？因为 12 月份正直西方圣诞节期间，犹太教不承认耶稣是神的儿子，因此大多数犹太人是不过圣诞节的。另外美国开展西进运动时，犹太人也从东部来到中西部，犹太社区也在中西部的新兴城市纷纷出现。但大多数犹太人仍然居住在美国的东部，中西部地区的犹太人保留传统更多一些。有了这样的背景知识，我们就能够理解 being Jewish in December in a small town in the Midwest 的意义了。兰登·多诺万（Landon Donovan）是美国国家足球队长期身披 10 号球衣的队员，2007 年他为国家队取得 9 个入球，在当年美洲金杯对厄瓜多尔的比赛中上演帽子戏法。但也有人批评他 2006 年世界杯期间表现欠佳，在世界杯后举办的美洲国家杯比赛中，他竟未能入选国家队。如果我们了解了这些 ups and downs of Landon Donovan's career，就能够更好地理解 bittersweet 一词的内涵。综上所述可以看出，译者对外部世界的认知有多么重要。

二、了解原语文本信息

除了对外部世界的认知，对原语文本信息的了解也很重要，看下面一段文字及图片：

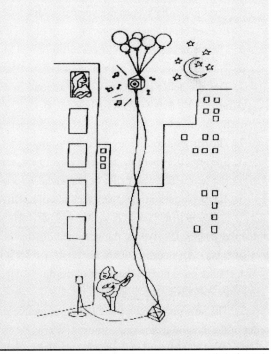

If the balloons popped, the sound would not be able to carry since everything would be too far away from the correct floor. A closed window would also prevent the sound from carrying since most buildings tend to be well insulated. Since the whole operation depends on a steady flow of electricity, a break in the middle of the wire would also cause problems. Of course the fellow could shout, but the human voice is not loud enough to carry that far. An additional problem is that a string could break on the instrument. Then there could be no accompaniment to the message it is clear that the best situation would involve less distance. Then there would be fewer potential problems. With face to face contact the least number of things could go wrong.

(Bransford & Johnson: "Contextual prerequisites for understanding". *Journal Of Verbal Learning And Verbal Behavior.* Volume 11, 1972.)

笔者在翻译课上曾就本段让学生猜一猜文章讲的是什么，结果给出的答案五花八门，其中竟没有一个答案是正确的，其实这丝毫也不奇怪。当把上文右侧的图给大家看时，所有同学都立刻明白了文中所讲的内容。由此可见，缺乏相关的文本信息常常会造成理解障碍。

再看另一个例子：

【原文】On the Indonesian resort island of Bali, the growing influx of Chinese tourists is not just changing the dynamics of the tourism market, it is also changing the face of God.

From the kerbside stalls of Kuta beach to the upscale galleries in Ubud, most of the popular wooden and stone statues and figurines on sale are now carved with the face of Guanyin, the Chinese Buddhist goddess of mercy.（Jamil Anderlini: Chinese join tourist trail...and head for the shops）（From http://www.ftchinese.com/story/001033029/ce）

【译文】在印尼度假胜地巴厘岛，中国游客越来越多，不仅在改变旅游市场的动态，也在改变神祇的模样。

从库塔海滩的路边摊，到乌布的高档画廊，随处可见的待售木雕与石像中，如今大多数都刻着中国佛教中大慈大悲的菩萨——观音。（何黎译）

经查阅 the face of God = divine countenance，指犹太基督教里神/上帝的脸。但真正理解文中的意义还要看第二段的内容。英语中 the face of God 固然有其特定的概念意义，但概念意义会随着语境的不同而不同。上面英语段落中"上帝的脸"已不再为西方人独有，而是泛指"一切神明"。

第三节　概念意义的重要性

第一节两段翻译给我们的启示是，联想意义的把握首先离不开对概念意义的准确理解，译者在理解概念意义时，对于没有把握的词语一定要查英英词典，这是因为英汉词典的解释有时不够清楚。例如，第一段中 raucous 一词英汉词典的解释大多为"粗声的；沙哑的"，而英英词典则解释为 disturbing the public peace; loud and rough; unpleasantly loud and harsh; characterized by loud noise, shouting, and ribald laughter。由此可见，将 raucous laughter 翻译为"粗野的笑声"比翻译为"沙哑的笑声"更贴近原文意义。一个词的概念意义往往有许多，译者必须结合语境找出最恰当的意义，下面例子中的 credit 意思都不一样：

1. Do liability accounts increase on the credit side?（贷方）
2. He deserves full credit for saving more than 150 lives.（名声）
3. No amounts have been drawn against this letter of credit.（信用证）
4. Even in bankruptcy, a company must obtain credit to operate.（信誉）
5. The merchants on Main Street refuse to sell him anything on credit.（赊账）
6. That led to the credit crunch and a lack of confidence by the consumer.（信贷）
7. This can help a student transfer academic credits from one U.S. institution to another.（学分）

Affair 一词下面也有诸多不同的概念意义：

1. She wore a long black velvet affair.（Velvet Affair：英国女士贴身服饰品牌）
2. The party turned out to be a quiet affair.（活动）
3. She organizes her financial affairs very efficiently.（事务）
4. Her love affair with ballet began when she was ten.（酷爱）
5. The book doesn't make any mention of his love affairs.（风流韵事）

有些词或短语虽然概念意义相同，但翻译时则必须根据语境给出不同的译文，例如，英语中 order of the day 的意思是：typical thing: something that is regularly done, offered, chosen, or experienced during a particular period（Encarta Dictionary），但在具体翻译时译入语必须有所变化，看下面的例子：

1. Murder and theft is the order of the day.
   凶杀和偷窃<u>大行其道</u>。
2. The new tax was the source of considerable public indignation, with marches, rallies and petitions the order of the day throughout the country.
   新税种的出台引起了公众的极大愤慨，举国上下<u>到处</u>是游行、集会和请愿。
3. The cost of developing new generations of chip technology are so high that collaboration is increasingly the order of the day.

开发新一代芯片技术成本昂贵，因此合作越来越成为时尚。

4. Mathematical knowledge is transmitted from teacher to pupil; telling, showing and explaining are the order of the day.

数学知识由老师传授给学生，讲解、演示和分析是通常的做法。

再举两个类似的例子，rain or shine 和 tight-lipped 的概念意义比较固定，前者意思是 regardless of the weather or circumstances; in any event，后者的意思为 having the lips firmly closed，但如何翻译要根据具体情况：

1. They were sent outside, rain or shine.
不管晴天雨天，他们都要被派出去。
2. I'm with you always. I'm with you rain or shine.
我永远和你在一起，有福同享，有难同当。
3. Debbie doesn't miss a day, rain or shine.
黛比风里来雨里去，没有耽误过一天。
4. He gave me a tight-lipped smile and reached for his prescription pad.
他抿着嘴儿向我笑了笑，伸手去拿他的处方簿。
5. Prosecutors are tight-lipped about any evidence they plan to present at the trial.
公诉人对于审判时提交的证据守口如瓶。
6. Charles was tight-lipped all the way to church.
查尔斯在去教堂的路上沉默不语。

看下面几个汉译英的例子，在不同的语境中，都可以使用 awash 来形象强调所指内容。
1. 市场上充斥着各种软件。The market is awash with all kinds of software.
2. 那个国家有的是石油。The country is awash with oil.
3. 她终日以泪洗面。She is awash with tears all day long.
4. 他站在那里，满脸是血。He stood there, his face awash with blood.
5. 小镇游客如织。The small town is awash with tourists.
6. 老师走了，教室里的人感到莫名其妙。The teacher was gone, leaving the classroom awash with confusion.

词语的意义有时会因外部环境的变化而改变，当年海明威乘坐的飞机被目击失事后，纽约《镜报》大字标题使用了"lost"，意指海明威已经去世。后来发现海明威依然活着时，《镜报》仍然使用这个标题，此时的"lost"变成了它本来的字面意义"失踪"。这说明词语的意义离不开相关背景，假如背景不明确意义则很难确定，看下面段中的两个译文：

【原文】All babies have a temporary lien on tenderness, of course: and therefrom children too receive a dwindling income, although on looking back, you will recollect that your childhood was upon the whole a lonesome and much put-upon period.（见"第二十一届韩素音青年翻译奖竞赛"，《中国翻译》，2009（6），第78页）

【译文一】婴儿当然都有权得到短期柔情贷款，而且在童年时期还会有逐日递减的柔情进账，然而你回忆往事时就会发现，童年大体上是一段孤独寂寞且屡屡受骗的时期。（曹明伦译）

【译文二】所有婴儿短期内自然都有获取温存的权力，他们在童年时期亦有逐渐减少的温存进账，尽管在长大后的回忆里，自己的童年大体孤单无助，全然是一段遭遇束缚的时期。

原文中的 put-upon period 到底是"屡屡受骗的时期"还是"遭遇束缚的时期"？【译文一】译者的根据是：put-upon also = impose upon or impose on (*A Dictionary of Slang and Unconventional English*); He knew he was imposed on.（他知道自己受骗了。）（《英汉大词典》p.881）；【译文二】译者的根据是：put-upon = having to do more than is fair in order to allow other people to get what they want in a situation (*Cambridge Advanced Learner's Dictionary*); put-upon = treated badly, especially by being taken advantage of or being asked to do an excessive amount of work. (*Encarta® World English Dictionary*)。前面我们强调过，对外部世界的认知可以帮助人们理解意义，但这里的问题是，当人们回忆自己的童年时，即可以有"屡屡受骗"的感觉，又可以有"遭遇束缚"的感觉。

词语意义的界定与法律有着密切的联系，法律语言准确的重要性不言而喻。然而，由于法律语言的不确定性造成的困难和问题并不鲜见。例如，法庭上的"言词证据"（verbal evidence）非常重要，但汉语"含义丰富"，有时"只可意会、不可言传"的特点，造成了"言词"的模糊、歧义和多义，给"言词"真实含义的确定带来很大麻烦，也造成了案件事实认定的困难。下面的对话来自一个真实的案例，这段对话是调侃还是性暗示？

笑笑：最近你好忙吧？	Xiaoxiao: How is everything going, busy?
老草：哈哈，不妨碍想你。	Laocao: Yes, but that won't stop me from missing you.
笑笑：哪天等你有空出来聚吧。	Xiaoxiao: Shall we have a gathering when you're free?
老草：不想出去，想你进来。	Laocao: I prefer not to, I want you to come in.
笑笑：太深奥了，我不懂。	Xiaoxiao: That's too difficult for me to understand.
老草：那就不懂吧。	Laocao: Forget it then.
笑笑：戏还是 8 月 15 日开吧？	Xiaoxiao: Will you start shooting the film on the 15th of August?
老草：当然了，拍戏又不是儿戏。	Laocao: Of course, we all have to be serious about serious things.
笑笑：我有希望和您一起合作吗？	Xiaoxiao: Do you think I'll be able to cooperate with you?
老草：你不进来，如何合作？	Laocao: If you don't come in, how can we cooperate?
笑笑：什么叫进来？	Xiaoxiao: What do you mean by "come in"?
老草：就是让我的"想"落实到实处。	Laocao: That means you have to translate "my idea" into practice.

上面的对话选自《法律语言学说》2007 创刊号中李振宇的一篇文章，题目是《浅说"言词证据"的认定》。对话的内容一般认为含义是清楚的，但也可以有不同的理解。对话的真实意图还要看对话双方的身份、熟悉程度、对话动机等等。因此，人们从不同角度进行解读时，既可以认为是性暗示，也可以认为是调侃。对于这样语义明确而有争议的对话，汉语本身的意义就难以确定，在翻译成英语时就更难说得清。

第四节　翻译中的对等

"对等"是翻译理论中的核心命题，西方翻译理论对于此多有论述。例如，奈达（Nida）区分了形式对等（formal equivalence）和动态对等（dynamic equivalence）；纽马克（Newmark）区分了语义对等（semantic equivalence）和交际对等（communicative equivalence）；豪斯（House）区分了显性对等（overt equivalence）和隐性对等（covert equivalence）。翻译界广泛接受的观点是，百分之百的对等是很难达到，译文在展示原文意义及内涵方面，普遍存在着有所增加、有所减少或有所歪曲的情况。因此，所谓好的译文不过是原文的最佳近似，译者的终极目标也只是不断贴近这一最佳近似。也有学者认为，每种语言都有特定的民族历史、民族文化和民族心理背景，不同语言之间在语言结构、思维方式和表达方法等方面均存在差异，因此"对等"的概念过于绝对化，并不适用于翻译研究。

翻译中的对应关系

Case	Source Language	Target Language
1 - Exact Equivalence (=) The word in the target language is identical in meaning and scope to the word in the source language	○	○
2 - Inexact Equivalence (≅) The word from the target language has a similar meaning but a different scope than the word from the source language.	◌	◌
3 - Single to Multiple (A=B+C) The concept in the source language combines two or more existing words in the target language.	○	◌◌
4 - Non-equivalence The target language does not contain a word which corresponds in meaning, either partially or inexactly, to the source language word.	○	◌

完全对等：指原语与目的语在意思及所指范围方面均相等。例如：WTO＝世界贸易组织；contract＝合同；Bill of Exchange＝汇票；Letter of Credit＝信用证。人们通常认为 Marxism＝马克思主义，而我们所理解的"马克思主义"与西方人所理解的 Marxism 实际上并不完全一样，但这并不影响我们把它们当作对等词语来翻译。

部分对等：如汉语中的"红"与英语中的 red 只在少数情况下对等。英语中的 in the red（赤字）和"红"可能有点儿关系，但 red tape（官僚习气）、red herring（转移注意力的话或事）、red dirt（大麻）、red eagle（海洛因）等则与"红"毫无关系；而汉语中的"红娘"（matchmaker）、"红榜"（honour roll）、"红利"（dividend）和"红运"（good luck）更是与英语中的 red 风马牛不相及。部分对等也包括下面的"多词同义"和"一词多义"两种情况。

多词同义：如英语中的 wife 一词在不同的语境下可分别翻译为"媳妇"、"老伴"、"爱人"、"妻子"和"夫人"等等，多词同义只是说词的基本意义相同，但其用法和在语境中的联想意义则差别很大。

一词多义：一词多义常与词义的宽窄有关。有些汉语词汇意义宽泛，如汉语中的"走"就包括英语中 walk, saunter, amble, stride, trudge, shamble, prance, scamper, clump, tiptoe 等词；有些英语词也具有意义宽泛的特点，如 carry 一词就具有"搬、运、送、提、拎、挑、担、抬、背、扛、搂、抱、端、举、夹、捧"等意思。

包含对等：指原语中一个词包含目的语中两个或多个词的意义，如汉语中的"门"就包含 door 和 gate 两个词的意义，"罪"也包含 crime 和 offence 两个词的意义，英语中的 cousin 包含汉语中"堂兄、堂弟、堂姐、堂妹、表兄、表弟、表姐、表妹"等词的意义。

零对等：指两种语言中不存对等词语，如英语中的 rubberneck（伸着脖子左顾右盼的好奇者）和 clock-watcher（总是看钟等下班的人）以及汉语中的"精气神儿、干打垒、海选"等词语。另外还有一种"交互对等"的情况，如英语中的 belief, faith, confidence, conviction, credit, trust 和汉语中的"信念、信任、确信、信赖、信誉、相信"，其中两个词之间的互译要看具体语境，它们相互之间不存在绝对的对等。

第五节 译文对比分析

由于翻译对等关系的多样性，在翻译实践中常会出现一些需要灵活处理的情况。下面是《简·爱》节选段的两种译文：

【原文】The chamber looked such a bright little place to me as the sun shone in between the gay blue chintz window curtains, showing papered walls and a carpeted floor, so unlike the bare planks and stained plaster of Lowood, that my spirits rose at the view.

【译文一】太阳从鲜艳的蓝印花布的窗幔间照射进来时，显出纸糊的墙和铺地毯的地板，和罗沃德的光板同褪色的粉墙很是不同，使得这房子在我看来是一个很愉快的小地方。（李霁野译）

【译文二】太阳从鲜艳的蓝色印花布窗帘缝隙间照进来，照亮了糊着墙纸的四壁和铺着地毯的地板，这跟劳渥德的光秃秃的木板和沾污的灰泥墙完全不同，这个房间看上去是个如此明亮的小地方，我一看见它就精神振奋起来。（祝庆英译）

【译文三】阳光从鲜艳的蓝色印花布窗帘缝隙照射进来，照亮了糊着墙纸的四壁和铺着地毯的地板，这与劳渥德学校宿舍裸露的木地板和脏兮兮的墙壁完全不同，阳光把这小屋变得如此明亮，我一见到它就精神振奋起来。（修改后学生译文）

原文 showing papered walls and a carpeted floor 中 show 的意义为：to be visible, or allow something to be seen easily, often inadvertently or against inclination（*Encarta® World English Dictionary*）。【译文一】仅仅给出了汉语中的对等词"显出"，不如【译文二】"照亮了"来得生动自然。【译文一】中"褪色的粉墙"不符合原文 stained plaster 的概念意义。根据《美国传统字典》，plaster = a mixture of lime or gypsum, sand, and water, sometimes with fiber added, that hardens to a smooth solid and is used for coating walls and ceilings.（灰泥：石灰或石膏、沙子和水的混合物，有时还加入纤维，变硬后成为光滑的固

体，用来涂墙壁和天花板）。可见 plaster 指的是墙壁最外层的涂刷层。有的词典干脆说 plaster 也是 a hardened surface of plaster (as on a wall or ceiling)，也就是我们所说的"墙皮"。把 bare planks 翻译为"光板"或"光秃秃的木板"都不够具体，其实 planks 就是指铺在地上的木板（木地板），bare 指的是裸露的，没有铺地毯。

再看下面《尤利西斯》节选段的两种不同译文：

【原文】Stately, plump Buck Mulligan came from the stairhead, bearing a bowl of lather on which a mirror and a razor lay crossed. A yellow dressing gown, ungirdled, was sustained gently behind him by the mild morning air.

【译文一】体态丰满而有风度的勃克·穆利根从楼梯口出现。他手里托着一钵肥皂沫，上面交叉放了一面镜子和一把剃胡刀。他没系腰带，淡黄色浴衣被习习晨风吹得稍微向后蓬着。（萧乾译）

【译文二】仪表堂堂、结实丰满的壮鹿马利根从楼梯口走了上来。他端着一碗肥皂水，碗上十字交叉，架着一面镜子和一把剃刀。他披一件黄色梳妆袍，没有系腰带，袍子被清晨的微风轻轻托起，在他身后飘着。（金隄译）

【译文三】体态丰满的勃克·穆利根庄严地出现在楼梯口，手里托着一碗肥皂沫，上面交叉放着一面镜子和一把剃须刀。他没系腰带，黄色浴衣在习习晨风的吹拂下轻轻向后托起。（修改后学生译文）

下面我们就译文中的一些语言点分析如下：

● 汉语中"楼梯口"可指楼梯的上端或下端，但英语中 stairhead 只有"楼梯顶"的意思。*Encarta*® *World English Dictionary* 对该词的释义是：top of stairs: the landing at the top of a flight of stairs。因此，Buck Mulligan came from the stairhead 意思是说，勃克·穆利根出现在了楼梯口，他如果"走了上来"，也应该从楼梯口的下端往上走。

● 英语中 to bear 和 to carry 意思差不多，如 *American Heritage Dictionary of the English Language* 对 to bear 的解释是：to carry from one place to another；*Encarta*® *World English Dictionary* 的解释是：to carry something: to hold or support and transport somebody or something。问题是无论 to bear 还是 to carry，其意义都比较宽泛，都包含汉语中"搬、运、搂、抱、托、端、举"等意义。当汉语中没有完全对等词语时，译者必须寻找其他相关信息。萧乾译文"他手里托着一钵肥皂沫"是有道理的，他本人在注释中说："这里，穆利根在模仿天主教神父举行弥撒时的动作。他手里托着的那钵肥皂沫，就权当圣餐杯。镜子和剃胡刀交叉放着，呈十字架形。淡黄色浴衣令人联想到神父做弥撒时罩在外面的金色祭披。……"课堂讨论中学生也认为，"托着"比"端着"应该更合理一些，既然那钵肥皂沫权当圣餐杯，为了圣物之神圣也应该"托着"或"捧着"，而不应该"端着"。

● lather 一词指"肥皂沫"，而不是"肥皂水"。词典释义很清楚：lather = soapy froth: foam that is produced by soap or detergent used with water（*Encarta*® *World English Dictionary*）。

● 关于 stately 一词大部分词典只列出形容词义项，但 *Webster's New World College Dictionary*（4th Ed.）不仅给出了该词作为形容词的两个义项：1) impressively weighty and dignified；2) grand and imposing in appearance，而且还称该词也是副词，其意义为 in a ceremonious or imposing manner（隆重而庄严地）。至此我们认为，上面的学生译文"体态丰满的勃克·穆利根庄严地出现在楼梯口"更合适，因为神父总应该庄严地出场。

● 上面译文还涉及到如何翻译 razor 和 dressing gown 的问题，英语中 razor 一词的意思是：an instrument with a blade or powered cutting head that is used for shaving hair off the face or body（*Encarta*® *World English Dictionary*），即"刮胡刀"、"剃须刀"或"剃胡刀"，汉语中"刮胡刀"口语中使用较多，"剃须刀"多为书面语，而"剃胡刀"则是较旧的说法。至于"剃刀"则常指"剃光头"时使用的刀具，当然也可以刮胡子。dressing gown 一词的意思是：a coat made of soft light material that is worn over nightclothes or before or after a bath（*Encarta*® *World English Dictionary*）。在课堂讨论中，多数同学认为把 dressing gown 译为"浴衣"或"睡袍"比较合适，"梳妆袍"的说法可能是方言。也有个别同学提出，萧乾译文"淡黄色浴衣被习习晨风吹得稍微向后蓬着。"中的"向后篷着"是北京方言，金隄译文"袍子被清晨的微风轻轻托起，在他身后飘着。"中的"飘着"有些过头，既然 the dressing gown was sustained，就不可能真正"飘起来"。

在汉译英时，原文同一词语的妙用会产生特殊的艺术效果，但译者想把其中的妙处翻译出来绝非易事。看老舍先生在《茶馆》中写下的一段精彩对白：

宋恩子：（我出个很不高明的主意：干脆来个包月，每月一号，按阳历算）你把那点……
吴祥子：那点意思!
宋恩子：对，那点意思送到，你省事，我们也省事!
王利发：那点意思得多少呢?
吴祥子：多年的交情，你看着办! 你聪明，<u>还能把那点意思闹成不好意思吗?</u>

上述对白使用了五个"意思"，正是这五个"意思"成就了对白的精彩，特别是"还把那点意思闹成不好意思吗?"令人拍案叫绝。翻译这句话的难点在于，如果按照原文的意思去翻译"意思"和"不好意思"，原文语言表达的妙处则损失怠尽。看下面的两种译文：

【译文一】

Song: ...you can send us this little....

Wu: Little expression of gratitude.

Song: Right. Just a little expression of gratitude. Save your time, and save us time.

Wang: This little expression of gratitude — how much will it come to?

Wu: We're old friends; do as you see fit. You understand these things — you wouldn't want to turn an expression of gratitude into ingratitude, would you? (Translated by John Howard)

【译文二】

Song: ...you'll hand in a....

Wu: A token of friendship!

Song: Right. You'll hand in a token of friendship. That'll save no end of trouble for both sides.

Wang: How much is this token of friendship worth?

Wu: As old friends, we'll leave that to you. You're a bright fellow. I'm sure you wouldn't want this token of friendship to seem unfriendly, would you? (Translated by Ying Ruocheng)

两个译文都很出色，尽管如此也无法将原文中的"妙处"全部体现出来，这就是两种语言中某些词语没有"完全对等"意义造成的。另外，台词翻译还有个是否适合演出的问题，John Howard 虽占据母语是英语的优势，但对戏剧及其特点不甚了解，因而其译文句子偏长、用词偏文，总体上并不适合演出。英若诚先生既是表演艺术家又是翻译家，他的译文更适合在舞台上表演。

再看下面一段赵本山《策划》台词：

牛：大叔大妈你们也吃，别光我一个人吃。你们吃。
赵：没有……我们吃不起。
牛：大叔，不能再喝了。无论如何啊，一会儿你得让我把那鸡抱走。
赵：<u>抱你是抱不走啦! 你可以端走。</u>
牛：端走?
赵：实话告诉你吧，你要得那只鸡让儿媳妇炖了，吃着就是。

上面台词中"抱"和"端"在翻译也很难处理，如完全照字面翻译则无法区分两个动词，其结果是原文中幽默的丧失，此时译者也必须考虑采用其他方式处理。例如：

Zhao: You can't take away the rooster alive, you can take away the plate instead.

Niu: Why is that?

Zhao: Right here in the plate is the rooster my daughter-in-law has cooked for you. You are enjoying it.

再看另一个汉译英的例子，我国 1996 年 3 月 17 日颁布的《中华人民共和国刑事诉讼法》第一百九十八条如下：

【原文】公安机关、人民检察院和人民法院对于扣押、冻结犯罪嫌疑人、被告人的财物及其孳息，应当妥善保管，以供核查。任何单位和个人不得挪用或者自行处理。对被害人的合法财产，应当及时返还。对违禁品或者不宜长期保存的物品，应当依照国家有关规定处理。

对作为证据使用的实物应当随案移送，对不宜移送的，应当将其清单、照片或者其他证明文件随案移送。

人民法院作出的判决生效以后，对被扣押、冻结的赃款赃物及其孳息，除依法返还被害人的以外，一律没收，上缴国库。

司法工作人员贪污、挪用或者私自处理被扣押、冻结的赃款赃物及其孳息的，依法追究<u>刑事责任</u>；<u>不构成犯罪的，给予处分</u>。

【译文】The public security organs, People's Procuratorates and People's Courts shall have the property, things of value of the criminal suspects and defendants, as well as the fruits accruing therefrom, that they have seized or frozen well kept for examination. No units or individuals shall misappropriate them or dispose of them without authorization. The lawful property of the victims shall be returned to them without delay. Prohibited articles and perishable things shall be disposed of in accordance with the relevant regulations of the State.

Things that serve as <u>tangible evidence</u> shall be transferred together with the case, but for things that are unsuitable to be transferred, their inventory and photos and other documents of certification shall be transferred together with the case.

After a judgment rendered by the People's Court becomes effective, all the seized or frozen illicit money and goods as well as the fruits accruing therefrom, except those that are returned to the victim according to law, shall be confiscated and turned over to the State Treasury.

Any judicial officer who embezzles or misappropriates or disposes of the seized or frozen illicit money and goods as well as the fruits accruing therefrom without authorization shall be investigated for <u>criminal responsibility</u> according to law; <u>if the offence does not constitute a crime, he shall be given administrative sanction</u>.

（http://www.lawinfochina.com/law/displayModeTwo.asp?id=347&keyword=）

上文中"作为证据使用的实物"即"物证"，我国法律翻译专家陈忠诚先生认为，"物证"在英语中的说法主要包括 physical evidence，real evidence 和 demonstrative evidence（陈忠诚：《法苑译谭》，中国法制出版社，2000年6月）。虽然语料库中可以找到 tangible evidence 意指"物证"的例子，但《美国法律数据库》（http://www.gpoaccess.gov/）中却没有相应的实例，《英国法律数据库》（http://www.opsi.gov.uk/）中也只找到一个例子（见 *Statutory Rule* 1999 No. 331），对于"物证"两个数据库大多采用 physical evidence 的说法，另外笔者对英语法律文本的调查显示，"作为证据使用的实物"采用 things (any thing) offered as physical evidence 的说法似乎更好些。

关于英语中"刑事责任"的说法，《美国法律数据库》中有两万多个 criminal liability 搭配，而没有 criminal responsibility 的搭配形式。《英国法律数据库》中的 International Criminal Court Act（2001）第104条中有如下文句：This section provides for an additional form of criminal responsibility, namely that of commanders and superiors for the acts of their subordinates. This is a well known concept of international law and was reflected in the jurisprudence of the Nuremberg and Tokyo Tribunals. 从中我们可以看出，上级指挥官所负的并非是直接的"刑事责任"。汉语中"责任"一词的意义相当宽泛，英语中与之相对应的词就有 obligation，duty，responsibility，burden 等等。在具体文本中如何找到两种语言中的对等词，看来仍需进一步调查和研究。

关于 crime 和 offence 的区别，布莱恩·加纳（Bryan Garner）指出：In BrE, and to a lesser extent in AmE, lawyers commonly distinguish crimes (at common law) from offenses (created by statute). It is common in both speech communities to use offense for the less serious infractions and crime for the more serious ones.（Bryan A. Garner: *Garner's Modern American Usage*, Oxford University Press 2003, p568.）加纳只是说广义上讲 crimes 指"重罪"，offenses（offences）指"轻罪"，一般立法文本中很少使用 crime，即使是"重罪"也用 offence 一词指代。因此，上面英译文 if the offence does not constitute a crime, he shall be given administrative sanction 依然值得商榷。下面是英国《武装部队法》（*Armed Forces Act 2006* (c. 52)）中有关 offences 定义的部分，从中可以看出 offence 一词完全可以指"重罪"。

chedule 2 offences

12 An offence under section 42 (criminal conduct) as respects which the corresponding offence under the law of England and Wales is—

(a) murder;

(b) manslaughter;

(c) kidnapping;

(d) high treason;

(e) piracy;

(f) cheating the public revenue;

由此看来，if the offence does not constitute a crime, he shall be given administrative sanction 的说法一定有问题。我们不妨把该句修改为：The person (judicial officer) whose conduct does not constitute a crime should be given an administrative punishment (administrative punishments).

本部分重点讨论了词语的概念意义及其翻译，这当然不是翻译对等的全部，实际上对等从词的对等开始一直贯穿翻译的全过程。翻译对等不仅要考虑词汇的概念意义，还要考虑其语境意义；不仅要考虑字面意义，还要考虑比喻意义；不仅要考虑所指意义，还要考虑言外之力。关于概念意义之外的翻译问题，本书将在其它章节中探讨。

本章主要参考文献：

陈忠诚：《法苑译谭》，中国法制出版社，2000年6月。

《美国法律数据库》（http://www.gpoaccess.gov/）

《英国法律数据库》（http://www.opsi.gov.uk/）

Bryan A. Garner: *Garner's Modern American Usage*, Oxford University Press, 2003.

翻译练习三

1. 将下面段落译成汉语：

Life and Death of a Hero

You were well advised to leave your pity at the door of Christopher Reeve's airy, sun-filled home, hidden amid the rolling meadows and white wooden barns of upstate New York. What struck you first, as he was steered into the room, was his commanding height: his throne-like wheelchair lifted his broad-shouldered bulk off the ground; sitting down, you found yourself tilting your head upwards to look at him.

The accident's power over him was diminishing, he said, as his ventilator sucked and hissed. He no longer snapped awake in the quiet hours, forced to confront, all over again, the fact that he had no sensation from the neck down. He didn't need to turn away when he was driven past the barn where he kept Buck, the thoroughbred horse from which he had been thrown in 1995, breaking his neck. But learning to live with his paralysis wasn't the same as resigning himself to it. "I've still never had a dream that I'm disabled," he said. "Never." He had vowed, controversially, to walk again by the age of 50. At the time, that deadline was three weeks away.

Walking by 50 had only ever been a hope, not a prediction, Reeve insisted. But what made the news of his death so acutely disorienting was the fact that, on some level, so many of us thought that, eventually—albeit a few years behind schedule—he might actually do it. Of course, he had always stressed that ordinary disabled people were the real superheroes in response to the inevitable movie-themed questions. But for the rest of us, the personal narrative was too seductive to resist: Superman, brought down to earth, ultimately triumphs again through sheer force of will. (China Daily Translation Contest)

2. 将下面段落译成汉语：

China on the Catwalk: Between Economic Success and Nationalist Anxiety

China's economic success has not been matched by recognition of Chinese fashion design on the world stage. One reason for this lies in the obstacles posed by the existing hierarchy of fashion capitals, which has proved notoriously difficult to subvert. Yet the Chinese fashion industry is also bedeviled by problems of its own. A high degree of national self-consciousness on the world stage is evident in national fashion shows featuring rather predictable pastiches of Chinese culture.

In 2002, Pierre Cardin was questioned about who was likely to lead the international fashion scene in the 21st century. He responded with heartening words for Chinese fashion designers. "I was sure Chinese fashion will become very strong," he said. "I know so much talent in China, maybe it will become one of the leading countries in the world for couture." He concluded, however, on a cautious note: "fashion is not about nationalities, it's just talent."

The latter observation begs questions about the semiotics of international fashion, and particularly about the signifying power of place names. Designs emanating from Paris, New York, London, Milan and Tokyo come with tags announcing their credentials. The cities lend their culture cachet to both established and emerging designers. This is especially true of Paris, a place so closely identified with fashion as to have become a by-word for it. Western reports on fashion in China routinely sound a note of surprise and discovery, as though Chinese people were still to be seen wearing Mao suits. "Fashion craze sweeps through a new China," announced the International Herald Tribune early in 2003, and "Chinese buy into the beauty myth," trumpeted Melbourne's The Age a year later. A quarter of century after the beginning of the reform era, it would appear, China is still "new". This newness is nothing very new. "New" China had been appearing on the horizon since the turn of the 20th century, and a fashion industry was apparent in Shanghai at least by the 1920s. （Antonia Finnane: "China on the Catwalk: Between Economic Success and Nationalist Anxiety,"*The China Quarterly*, September 2005）

第四章

英汉句法结构差异与翻译

翻译理论界长期以来争论的一个话题是，译者在翻译时应采用归化法还是异化法。归化法主张恰当使用目的语中的表达方式，利用目的语自身语言文化素材体现源语意义，以尽量减轻读者对译入文化的异质感。异化法则倡导适度放弃目的语中的习惯表达，以保留源语文化的异域性和原文风貌。本章所讨论的问题与两种翻译法有着密切的联系，但并非是文化因素的移植问题，而是两种语言之间句法结构转换的问题。我们先来看一段翻译实例：

【原文】The implied inclusion of books among the world's perishable goods is hardly made more agreeable by the reflection that increasing numbers of books these days do seem to be written with just such consumption in mind, and that most book-stores have become little more than glorified news stands for hardcover publications of this sort, which are merchandised for a few weeks—sometimes only as long as they remain on the best-seller lists—and are then retired to discount stores (those jumbled graveyards of books, so saddening to the hearts of authors) shortly before dropping out of print altogether. （英语高级口译资格证书考试《翻译教程》第二版第180页）

【原译】不言而喻地把书籍归入世界易损商品之列，一点不会因为人们想到如今越来越多的书确实是为了这样的消费而写的就令人感到舒心，也一点不会因为人们想到大多数书店已经变成仅仅是出售这类精装书的花里胡俏的书报摊就令人感到舒心，这类书卖不到几个星期——有时候只能维持到仍列入畅销书单这段日子——就会被打入折扣书店里（也就是令作者深感伤心的杂乱不堪的书堆），紧跟着也就完全绝版了。

【改译】现在越来越多的书籍确实似乎是脑子里想着把它们当作应时消费品写出来的。现在大多数书店已经变成只不过是出售这类精装出版物的门面漂亮的书报摊。这类精装出版物只当几个星期的商品，有时只在它们还列在畅销书名单上时当作商品，然后退到折价书店（那些令作者们伤心的拥挤的书籍坟场），很快就彻底绝版了。想到上述情景而把书籍不言而喻地把归入世界易腐商品之列很难使人心情舒畅。（解伯昌改译）

【分析】在英语句子中，by the reflection 是主句的方式状语，reflection 后面是两个 that 连接的并列的同位语从句。按汉语的思维逻辑，通常是先状语，然后才是句子其他成分，所以翻译时首先考虑把方式状语 by the reflection that...and...that 先翻，再翻主句的主语和谓语部分。可是方式状语中 reflection 有两个同位语从句，而且很长。因此先翻两个同位语从句，再翻介词短语状语。具体翻译的时候，注意使用分句法，词性转译法等各种翻译技巧使译文通顺流畅。（解伯昌分析）

上面原译紧随原文句法结构，结果是读者需付出极大努力才能理解。改译和分析无可挑剔、可谓精当，但读起来仍需付出不少努力。两译文的问题在于过多地考虑了原文的句法结构，而忽视了汉语中固有的表达习惯。汉语的句法结构与英语完全不同，汉语的逻辑关系并非体现在句法结构层面，而是以语义关系为纲，不大计较名、动、形的词类划分和它们与句子结构成分的关系。如果我们从这一视角看待问题，就会产出完全不同的译文。

【另译】人们心照不宣，如今已把书籍归于易耗消费品之列，越来越多的书籍作者就是为了满足这种消费而写作的。现在大多数书店只重外表装饰，已同街面上出售精装本的书报摊儿相差无几，摊儿上的东西只销售数周而已，一旦从排行榜上消失，便被打入折扣书店（即杂乱不堪、令作者心碎的书籍坟场），不久也就绝版了。此情此景不免令人心灰意冷、难以接受。

英汉互译中的句法结构转换是个值得深入探讨的问题。一方面，在全球化日益深入发展的今天，一味地采用归化法显然是不适当的。另一方面，无节制地采用异化法也会带来诸多问题。对于译者来说，最重要的是根据不同的情况灵活使用两种翻译方法。

第一节 英汉句法结构的特点

一、"形合"与"意合"

由于文化传统及思维方式的不同，英汉两种语言在词法、句法、篇章结构诸方面都存在较大差异。陈定安（1998）在对英汉两种语言句式比较之后，把英汉句式形象地比喻为大树和竹竿。英语句法结构如同一棵多枝共干的大树，其排列不是简单句与简单句的相加，而是先确立主句，然后设法将分句、从句、附加成分往主句上搭，搭建的工具是各种关系代词、介词、分词等。汉语的句式就像竹竿一样，一个分句接着一个分句展开，不受主谓结构框架的限制，形式上没有显性的衔接手段，虽然采用相同的句式，但句子之间的关系却多种多样。英语句式这种环环相扣、逻辑紧密的特点就是人们常说的"形合"，而汉语句子依次展开、句子之间关系须通过语义分析才能确定的特点就是人们常说的"意合"。英汉两种语言的差别涉及的方面很多，但最重要的差别就是"形合"与"意合"的差别。正如奈达所说："就汉语和英语而言，也许在语言学上最重要的一个区别，就是形合和意合的对比。"(Eugene Nida: *Translating Meaning*. California: English Language Institute. 1982, p16.)

二、英语中的句法结构

英语中有七种基本句型，任何繁杂的英语句式均由这七种句型演变而来，每一种句型都有其特定的限制条件：

Basic Sentence Patterns	Examples
1.Subject-Verb (S-V)	Angry customers complain.
2.Subject-Verb-Object (S-V-O)	The manager helped us gladly.
3.Subject-Linking Verb-Noun (S-LV-N)	Her decision was a terrible mistake.
4.Subject-Linking Verb-Adjective (S-LV-A)	My friend suddenly looked pale.
5.Subject-Verb-IndirectObject-Object (S-V-IO-O)	Her cousin often showed visitors the capital.
6.Subject-Verb-Object-Object Complement (S-V-O-OC)	They called the anonymous benefactor a saint.
7.Subject-Verb-Object-Adjective (S-V-O-A)	We painted the house green again.

其他句型还包括：

Sentence Patterns	Examples
1.Passive Voice Patterns	Rome was not built in a day.
2.Compound Sentences	Max maintained that the database needed restructuring, but Laura disagreed.
3.Complex Sentences	If the temperature stays at about freezing, then we can join the polar bear club for a dip in the lake.
4.Compound-Complex Sentences	In America everybody is of the opinion that he has no social superiors, since all men are equal, but he does not admit that he has no social inferiors, for, from the time of Jefferson onward, the doctrine that all men are equal applies only upwards, not downwards. (Bertrand Russell)

综观以上各类句型我们不难发现，英语中所有句型的核心就是主谓结构，主谓结构和与之相配套的一致原则是英语中最基本的原则。英语作为形态语言的特征，最集中地表现在主谓一致的严格要求上。英语中做主语的主要是名词和代词。名词有数的变化，代词有人称、性、数、格的变化。作谓语的是动词，有人称、数、时、体、态的变化。在人称和数的问题上，英语的主谓必须保持一致，不同人称和数的主语要配备不同的动词形式。总之，英语中的基本句型是句子的主干，就如同一棵树的树干，其他枝叶无论多么茂盛都是从主干中生长出来的。由此我们可以看出，英语的句法结构就如同一个龙骨框架，支撑着英语语法体系的全面展开，在纷繁复杂的句子结构中，每一个词或短语都可以找到属于自己的坐标点。

三、汉语中的句法结构

汉语句子结构与英语相比截然不同，赵元任在《汉语口语语法》(1979)一书中说："主语和谓语的关系可以是动作者和动作的关系。但在汉语里，这类句子的比例是不大的……因此在汉语里，把主语和谓语当做话题和说明来看待，比较适合。"也就是说汉语中的话题虽然是一个句子谈论的中心，但未必是该句的主语；换言之，一个汉语句子当中未必一定要有主语。实际上，当主语在特定的语境中明白无误时，往往被省略。由此可见，汉语的行文特征并非靠词语之间结构上的逻辑，而是靠语义上的连接。根据潘文国（2003）的观点，汉语句子是"话题+说明"结构的层层推进，犹如一节一节的竹子。汉语的竹式结构相对于英语的树式结构主要有两个区别性特征：1）汉语中不存在一个主干结构，也没有主干和枝叶之分。2）汉语的句式就像节节攀升的竹子，竹节可多可少，是开放性的，正好符合汉语句子界限不定的特点。

四、英汉句式中的施事与受事

施事和受事是一对相对的概念。施事是指句中发出动作的人或事物，在语义上，施事意味着主语和谓语、宾语和动词的施动关系。受事指句子中受动作支配的人或事物,语义上一般指主语和谓语、宾语和动词的受动关系。潘文国在《汉英语对比纲要》中把英语的主语分为四种:

1. 施事主语:She quit her job.
2. 受事主语:Slavery was abolished in New York State in 1827.
3. 形式主语:It is good to be rich.
4. 主题主语:The event is historically of great significance.

汉语中的主语问题非常复杂,如有零位主语(下雨了、刮风了)、时间主语(昨晚抓住三个小偷)和工具主语(一把菜刀闹革命)等十几种。不过对于译者而言,在英译汉时,重要的是运用英语句法知识理解好原文;而在汉译英时,重要的是选用适当的英语结构,将汉语意义恰当地表达出来。看下面汉译英的例子:

1. 回家的感觉真好。It feels good to be back home.
2. 这姑娘长得鼻子是鼻子,眼睛是眼睛。The girl has delicate facial features.
3. 这么一小段路就骑了一身汗。I got a good sweat from such a short-distance cycling.
4. 这药吃了准好。Take the medicine and you will recover soon.
5. 我的法语看报很吃力。My French is so poor that I can hardly read French newspapers.
6. 剧本把我写伤了,电视剧完全把我给写坏了。(王朔)I am sick of scriptwriting, and I am fed up with writing TV series.

第二节 英汉句法结构对比

一、文学语篇结构对比

英汉两种语言句法结构完全不同,英语中主谓结构必须明确,而汉语中不仅主语可以省略,甚至动词也可以省略,这一特点在诗歌中表现得尤为突出。在翻译时,译者必须考虑这样的结构差异:

《天净沙·秋思》 马致远 枯藤老树昏鸦, 小桥流水人家, 古道西风瘦马, 夕阳西下, 断肠人在天涯。	Tune: Tian Jing Sha By Ma Zhiyuan Withered vines hanging on old branches, Returning crows croaking at dusk. A few houses hidden past a narrow bridge, And below the bridge quiet creek running. Down a worn path, in the west wind, A lean horse comes plodding. The sun dips down in the west, And the lovesick traveler is still at the end of the world. (Translated by Ding Zuxin & Burton Raffel)

英语主谓结构分明、汉语主语及动词可省略的情况在歌词中也有反映:

一个太阳满天亮, 五月里来槐花香, 槐花香啊柳丝长, 思念的人儿在何方。 (邹静之:电视剧《五月槐花香》歌词)	The sun brightens the sky. With fragrant flowers, Pagoda trees bloom in May. And willow trees are dancing, With their drooping branches. Oh, where is my beloved now?

不过歌词的翻译有其特殊的困难,上面的歌词英译已无法和曲调相配。因此,歌词的翻译有时不得不另起炉灶,所谓翻译其实就是重新创作。例如,张学友《吻别》的歌词已和Jascha Richter "翻译"的歌词大相径庭:

我和你吻别在无人的街, 让风痴笑我不能拒绝。 我和你吻别在狂乱的夜, 我的心等著迎接伤悲。 (何启弘:《吻别》歌词)	Take me to your heart, take me to your soul, Give me your hand and hold me, Show me what love is - be my guiding star, It's easy take me to your heart. (Words by Jascha Richter)

也有个别例外的情况,下面英译文中就没有动词:

《江雪》	**River Snow**
柳宗元	A hundred mountains and no bird,
千山鸟飞绝，	A thousand paths without a footprint;
万径人踪灭。	A little boat, a bamboo cloak,
孤舟蓑笠翁，	An old man fishing in the cold river-snow.
独钓寒江雪。	(Translated by Witter Bynner)

另外，汉语中一些顺口溜式的表达具有结构整齐、朗朗上口的特点，译者在翻译时也要考虑句法结构的差异问题。下面是《中国公民出境旅游文明行为指南》（Tourism Etiquette Rules for Chinese Citizens Traveling Abroad）的部分原文及译文：

中国公民，出境旅游，	Chinese citizens traveling abroad must observe the local standards of propriety while keeping their own national dignity.
注重礼仪，保持尊严。	Keep the place clean and tidy, and protect the environment. Be dressed appropriately. Don't yell or talk loudly.
讲究卫生，爱护环境；	Respect senior citizens and care for children. And be ready to help others in need. To the female practice "lady first"; to others follow the rule "after you, please".
衣着得体，请勿喧哗。	Keep track of the time difference and arrive at appointments on time. Wait in a queue to get your turn and stand behind the yellow line.
尊老爱幼，助人为乐；	Be a welcome guest in a hotel. Don't damage objects in hotel rooms.
女士优先，礼貌谦让。	Wine and dine quietly, and don't waste food.
出行办事，遵守时间；	Go in for healthy and cultured entertainments,
排队有序，不越黄线。	and say no to pornography, gambling and drugs.
文明住宿，不损用品；	Follow the rules and tips on sightseeing tours.
安静用餐，请勿浪费。	Be careful to observe the local customs or taboos. Don't violate or offend against them.
健康娱乐，有益身心；	When in doubt or difficulty, make enquiries to the Chinese embassy or the consulate.
赌博色情，坚决拒绝。	Be a responsible traveler and enjoy a safe and pleasant trip.
参观游览，遵守规定；	（丁衡祁、陈小全译）
习俗禁忌，切勿冒犯。	
遇有疑难，咨询领馆；	
文明出行，一路平安。	

汉语竹节句依次展开，不受主谓结构框架限制的特点，一般在小说等语篇中反映的最为突出。因此，在将英语小说翻译成汉语时，不同译者在翻译时采用的竹节顺序往往不同。看下面的例子：

【原文】It was a typical summer evening in June, the atmosphere being in such delicate equilibrium and so transmissive that inanimate objects seemed endowed with two or three senses, if not five. There was no distinction between the near and the far, and an auditor felt close to everything within the horizon. The soundlessness impressed her as a positive entity rather than as the mere negation of noise. It was broken by the strumming of strings. (*Tess of the d"Urbervilles*, Chapter 19)

【译文一】那是六月里一个典型的夏季黄昏。一片大气，平静稳定，都到了精密细致的程度，而且特别富于传送之力，因此那些没有生命的东西，也都变得仿佛有了两种或者三种感官，即便不能说有五种。远处和近处，并没有什么分别，凡是地平线以内的东西，听的人都觉得，好象近在眼前。那种静悄无声的情况给她的印象是：与其说它单纯音响绝灭，不如说它积极具有实体。这种寂静，忽然叫弹琴的声音打破了。（《德伯家的苔丝》，人民文学出版社，第185页）

【译文二】这是六月里一个典型的夏日黄昏，空气非常平静怡人，又是如此能传播的声音，以致没有生命的东西仿佛也具有了两三种官能，如果说不是五种的话。远处和近处没有分别，地平线以内的一切对于听者来说都近在咫尺。寂静无声使苔丝产生的印象与其说是声音的不存在，不如说是感觉到一个明确的实体。有人拨动琴弦，打破了寂静。（《苔丝》，上海译文出版社，第113页）

【译文三】那是一个典型的六月黄昏。大气的平衡如此精致，传导力如此敏锐，就连冥顽的无生物也有了知觉——如果不是五种知觉的话，也有两三种。远和近已失去了差异，地平线以内的声音都仿佛是一种积极的实际存在。而这寂静却被拨弄琴弦的声音打破了。（《苔丝》，译林出版社，第108页）

【译文四】这是六月里一个典型的夏天的傍晚，空气柔和均衡，特别具有传导性能，因此，没有生命的东西也仿佛有了感觉，即使不是五种，至少也有两三种。远方和近处没有了区别，凡是在地平线以内，任何东西听起来仿佛就在身边。万籁俱寂。她顿时觉得，这寂静本身就是一个积极的实体，而并非只是声音的消失。接着，这寂静忽然被琴声所打破。（《苔丝》，浙江文艺出版社，第144页）

【译文五】这是六月里特有的夏日黄昏。暮色格外柔和静美且极富感染力，连那些冥顽之物都仿佛平添了几分灵性，有了各种知觉。远近一切，难分彼此；天际间任何一丝声息，听来都恍如近在耳畔。她觉得这静寂并非单纯的悄无声息，而是一种实实在在的感受。不想这静寂却被瑟瑟的琴声打破了。（马红军 改译）（原文和五段译文选自马红军：《翻译批评散论》，中国对外翻译出版公司，2000，第119—121页）

五段译文原本用于比较译文的优劣，这里可比较一下译文句法结构。你会发现无论质量如何，译文各具特色。这说明汉语句法结构松散、不受主谓框架限制的特点非常突出。

再看另外两个例子：

【例1】As the oldest son of a nearly impoverished Jew with a distinct German accent, Adolph, with his black curls and "round Jewish face," learned to value compromise, work harder than anyone else, and seek harmony whenever possible.（Susan Tifft: *THE TRUST*）

【译文一】作为一个穷困潦倒、说话带有明显德国口音的犹太人的长子，长着黑色卷发和一张"犹太圆脸"的阿道夫认识到了妥协的重要，他比任何人都勤奋努力，绝不放过任何寻求和谐的机会。

【译文二】阿道夫的父亲是个穷困潦倒的犹太人，说话带有明显的德国口音。阿道夫是家中的长子，长着一头黑色卷发和一张"犹太圆脸"，他认识到了妥协的重要，比任何人都勤奋努力，绝不放过任何寻求和谐的机会。

显而易见，【译文一】更贴近原文的句式结构，【译文二】则更具竹节的特点。笔者在翻译课上讨论两个例子时，多数同学更喜欢【译文一】。

【例2】There is a housing project standing now where the house in which we grew up once stood, and one of those stunted city trees is snarling where our doorway used to be.（Source Unknown）

【译文一】眼前是一片如今占据我们童年时代老屋位置的建筑群，一棵矮墩墩的树在原来我们屋门口的位置长得枝盘叶绕。

【译文二】眼前是一片新建筑群，我们童年时代的老屋原来就在这儿。原来的屋门口，现在是一棵矮墩墩的树，长得枝盘叶绕。

同样是【译文一】更贴近原文的句式结构，【译文二】更符合竹节的特点。这一次同学们的反应恰恰相反，绝大多数同学更喜欢【译文二】。

通过以上两个例句四个译文的对比我们可以看出，就句法结构转换而言，译者在将树型结构变为竹节句式时，应当把握好一个"度"的问题。

虽然英汉文学翻译句法结构转换灵活多变，但也有非常类似的情况。下面一段英语在翻译成汉语时，句法结构转换就非常简单。

【原文】It was the best of times, it was the worst of times, it was the age of wisdom, it was the age of foolishness, it was the epoch of belief, it was the epoch of incredulity, it was the season of Light, it was the season of Darkness, it was the spring of hope, it was the winter of despair, we had everything before us, we had nothing before us, we were all going direct to Heaven, we were all going direct the other way, ... (Charles Dickens: *A Tale of Two Cities*)

【译文】那是最美好的时代，那是最糟糕的时代；那是智慧的年头，那是愚昧的年头；那是信仰的时期，那是怀疑的时期；那是光明的季节，那是黑暗的季节；那是希望的春天，那是失望的冬天；我们拥有一切，我们一无所有；我们全都在直奔天堂，我们全都在直奔相反的方向……（霍锋利译）

下面看两个汉译英的例子，汉译英的过程即是将竹节句式转为树型结构的过程，译者同样需要考虑两种语言的句法结构差异。

【例1】

【原文】一九三九年古历八月初九，我父亲这个土匪种十四岁多一点。他跟着后来名满天下的传奇英雄余占鳌司令的队伍去胶平公路伏击敌人的汽车队。奶奶披着夹袄，送他们到村头。余司令说："立住吧。"奶奶就立住了。（莫言：《红高粱》）

【译文】NINTH DAY of the eighth lunar month, 1939. My father, a bandit's offspring who had passed his fourteenth birthday, was joining the forces Commander Yu Zhan'ao; a man destined to become a legendary hero, to ambush a Japanese convoy on the Jiao-Ping highway. Grandma, a padded jacket over her shoulders, saw them to the edge of the village. "Stop here," Commander Yu ordered her. She stopped.（Translated by Howard Goldblatt）

第一句译文将原文中的两句合为一句，将汉语中的竹节句式变为了英语中的树型结构，是个包含多种成分的复合句。这样的句式符合英语为母语人士的思维方式，读来流畅自然。如果我们完全按照汉语的句式翻译，译文则会显得支离破碎，毫无文采可言。例如：It was the ninth day of the eighth lunar month. My father had just passed his fourteenth birthday. He was a bandit's offspring...

【例2】
【原文】陈博士：这个胖子为什么捆着铁链？

丁保罗：这叫仿同情结，是一种潜意识过程，模仿他所崇拜的人，同时还具有移情仿同，从崇拜某个人，到崇拜某个人用过的东西。这副铁链就是这位胖子非常崇拜的，这个戴眼罩人用过的京剧道具，胖子戴上它，通过模仿，来抚慰自己，一下就觉得他自己就是他崇拜的那个人。（过士行《鸟人》）

【译文】*Dr. Chen*: Why is Fatty shackled with the metal chain?

Ding Baoluo: This is called sympathetic transference. It is a subconscious process in which one imitates an idol. At the same time, one transfers the feelings one has for the idolized to things used by the idol. This metal chain is greatly admired by Fatty. As soon as Fatty puts on the prop used by San Ye, the one whom he idolizes, Fatty feels as if he actually turns into San Ye.（Translated by Jonathan Scott Noble）

虽然是口语化的台词翻译，译文中也反映出英语树型结构的特征，例如 It is a subconscious process in which one imitates an idol 以及 At the same time, one transfers the feelings one has for the idolized to things used by the idol。这样翻译是充分考虑到了英汉两种语言句法结构差异的结果。

二、非文学语篇结构对比

非文学翻译中的句法结构转换与文学翻译相比总体上要简单一些，但非文学翻译的类别繁杂，因此，不同的语篇往往有着各自的特点。例如，演说的翻译特别强调朗读时的节奏感，如果译文的节奏感与原文不符，则很难称得上是好的译文。通常的情况是，译者不能遵从原文的句法结构，必须考虑两种语言各自的句法特征。看下面的两个例子：

【例1】Four score and seven years ago, our fathers brought forth upon this continent a new nation, conceived in Liberty, and dedicated to the proposition that all men are created equal.

Now we are engaged in a great civil war, testing whether that nation, or any nation so conceived and so dedicated, can long endure.

We are met on a great battlefield of that war. We have come to dedicate a portion of that field as a final resting place for those who here gave their lives that this nation might live. It is altogether fitting and proper that we should do this.（Lincoln's Gettysburg Address）

【译文】八十七年前，我们的父辈在这块大陆上创建了一个新的国家。这个新的国家在自由中孕育，信奉人人生而平等的主张。

现在我们正在从事伟大的国内战争，来考验这个国家，或任何在自由中孕育，信奉人人生而平等的主张的国家，能否长久存在下去。

我们今天相聚在这场战争的一个伟大的战场上。<u>我们相聚在这里是为了把这伟大战场的一部分奉献给那些为了我们国家的生存而献出了生命的烈士们作为最后的安息地</u>。我们这样做完全是合情合理的。（解伯昌译）

林肯的《葛底斯堡演说》是政治演说中精品之精品，一百多年来在全世界广为流传，绝对称得上是传世佳作。在我国有许多这篇演说的中译文，所有译文都会考虑到英汉两种语言的句法结构差异，而不会完全按照英语的句式进行翻译，因为那样会破坏原文铿锵有力、富于节奏感的风格。如把演说第一句译为"八十七年前，我们的先辈在这个大陆上建立了一个孕育于自由之中、信奉人人生而平等主张的崭新的国家。"就不是很好。上例译文中的下划线部分略长，也可将其结构调整一下，如翻译为："烈士们为使这个国家能够长存，献出了自己的生命，我们要把这个战场的部分土地奉献给他们，作为他们最后的安息之所，我们这样做是理所应当的。"

【例2】讲到长征，请问有什么意义呢？我们说，长征是历史纪录上的第一次，长征是宣言书，长征是宣传队，长征是播种机。自从盘古开天地，三皇五帝到于今，历史上曾经有过我们这样的长征吗？（毛泽东《论反对日本帝国主义的策略》）

【译文】Speaking of the Long March, one may ask, "What is its significance?" <u>We answer that the Long March is the first of its kind in the annals of history, that it is a manifesto, a propaganda force, a seeding-</u>

machine. Since Pan Ku divided the heavens from the earth and the Three Sovereigns and Five Emperors reigned, has history ever witnessed a long march such as ours? (*Selected Works of Mao Tse-tung*, People's Publishing House, Peking, April 1960)

汉语原文朗朗上口、节奏鲜明、掷地有声。译文也很精彩。不过划线部分似可调整一下，如译为：We say the Long March — the first of its kind in recorded human history — is a manifesto, (is) a publicity campaign, and (is) a seeding-machine。

就句法结构转换而言，非文学语篇翻译变化相对较小，与文学语篇翻译形成对比。一些英汉句子的结构几乎完全一样，看下面的例子：

【例1】Religious faith has much to contribute to the public sphere; is still a thriving part of what makes a cohesive community; is a crucial motivator of millions of citizens around the world; and is an essential if non-governmental way of helping to make society work.（Tony Blair's speech to the "Islam and Muslims in the World Today" conference, 4 June 2007）

【译文】宗教信仰对于公共领域贡献巨大；是促成社区凝聚力的活跃成分；是世界上数以千万计公民赖以前进的关键动力；是促成社会运行必不可少的非政府手段。

【例2】我们有着一个和谐融洽的企业氛围；我们拥有一支高素质、久经市场锻炼的优秀团队；我们具有先进的管理理念、扎实的业务基础和丰富的市场经验；我们拥有国内外广泛的客户、市场资源和营销网络。（公司讲演稿）

【译文】We have cultivated a harmonious corporate culture; established an outstanding team consisting of high-caliber people with superior market savvy; equipped ourselves with modern management philosophy, excellent skills in business and sophisticated market expertise; and have developed across the globe a broad network of customers, market resources and channels of distribution.

再看下面的两个例子，英语原文虽是个复合句，但其分句同汉语中的竹节句式也很类似。

【例1】The United Kingdom has been through 13 years in which unemployment has more than doubled, irreplaceable assets have been wasted, markets at home and abroad have been lost, manufacturing investment has fallen, poverty has increased, the crime rate has rocketed, and talents have been neglected. (It's time to get Britain working again. London: The Labour Party, 1992.)

【译文】过去的十三年中，英国的失业率增长两倍多，不可替代资产遭到浪费，国内外市场丢失，制造业投资下降，贫困人口增加，犯罪率直线上升，各类人才得不到重用。

【例2】人民生活显著改善。城乡居民收入较大增加，家庭财产普遍增多。城乡居民最低生活保障制度初步建立，贫困人口基本生活得到保障。居民消费结构优化，衣食住行用水平不断提高，享有的公共服务明显增强。（十七大报告）

【译文】Living standards improved significantly. Both urban and rural incomes increased considerably, and most families had more property than before. The system of subsistence allowances for urban and rural residents was basically in place, guaranteeing basic living conditions for the poor. Residents improved their consumption patterns, had increasingly better food, clothing, housing, transport and other daily necessities, and enjoyed markedly improved public services.（官方译文）

下面一段英语划线部分与相对应的中译文比较，句法结构变化很大。为了使译文流畅易懂，这样的结构调整是完全必要的。

【原文】The World Bank, which also raised its forecast for Chinese growth this year, said the current account surplus was likely to drop from 9.8 per cent of gross domestic product last year to 5.6 per cent of GDP this year, and to 4.1 per cent in 2010. In absolute terms, the bank forecast that the surplus would fall from $426bn in 2008 to $261bn (€176bn, £158bn) this year and $213bn in 2010. At its peak in 2007 — when, some economists argue, a large imbalance in China's favour contributed to the glut of liquidity in western financial markets that precipitated the global crisis — the current account surplus was equivalent to 11 per cent of GDP.

【译文】世行上调了对中国今年增长率的预期，并表示，经常账户盈余占国内生产总值(GDP)

的比例可能从去年的9.8%下降至今年的5.6%,2010年将降至4.1%。世行预测,盈余绝对值将从2008年的4240亿美元下降至今年的2610亿美元,2010年将降至2130亿美元。<u>中国经常账户盈余在2007年达到峰值,规模相当于GDP的11%。一些经济学家认为,当时,有利于中国的严重失衡局面,助长了西方金融市场的流动性泛滥,进而导致了全球危机。</u>(章晴译)(http://www.ftchinese.com/story/001029542/ce)

以上所谈为两种极端的情况,就大部分非文学语篇而言,翻译过程是个适当调整结构的过程。看下面的例子:

【原文】<u>Under the overarching theme of supporting China in making two historic transitions</u> from a rural, agricultural society to an urban, industrial society, and from a centrally-planned economy to a more globally integrated market-based economy—<u>the Bank Group's assistance strategy is designed to help China:</u> (a) improve the business environment and help accelerate the transition to a market economy, mostly through an array of knowledge transfer activities; (b) address the needs of the poorer and disadvantaged people and lagging regions, through investment lending in rural development, infrastructure and social sectors, as well as AAA and training; and (c) facilitate an environmentally sustainable development process, through investment lending in natural resource management, watershed rehabilitation and wastewater treatment, energy, global environment projects supported by the Global Environment Facility and Montreal Protocol, and policy work. (World Bank Document, Report No. 25141)

【译文】<u>中国正在经历两个最重要的历史性转型</u>,即:从农村和农业社会向城市和工业社会转型,从中央计划经济向全球一体化的市场经济转型。<u>在实现这两个转型的主题下,世行的援助战略旨在帮助中国:</u>(1)以知识传播活动为主改善经营环境并加快向市场经济转轨;(2)通过向农村发展、基础设施和社会部门贷款投资,以及分析咨询和培训活动,满足贫困和弱势人口及落后地区的需求;(3)通过对自然资源管理、小流域治理、污水处理、能源、全球环境基金和蒙特利尔议定书支持的全球环境项目贷款投资,以及政策研究工作,推动环境可持续发展进程。(官方译文,略有改动)

译文没有按照原文的句法结构把第一句话翻译为:"在支持中国实现最重要的两个历史性转型的主题下,即从农村和农业社会向城市和工业社会转型及从中央计划经济向全球一体化的市场经济转型,世行的援助战略旨在帮助中国:……",而是将原句的句法结构拆分成汉语中的竹节句式,目的是使译文读者更加容易理解。

应当指出,有经验的译者在将英语复杂的句法结构转换成竹节句式的过程中,依靠的是对原文的准确理解以及对汉语的有效把握,他们未必对英汉两种语言的句法结构差异进行过多少研究。这是因为译者在理解原文之后,会按照汉语的思维习惯将原文意义进行重新整理,此后的翻译不过是将原文意义进行重新书写,在这一过程中对汉语的熟练把握起到了关键的作用。因此,对于一个熟练掌握了汉语的译者来说,最重要的就是理解好英语原文的意义。正如奈达所言:"有人想象,翻译工作最大的难题是在接受语或译语中找出恰当的词和结构。恰恰相反,对于译者来说,最大的困难是透彻理解所译文本的所指意义和联想意义,这就不仅需要理解词语的意义和句法关系,而且还要对各种文体手段的细微差别感觉敏锐。正如一位辛勤耕耘的译者在总结他的困难时所说的:'如果我真正理解了原文的意思,我就能够得心应手地进行翻译。'"(Eugene A. Nida: *Language, Culture, and Translating*. 上海外语教育出版社,2001。)

第二节 汉英句法结构转换

译者真正理解了原文的意思,就能够得心应手地进行翻译。这话一般只适用于译者将外语译成母语的情况。例如,我们在将英语译成汉语时,在完全理解了原文的基础上,我们会凭直觉将原文意义重新整理,产出的译文在句法结构上通常不会有问题,如果有问题通常是因为我们对原文的理解有误。在将汉语译成英语时,母语是英语的译者同样不会在句法上出问题,如果出问题,同样是因为对汉语原文的理解有误。看下面的例子:

【原文】胖子:那叫凤凰台。百灵爪子抓不住杠,天生来是沙子,地上跑的玩艺儿。你想啊,沙漠

哪有树哇？<u>不像人，老想着攀高枝儿</u>，所以得造一个台儿，让它台上露脸。（过士行：《鸟人》）

【译文】Fatty: It's called the Phoenix Rostrum. The feet of the lark can't grab onto bars. From birth it was this little critter running on the sand. Just think, are there any trees in the desert? <u>They are not like us, always thinking about climbing to higher branches</u>. Therefore, we have to give them a rostrum, a stage for them to strut on and show off their stuff.（Translated by Jonathan Scott Noble）

原文中"不像人，老想着攀高枝儿，"一句是指谁老想着攀高枝儿？当然是人而不是鸟儿。但英译文 They are not like us, always thinking about climbing to higher branches. 中的主语 They 指的却是鸟儿，因此 always thinking about 的逻辑主语也是鸟儿。这样一来该句的意思就成了"鸟儿老想着攀高枝儿"。可以把这句话改为：They are not like people, who are always thinking about climbing to higher branches。我们没有理由相信译者的错误是由于句法结构转换出了问题。

然而，对于我们这些英语是外语、汉语为母语的译者来说，汉英翻译几乎是个无法做好但又必须去做的工作，此时，对于汉英句法结构差异的自觉认识，便有着极其重要的意义。就目前情况来看，汉语句法结构语义关系多样化如何在英译文中得以实现的问题，是个远未得到很好解决的问题，即使是专业人士的高层次译文，也难免存在这样或那样的问题。汉语竹节句式层层展开的特点，如何经过语义分析，最终搭建英语句式框架，是每个译者都无法回避的问题。看下面的例子：

【原文】
1. 中国的改革开放取得了重大成果。
2. 中国加入世界贸易组织的协定范围广泛，从农业到知识产权涵盖八个领域。
3. 该词典内容详实，资料丰富，融学术性、知识性、实用性于一体。

【译文】
1. China's economic reform and opening-up have made great achievements.
2. The agreement for China's entrance into WTO has a broad scope and also has eight fields from agriculture to intellectual property rights.
3. Detailed and reliable in content(s) and rich in references, the dictionary embodies a combination of academic authenticity, informativeness and practicability.

【改译】
1. China has made great achievements in its economic reform and opening up to the outside world.
2. Broad in scope, China's WTO accession agreement covers eight areas, ranging from agriculture to intellectual property rights.
3. This dictionary provides an authoritative and practical guide to translation studies and brings together a wealth of accurate information with a comprehensive coverage of all aspects of translation.（孙艺风改译）

上面三个译文存在着句法结构转换和语言表达两方面的问题。第一句中的主语在英语中不能被接受；第二句将汉语竹节句式直接植入译文，让人感觉到中式英语的味道。另外 China's entrance into WTO 应为 China's entry into the WTO。第三句主要是表达方面的问题，如把"内容详实"表述为 rich (and grounded) in content，把"资料丰富"表述为 comprehensive (broad) in reference 情况会好得多。

再看下面一些翻译段落实例：

【例1】中国西部地区资源丰富，产业基础好，政策优惠，发展潜力大，投资机会多，市场前景广阔。（商务部副部长姜增伟在国际投资环境暨项目推介会上的致辞）

【译文】Western China enjoys abundant resources, solid industrial infrastructure and preferential policies, which boasts tremendous investment opportunities and a broad and promising market outlook.
（http://english.mofcom.gov.cn/aarticle/translatorsgarden/）

【另译】With its abundant resources, solid industrial infrastructure and preferential policies, Western China has gained a considerable development edge, more opportunities for investment and a growing market with huge potential.

分析一下原文我们会发现，"资源丰富，产业基础好，政策优惠"是条件，在此基础上中国西部才"发展潜力大,投资机会多,市场前景广阔"。按照这样的思路,我们可以把"中国西部发展潜力大……"确立为主干句。

【例2】我们有决心、有信心,通过深化改革、扩大开放,变压力为动力,迎接加入世贸组织带来的挑战,促进国民经济不断取得新的发展。(石广生中国加入WTO和参与经济全球化演讲)

【译文】We have the determination and confidence that through the deepening of reform and opening wider to the outside world, we can turn pressure into motive force to take the challenges arisen from our accession to the WTO and enable the national economy to achieve new progress on a continuous basis.

(www.cofortune.com.cn/moftec_cn/fyyd/)

【另译】With confidence and determination, and through further reform and opening wider to the outside world, we will respond positively to the pressure upon us, meeting challenges arising from China's accession to the WTO, and pushing forward the development of our national economy.

先确立了主句,然后在主句上搭建介词短语和分词短语,使英译文结构及语义层次变得清晰起来。译文 challenges arisen from our accession to the WTO 中的 arisen 应改为 arising。另译中的 to respond positively to the pressure 是英语中的常用表达,当然也可以用 to turn pressure into motivation 之类的表达。

【例3】为了实现我们的发展目标,中国根据本国国情和时代要求明确了自己的发展理念,这就是树立和贯彻以人为本、全面协调可持续发展的科学发展观,<u>统筹</u>城乡发展、<u>统筹</u>区域发展、<u>统筹</u>经济社会发展、<u>统筹</u>人与自然和谐发展、<u>统筹</u>国内发展和对外开放。(胡锦涛在美国耶鲁大学的演讲)

【译文】To realize these goals, China has adopted a new concept of development in line with its national conditions and the requirement of the times. That is, to pursue a scientific outlook on development that makes economic and social development people-oriented, comprehensive, balanced and sustainable. We will work to strike a proper balance between urban and rural development, development among regions, economic and social development, development of man and nature, and domestic <u>development</u> and opening wider to the outside world.

(http://www.eduzhai.net/yingyu/618/795/yingyu_253399.html)

译文对五个"统筹……发展"的英译不妥,英译文重复了五次 development,而应该重复的词是 between 而不是 development。上段最后一句可翻译为:China will promote a balanced development <u>between</u> urban and rural areas, <u>between</u> different regions across our country, <u>between</u> our economy and society, <u>between</u> man and nature, and <u>between</u> China's domestic development and its opening up to the outside world.

【例4】今天的香港,社会保持稳定,经济更加繁荣,民主有序发展,民众安居乐业,展现出一派欣欣向荣的景象。(胡锦涛主席在庆祝香港回归祖国10周年大会上的讲话)

【译文】Today's Hong Kong enjoys stability and has a dynamic economy, and its democracy is growing in an orderly way. The Hong Kong people enjoy their lives and everywhere in the city one sees a scene of prosperity.

(http://www.ebigear.com/news-54-30995.html)

【另译】We see a Hong Kong with signs of growing prosperity today — a stable society, a dynamic economy, a democracy growing in an orderly fashion, and a people enjoying their life and work in peace and comfort.

首先,【译文】频繁变换主语及谓语动词不是英语的句法特点,也不符合英语多枝共干的结构特征;其次,【译文】的风格未能展示出汉语原文节奏鲜明、铿锵有力、朗朗上口的特点。其中的原因显而易见:【译文】几乎完全套用了汉语原文的结构。

本章主要参考文献:

陈定安:《英汉比较与翻译》,商务印书馆,1992年。

连淑能:"论中西思维方式",《外语与外语教学》,2002(2)。

潘文国:《汉英语对比纲要》,北京语言大学出版社,2003年。
赵元任:《汉语口语语法》,吕叔湘译,商务印书馆,1979年。
Nida, Eugene: *Translating meaning*. California: English Language Institute, 1982.

翻译练习四

1. 将下面段落译成汉语:

That must be the story of innumerable couples, and the pattern of life it offers has a homely grace. It reminds you of a placid rivulet, meandering smoothly through green pastures and shaded by pleasant trees, till at last it falls into the vasty sea; but the sea is so calm, so silent, so indifferent, that you are troubled suddenly by a vague uneasiness. Perhaps it is only by a kink in my nature, strong in me even in those days, that I felt in such an existence, the share of the great majority, something amiss. I recognised its social values, I saw its ordered happiness, but a fever in my blood asked for a wilder course. There seemed to me something alarming in such easy delights. In my heart was a desire to live more dangerously. I was not unprepared for jagged rocks and treacherous shoals if I could only have change-change and the excitement of the unforeseen. (Somerset Maugham: *The Moon and Sixpence*)

2. 将下面段落译成英语:

如何克服出口低迷的局面

近年来,中国出口厂商受到了亚洲金融危机的冲击。该地区许多国家的经济不景气引起消费市场萎缩,货币疲软使购买力下降。有的国家政局不定、经济不稳,贸易保护主义升级,外交磨擦抬头。这些使得对该地区的出口十分困难。我们必须采取有效措施来对付这种局面。

我们要大力推进外贸体制改革,走集团化的道路,组建以外贸为龙头的工贸、农贸、技贸相结合的企业集团,以增强企业的竞争力。老的大中型国有企业必须进行技术改造以增强活力,对有条件的大中型企业应授予其进出口经营权。工业企业自营出口这是我国外贸体制改革的一个重大步骤。

必须优化传统的出口商品结构,靠价格和数量竞争的时代已一去不复返了。在当今激烈竞争的世界上,只有以质取胜和改善售前售后服务才能行得通。要通过精加工和深加工提高出口商品的附加值;要努力生产适销对路的名特优新产品和"拳头"产品打入国际市场。由于市场形势千变万化,出口产品必须不断地更新换代,做到你无我有,你有我优,胜人一筹。

要全方位地开拓国际市场,市场多元化是立于不败之地的关键。俗话说:"不能在一棵树上吊死。"在选择新辟市场时要权衡其风险与机会,并且要反应迅速;要随时跟踪市场变化情况,以便选择有利时机和地点抓紧出口。只有那些富有活力、洞察力和应变力的企业才能在市场景气时大显身手,而在市场萧条时也能站稳脚根。当某些市场疲软时,总还有另一些市场坚挺,所以能够做到"东方不亮西方亮"。

出口商品必须有一流的品质,样式,包装和装潢,但行之有效的广告宣传和促销活动也很重要,尤其要提高用外语针对国外市场进行宣传的能力。赴国外参展,派人员出国推销,在国外建立生产或销售点等等,一定要讲求实效。最后,引进国外的技术和资金以提高我国出口商品的质量和劳动生产率,通过加强管理降低成本,通过加强培训以提高人员的素质,等等,都是不可忽视的方面。通过落实各项优惠政策,搞好基础设施建设,完善配套服务,掀起一个吸引外资的新高潮。

第五章

翻译中的文化与修辞

长期以来，翻译研究主要关注两种语言文字层面上的转换，如翻译策略、翻译技巧、翻译标准、可译性、不可译性及译者风格等。从 20 世纪 70 年代开始，国际译学界一批著名的翻译理论家，如詹姆斯·霍尔姆斯（James S Holmes）、苏珊·巴斯奈特（Susan Bassnett）、安德烈·勒菲弗尔（Andre Lefevere）、劳伦斯·韦努提（Lawrence Venuti）、西奥·赫曼斯（Theo Hermans）等，他们跳出了语言文字层面的转换，从更加广阔的文化视野去审视翻译和翻译研究，这就是所谓译学研究的"文化转向"。以苏珊·巴斯奈特为代表的文化学派，对当代社会需求和翻译现状进行了思考，提出了文化翻译观。文化翻译观以文化为大背景对翻译进行考察，关注文化语境、历史渊源、意识形态等宏观问题，让人们以新的视角看待翻译的性质、功能、译者地位等问题。对文化学派而言，翻译的基本单位不是单词，不是句子，甚至不是语篇，翻译的本质就是文化翻译。

文化翻译观强调译文读者努力理解和吸收异域文化，强调文化的移植。因此，译者应当尽量保留差异，保留原语中的原汁原味，翻译的目的不是消除差异，而是将其显现，以达到两种文化进行交流的目的。另一方面，由于地理环境、动植物品种、文化习俗、神话传说、历史渊源、思维方式、文化价值观等方面的差异，文本意义及所传达的情感往往超越字面意义，译者必须在两种文化之间进行对比，然后做出最恰当的选择。

第一节 文化与翻译

一、词语中的文化信息

语言是文化的载体，语言中的大量固定短语（set phrases）、惯用语（idioms）、典故（allusions）、俚语（slangs）、俗语（colloquialisms）、谚语（proverbs）、格言（sayings）、歇后语（enigmatic folk similes）、套话（routines）等都蕴含着丰富的文化信息，都带有浓烈的民族色彩和地域特征。例如：

【例 1】And that's flat-unless I see Amelia's ten thousand down you don't marry her. I'll have no lame duck's daughter in my family. Pass the wine, sir — or ring for coffee.（Thackeray: *Vanity Fair*）

【译文】反正除非他把爱米丽亚的十万镑嫁妆拿出来给我瞧过，你就不准娶她。这件事是不能含糊的。我可不要娶个破产经纪人的女儿进门作媳妇。把酒壶递给我，要不，打铃子让他们把咖啡送上来也好。（杨绛译）

【例 2】Still, Clinton is far from being a lame duck and the Republicans have yet to establish themselves as the new majority party.（*U.S. News & World Report*, 1994 November 21）

【译文】尽管如此，克林顿还远不是一只"跛脚鸭"，共和党人仍然需要成为新的多数党。

英语原文中 lame duck 字面意为"跛脚鸭"，原指一些失魂落魄的股票破产人，指他们精神溃散、步履蹒跚，状似"跛脚鸭"，该词在英文中已存在 100 多年了。后来 lame duck 进入美国英语，成了一个政治术语，用以指代即将下台的政界人物，尤其指第二任期已到最后两年的美国总统。

【例 3】"Since October, economic indicators have deteriorated at a pace that defies any rule of thumb," Tetsufumi Yamakawa, chief Japan economist at Goldman Sachs, said in a recent report. "There has been an unprecedented large decline in exports and production-related indicators in particular."

【译文】高盛公司首席日本经济学家彻文山川在近日公布的报告中称："自去年十月始，诸多经济指标严重下滑，速度之快有违任何经验法则。特别是出口和生产相关指标严重下跌。"

上例中 rule of thumb 可翻译为"经验法则"或者"拇指规则"，意指单凭经验来做的方法，较为通用的原则，但并非放之四海而皆准。关于这个短语的起源有两种说法。其一是旧时人们习惯用大拇指的最后一个关节到指甲之间的这一段作为天然的测量工具，因为成年男子这一段的平均长度是一英寸。另外一种说法是，当年有经验的酿酒师习惯用大拇指伸进酿酒池测量发酵温度，以了解酿造的进展情况。（本例子选自《英语点津》http://www.chinadaily.com.cn/language_tips/news/2009-02/17/content_7483149.htm）

下表中是一些富含文化信息的英语习惯表达，这些表达与其字面意思相差甚远，在翻译过程中，译者需要认真查证和仔细揣摩，这样才能够准确理解其中的内涵。

the bee's knees（微不足道的事物） nine days' wonder（昙花一现） never-never land（想像中的地方；偏远地区） paint the town red（狂欢；痛饮；胡闹） lock, stock and barrel（全部） dead ringer（与另一个人或物一模一样的人或物） the whole nine yards（在各个方面，应有尽有） ship-shape and Bristol fashion（整整齐齐） head over heels（彻头彻尾，神魂颠倒） shake a leg（迅速行动） taken aback（吓一跳）	shanks' mare（步行） heard it through the grapevine（道听途说） eat humble pie（忍辱含垢；忍气吞声） thumbs up（赞许） helter-skelter（慌慌张张） flotsam and jetsam（流浪者；无价值物） knuckle down（开始认真工作） a cock and bull story（无稽之谈） saved by the bell（脱离窘境） below the salt（处于无足轻重的地位） local derby（同城两队之间的比赛） （选自：http://www.phrases.org.uk/）

二、修辞的翻译

修辞与社会文化相适应，不能脱离社会文化而存在，修辞的表达体现了不同的文化心理和文化内涵。由于不同语言中修辞手法带有明显的差异性，译者必须透视修辞手法背后的丰富文化，才能够把握好原文的意义，顺利完成翻译任务。

（一）明喻 (Simile)

一种将具有某种共同特征的两种不同事物连接起来的修辞手法。英语中常使用 like, as 等词语。

1. My love is like a red, red rose.（Robert Burns: *A Red, Red Rose*）

啊，我的爱人像一朵红红的玫瑰。（王佐良译）

2. The atmosphere at World Cups is joyous, not hostile; more like a carnival than a war.

世界杯的气氛是欢乐的，没有任何敌意；它更像是狂欢节，而不是战争。

3. Big banks are like nuclear power stations. They provide valuable services, such as channeling capital from savers to entrepreneurs. Occasionally, they blow up, causing damage to the rest of the economy and necessitating spending vast sums of taxpayers' money on clean-up operations.

（http://www.ftchinese.com/story/001031787/ce）

大银行就像核电站。它们提供着有价值的服务，比如把资本从储户输送到企业家手中。偶尔，它们也会崩盘，对其他经济领域造成破坏，并迫使政府拿出巨额纳税人资金来收拾残局。（君悦译）

（二）暗喻（Metaphor）

暗喻是本体和喻体同时出现，它们之间在形式上是相合的关系，说甲（本体）是（喻词）乙（喻体）。

1. You are the cream in my coffee.

你是我咖啡中的奶油。（意思是"你使我的生活更美。"）

2. You are my oxygen.

你是我的空气。（意思是"我离不开你。"）

3. I have sacrificed a pebble, and saved a diamond.

我失去了一块卵石，却收获了一枚钻石。（意思是"得到的远比失去的宝贵得多。"）

4. He has been a tower of strength for all of us who were frightened, shaken, sorrowful and depressed.

对于我们这些饱受威胁、惊恐不安、悲伤沮丧的人来说，他就是我们大家的主心骨。（a tower of strength: 力量之塔 = 危难时刻可以信赖的人）

（三）拟人（Personification）

拟人是指把物（包括物体、动物、思想或抽象概念）拟作人，使其具有人的外表、个性或情感的修辞手段。拟人可以通过形容词、动词或名词表现出来。

1. I kissed the hand of death. 我吻过死亡之手。（我和阎王爷握过手。）

2. a promising morning 充满朝气的早晨

3. a treacherous sea 背信弃义的大海

4. Sometime too hot the eye of heaven shines,/And often is his gold complexion dimm'd;（Shakespeare）

有时候当空照耀着烈日，/又往往它的光彩转阴淡。（戴镏龄译）

（四）对比（Contrast）

对比是把具有明显差异、矛盾和对立的双方安排在一起，进行对照比较的表现手法。写作中的对比手法，就是把事物、现象和过程中矛盾的双方，安置在一定条件下，使之集中在一个完整的艺术统一体中，形成相辅相成的比照和呼应关系。运用这种手法，有利于充分显示事物的矛盾，突出被表现事物的本质特征，加强文章的艺术效果和感染力。

1. He wept for joy. 他喜极而泣。
2. Speech is silver; Silence is golden. 言语是银，沉默是金。
3. To err is human, to forgive is divine. 失误人皆有之，宽恕乃圣贤之举。
4. The evil that men do lives after them; the good is often interred with their bones. 好事不出门，坏事传千里。

（五）矛盾修辞法（Oxymoron）

矛盾修辞法是指将语义截然相反对立的词语放在一起使用，来揭示某一项事物矛盾性质的一种修辞手法。换言之，它使用两种不相协调、甚至截然相反的特征来形容一项事物，以增强语言的感染力。

1. Life is a bitter sweet symphony.
生活是苦乐参半的交响曲。
2. Unrequited love is such sweet sorrow.（《罗密欧与朱丽叶》，莎士比亚）
单相思是甜蜜的忧伤。

（六）委婉语（Euphemism）

对于不愉快的、粗鲁无礼的、令人尴尬的、伤人伤感的或具有侮辱性质的词语或句子，人们往往都采用迂回婉转的说法，即委婉语。就是用好听的、使人感到愉快的说法，代替令人不悦的或不敬的表达方式。

1. I'm afraid that he has misrepresented the facts. (= lied)
恐怕他误传了事实。（= 撒谎）
2. You drove there in your fancy Jaguar, and you took a lady friend.
你开着高档捷豹车到了那里，还带上了你的红颜知己。（lady friend= 情妇）
3. 关于死亡的委婉语：
to go west 归西去了
to go to glory 升天了
to go to one's account 逝去
to go to one's last home 回老家去
to go to a better world 去了极乐世界

（七）双关语（Pun）

利用词的多义及同音（或近音）条件，有意使语句有双重意义，言在此而意在彼，就是双关。双关可使语言表达得含蓄、幽默，而且能加深语意，给人以深刻印象。对双关语做过深入研究的修辞学家王希杰曾说，双关语虽然是各民族都普遍使用的修辞格，但它具有浓厚强烈的民族色彩，是很难翻译成别种语言的。例如：

1. On Sunday they pray for you and on Monday they prey on you.
意思为"他们星期天为你祈祷，星期一剥削你"，但发音相同的 pray 和 prey 构成的双关难以体现。
2. More sun and air for your son and heir.
意为"给子孙后代留下更多的阳光与空气"，无法翻译出"sun and air"和"son and heir"所构成的双关。
3. Money doesn't grow on trees. But it blossoms at our branches.
钱没有长在树上，但在我们的枝头开花。

在双关语的翻译中，如果能够既传达原文的内容，又保存原文的形式和文化特色，内容形式浑然一体，"形""神"俱备，当然为上上之策。英汉语言中带有共同认知特征的比喻型双关语往往相对容易，一些其他类型的双关语在翻译实践中也不乏成功的例子。

4. That home is home though it is never so homely. 家虽不佳仍是家。（刘炳善译）
译者选择"家"、"佳"、"家"这三个音同的字来对应原语中"home"、"home"、"homely"这三个形、音相同（似）的词，将原句中不可传达的形美化成了译句中的音美，既保持了原语的语言特征，又准确地传达了文本信息。

5. *First Gentleman*: Thou are always figuring diseases in me, but thou are full of error, I am sound.
Lucio: Nay, not as one would say, healthy, but so sound as things that are hollow, impiety made a feast of thee.（William Shakespeare, *Measure for Measure*）
绅士甲：你总是认为我有那种病，其实你大错特错，我的身体响当当。
路奇奥：响当当，可并不结实，就像空心的东西那样响当当的，你的骨头都空了，好色的毛病把你掏空了。（英若诚译）

原语中"sound"一语双关，兼有"身体健康"和"听起来"之意。译者把"sound"译为"响当当"，是一个非常恰当的选择。在汉语里，"响当当"也有双重意思，既有"健康结实"之意，也有"中空的，发出声音"的意思。这样，译者通过巧合的双关语，最大限度地实现了和原文从形式到内容的吻合。

（八）讽刺（Sarcasm）

讽刺是用比喻、夸张等手法对不良的或愚蠢的行为进行揭露或批评。讽刺效果离不开具体的语境，离不开讲话者的口吻。

1. See how these Christians love one another.
看这些基督徒是怎样相爱的！
2. He is a perfect Solomon.
他是不折不扣的所罗门。（他真是绝顶聪明。）
3. Sometimes I need what only you can provide: your absence. (Ashleigh Brilliant)
有时候我只需要你能提供的东西：你离开这里。
4. I find television very educating. Every time somebody turns on the set, I go into the other room and read a book. (Groucho Marx)
电视这玩意儿还挺教育人的。每当有人打开电视机时，我就会到另一个房间去读书。

第二节 文化翻译策略

一、熟悉约定俗成的译法

（一）翻译中的文化差异大多需要译者在理解语篇的基础上灵活处理，但由于文化之间的不断融合，许多文化负载词汇已经约定俗成，译者应当熟悉并使用它们。看下表：

英译汉	汉译英
armed to the teeth 武装到牙齿	阴阳 Yin yang
domino 多米诺骨牌	风水 Feng shui
Trojan Horse 特洛伊木马	太极 Tai chi
crocodile tears 鳄鱼眼泪	功夫 Kung fu
Aladdin and His Lamp 阿拉丁神灯	叩头 Kowtow
Pandora's Box 潘多拉的盒子	军阀 war lords
Cupid's Arrow 丘比特箭	杀手锏 assassin's mace
shylock 夏洛克式的人物（吝啬鬼）	扫墓 sweeping graves
sword of Damocles 达摩克利斯之剑	红卫兵 Red Guards
Achilles' heel 致命的弱点	走资派 capitalist roader
Helen of Troy 红颜祸水	铁饭碗 iron-rice bowl
Electra Complex 恋父情结	百花齐放 hundred flowers
Oedipus Complex 恋母情结	纸老虎 paper tiger
Odyssey 漫长旅程	爆竹 fire cracker
Prometheus 普罗米修斯	砚台 inkstone
Venus (the Queen of love) 维纳斯	丢脸 to lose face
Saint Valentine's Day 情人节	锅 wok
Arcadia 阿卡狄亚(世外桃源)	福娃 Fuwa

（二）由于文化重合或文化融合，英汉两种语言中存在着一些对等说法，这些译者只需学习和使用，不必另起炉灶创造新的说法。

1. Blood is thicker than water. 血浓于水。

2. Long time no see. 好久不见。

3. Where there is a will, there is a way. 有志者，事竟成。

4. The older the ginger the hotter the spice. 姜还是老的辣。

5. to do something through the back door 走后门。

6. What is said can not be unsaid. 一言既出，驷马难追。

7. Misfortunes never come alone. 福无双至，祸不单行。

8. Actions speak louder than words. 事实胜于雄辩。

9. A rolling stone gathers no moss. 流水不腐。

10. When in Rome, do as the Romans do. 入乡随俗。

二、文化中比喻修辞的翻译

（一）英语中有些比喻容易理解，翻译起来也不难，但需要灵活处理。

1. This dream is no castle in the air. 这梦想绝非空中楼阁。

2. His feet were as big as boats. 他的双脚像两只大船。

3. The clouds were fluffy like cotton wool. 云朵像棉絮一样蓬松。

4. She is as pretty as a picture. 她美得像一幅画。

5. The moon was a misty shadow. 月色朦胧。

6. The striker was a goal machine. 前锋是个进球机器。

7. He is as slippery as an eel. 他像泥鳅一样狡猾。

8. Encyclopedias are like gold mines. 百科全书像金矿。

9. He doesn't have an idea of his own. He just parrots what other people say.
他没有自己的观点，只会鹦鹉学舌。

10. Economists set themselves too easy, too useless a task if in tempestuous seasons they can only tell us that when the storm is past the ocean is flat again.（J.M. Keynes: *A Tract on Monetary Reform* 1923）
经济学家们为自己设定的任务太容易也太无用，他们只是在风暴来临时告诉我们：风暴结束后海洋将恢复平静。

（二）英语中有些比喻容易理解，但翻译起来有难度；另外一些理解比较困难，翻译时有难有易，有时需要变换喻体。先看两个例子：

【例1】

【原文】Once the embargo ends, American tourists will <u>flood</u> the tiny country of 11 million people that long has been travelers' <u>forbidden fruit</u>.

【译文】一旦解除禁令，美国游客将如洪水一般，涌入这个只有1100万人口的小国。这个国家长期来一直都是旅行者梦想前去的地方。

原文中 flood 在这里是比喻义，直接用字面意思翻译即可让汉语读者理解。而 forbidden fruit 的意思是：banned object of desire: something desired or pleasurable that somebody is not allowed to have or do, especially some form of sexual indulgence that is illegal or considered immoral（*Encarta® World English Dictionary*）forbidden fruit 汉语中有现成的说法"禁果"，但这里不能直接引用，需按照原文的意思换个说法，这样才能使读者更容易理解。

【例2】

【原文】I think if the police department had done what I asked them to do, they could have <u>nipped this in the bud</u>.

【译文】我想如果警方按照我所说的去做，他们或许已把事件扼杀在摇篮之中。

原文中 nipped this in the bud 指的是在 this 尚处于蓓蕾状态就将其掐掉，不至于开花结果。根据汉语习惯，应调整喻体将其翻译为"扼杀在摇篮之中"，这样才能让译文读者更容易理解。

下面的例子翻译时大多需要改变喻体：

1. I <u>hit the wall</u> and was pretty much <u>a limp dishrag</u> for the next several days.

我<u>遭受到重创</u>，在随后的几天中，我像<u>一块软抹布</u>那样无精打采。

2. With exports and investment both <u>under large clouds</u> in the next couple of years, the performance of Chinese consumers has become much more important.

由于未来几年出口和投资的情形都<u>不容乐观</u>，中国消费者的表现变得更为重要。

3. No one invites Harold to parties because he's <u>a wet blanket</u>.

没有人邀请哈罗德参加聚会，因为他是个<u>令人扫兴的人</u>。

4. Carmen was <u>a ride-or-die chick</u> to the bone — a five-foot-seven Puerto Rican beauty with pretty almond-shaped eyes and thick black lashes to complement them.

卡门是个<u>与生俱来无所畏惧的女孩</u>，这位波多黎各佳丽身高五英尺七英寸，浓黑的睫毛下映衬着一双美丽的杏眼。（ride or die chick 指女孩不管好事坏事都敢做敢为。）

5. In the darkest hour of winter, when all the starlings had flown away, Gretel Samuelson fell in love. It happened the way things are never supposed to happen in real life, <u>like a sledgehammer, like a bolt from the blue</u>.

在漆黑的冬夜里，当所有的椋鸟飞走时，格勒泰·萨缪尔森坠入了情网。事情的发生如此突然，<u>犹如雷霆万钧，又如晴空霹雳</u>，这在真实的生活中是难以想象的。

三、翻译中的"假朋友"

Mona Baker 这样定义"假朋友"（false friends）：False friends are words or expressions which have the same form in two or more languages but convey different meanings。"假朋友"看似相符，实则有别，所以在翻译时要特别小心。看下表的例子：

英文	"假朋友"	"真朋友"
capital idea	资本主义思想	好主意
morning glory	晨光	牵牛花
Spanish athlete	西班牙运动员	吹牛的人
liberal arts	自由艺术	文科
English disease	英国病	软骨病
pull one's leg	拖后腿	开玩笑
You don't say!	你别说！	是吗！
pigtail	猪尾巴	辫子
marriages go off the rails	婚姻出轨	家庭出现小矛盾

翻译中的"假朋友"常常使译者误入歧途，有些"假朋友"常常被当作"真朋友"。例如，out of sight, out of mind. 常被译为"眼不见，心不烦"，而其真正意义是"久别情疏"。lady killer 常被认为是"少奶杀手"，但其主要意义是"爱情骗子"。汉语中"避雷针效应"的寓意是："善疏则通，能导必安。"而英语中 lightening rod 则有"招惹麻烦、众矢之的"等意义。看下面的两个例子：

【例1】

【原文】Microsoft's decision to offer new employee perks, initially only at its headquarters campus near Seattle but eventually also in other sites around the world, marks a reversal of an earlier, unpopular cost-cutting policy. A decision to scrap the free towel service two years ago became a lightening rod for employee dissatisfaction.（Microsoft plans perks to retain staff, May 20 2006）

【译文】美国微软公司决定向新员工提供福利，起初仅限于临近西雅图总部的员工，后来扩展到全球的所有员工，这标志着该公司对此前不受欢迎的节约成本政策的彻底否定。两年前微软曾取消向员工免费提供毛巾，<u>此举成为了员工不满的导火索</u>。

【例2】

【原文】 The Passion of the Christ, which has so far been seen by tens of millions of people in the U.S. alone, proves again what we have long known about movies: artists should write about and direct what they know. They should produce from their passion. But too often pictures made by Christians have been <u>thinly veiled propaganda vehicles</u>.（JERRY B. JENKINS：*Mel Gibson: Passionate Art From the Gut*. TIME, Apr. 26, 2004）

【译文】《耶稣受难记》目前仅在美国就拥有了数千万观众,再次证明了人们对电影本质的长久认识:作家要写自己熟悉的东西,导演要执导自己熟悉的内容,艺术家的创作必须发自内心的激情。然而通常的情况则是,基督徒生产的影片总是<u>蒙上一层虚伪的面纱</u>。

原文中 propaganda vehicles 直译成汉语是"宣传工具",但这里不能采用这种译法。首先汉语中"蒙上……宣传工具"不构成搭配,另外 propaganda 通常是个贬义词,作者使用 propaganda vehicles 旨在说明,督徒生产的影片往往不够真实,里面含有许多宣传成分。因此,译者可以通过改变喻体把原文的意思表达出来。"蒙上一层虚伪的面纱"即能将原文的意思表达出来,同时又符合汉语的表达习惯。

"假朋友"在母语环境中也可以骗人,这与不同地域之间的文化差异有关。比如,初次听到上海人讲"一只碗不响,两只碗叮当"时就不得要领,经解释后才明白是"一个巴掌拍不响"的意思。王朔曾说过这样一段话:"出版社跟报社一样的,《看上去很美》给我删掉两万多字呢。校对说你写字不规范,有个关于正确使用汉字的正确用法,你不符合规范用法,我多少新词在里头啊,他全给我调整过来了,我都不认识了,'找不着北'全给改成'不知道北在哪里'了。"（李振忠:《王朔"找不着北"》,南方周末,2007-01-21。）对此有人挖苦说:"这一改,倒是改得绝对规范了,但规范之外,就好像把一个十七八岁女郎,硬生生给掰成一个更年期家长里短的老太太。"（林如敏:《缺乏幽默感比"不规范"更不是滋味》,羊城晚报,2007-01-20。）

本节重点讨论了文化翻译策略的问题,就翻译操作层面而言,对于文化负载词语的翻译,可遵循下列原则:

（1）当原文语言表示的形象、意义和感情色彩对译文读者不难理解时,尽量采取对等译法保留原文说法。

（2）当对等译法不便于译文读者的理解,但可能保留原文的文化色彩时,可以采用增译法适当添加解释原文内涵的词语,这样既可以在译文中保留原语特征和风格神韵,又可以使译文意思明确,便于读者理解。

（3）当保留原文的字面意象不能表达原文的真正意义时,可以采取换译法适当转换原文的形象,根据译文读者的心理,采用内涵相似的说法再现原文的意思。

（4）对于一些具有独特原语文化的词句,可以直接译出隐含意义,这样可以避免读者在阅读过程中产生费解甚至误解。

第三节 翻译中的文化失真

王佐良先生在翻译苏格兰诗人罗伯特·彭斯 "A Red, Red Rose" 一诗时,综合考虑了词语的联想意义以及比喻的处理,给后人留下了精彩之笔:

原文	译文
Till a' the seas gang dry, my Dear,	纵使大海干涸水流尽,
And the rocks melt wi' the sun:	太阳将岩石烧作灰尘,
And I will luve thee still, my Dear,	亲爱的,我永远爱你,
While the sands o' life shall run.	只要我一息犹存。

本段前两句汉语中有现成的说法:"海枯石烂不变心"。如果把这一毫无新鲜之感的说法套入译文中,诗的意境则会大打折扣。诗中 sands o' life 如果直译应该是"生命之沙漏",在时钟发明以前,人

们用某种器皿盛沙,使沙从小孔中漏过,以此计时。如果把人生比作沙子,沙子一经漏完人生也就结束了。由于汉语中没有类似的表达,采用直译的方法无法传递信息,译者必须换一种方式把原诗的意义和意境表达出来。王佐良的译文质量是译界所公认的,对于 sands o' life 的翻译达到了近乎完美的最佳近似,但翻译中的文化失真也在所难免。

所有诗歌都用来表达人们的内心感受,但东西方诗歌在表达方法上却存在着差异,正如美国学者孙珠琴(Cecile Chu-chin Sun)所说:

"事实上,不管是中文诗歌还是西方诗歌,所有诗歌都会寻找各种生动的方式来表达内心感受。然而,诗人的内心感受与外部世界的联系,却总和诗人的个性及文化制约紧密相连。

在中文诗歌中,借助外界景物既可以展现场景,又可以表达诗人的情感。如描写人垂垂老矣的诗句:"雨中黄叶树,灯下白头人"。中文诗歌中大多经久不衰的活力,便来自外界景物与诗人情感之间的相互呼应。

然而在西方,外界景物一般都没有这样的双重功能,不管从语法或是语义上讲,都没有情感本身的表达那样重要。外界景物总体上不过是客观场景,并不属于诗人内心情感的一部分,除非诗人将其内化。"[1]

由于东西方之间的这种文化差异,中文诗歌英译的接受程度便会打折扣。杜甫《登高》名句"无边落木萧萧下,不尽长江滚滚来"有许多英译文。我们看下面三个不同的翻译版本:

1. Everywhere the leaves fall rustling from the trees, while on for ever rolls the turbulent Yangtze.(杨宪益、戴乃迭译)

2. The boundless forest sheds its leaves shower by shower; The endless River rolls its waves hour after hour.(许渊冲译)

3. In the boundless forest, rustling leaves are falling down, swirling and twirling all around;
　On the endless river, rolling waves are surging away, crashing and rushing all along.(丁衡祁译)

三位译者都是高手,三种译文各有各的精彩。但英语读者阅读译文的感受同汉语读者阅读原文的感受却不尽相同。这里涉及到人格风景双重功能的问题,也就是美学和心理学里所说的"审美通感"和"移情"。这也是 Robert Frost 为什么说"Poetry is what gets lost in translation"(诗,在翻译中失去)的原因。

再举一个更为典型的例子,是关于 A. C. Graham 翻译杜甫《登岳阳楼》时的一则轶事,我们先来看原文:

> 昔闻洞庭水,今上岳阳楼。
> 吴楚东南坼,乾坤日夜浮。
> 亲朋无一字,老病有孤舟。
> 戎马关山北,凭轩涕泗流。

A. C. Graham 译完此诗决定不予发表,原因是他不满意自己译文的最后一句 As I lean on the balcony my tears stream down,用他自己的话说: Tu Fu will on occasion speak of his feelings or at any rate his tears, with a simplicity which falls flat in English. 汉语中的"涕泗"与英语中的 tears 无疑是对等词语,但由于文化传统、社会风俗等方面的原因,这两个几乎完全对等的词语在不同的文化语境下却产生了截然不同的效果。

我们再看葛浩文(Howard Goldblatt)翻译的莫言小说《红高粱》中的一段:

【原文】父亲听着河声,想着从前的秋天夜晚,跟着我家的老伙计刘罗汉大爷去河边捉螃蟹的情景。夜色灰葡萄,金风串河道,宝蓝色的天空深邃无边,绿色的星辰格外明亮。北斗勺子星——北斗主死,南斗簸箕星——南斗司生、八角玻璃井——缺了一块砖,焦灼的牛郎要上吊,忧愁的织女要跳河……都在头上悬着。刘罗汉大爷在我家工作了几十年,负责我家烧酒作坊的全面工作,父亲跟着罗汉大爷脚前脚后地跑,就像跟着自己的爷爷一样。

---

[1]（Cecile Chu-Chin Sun: *Limits of Translation and Their Cultural Implications: The Case of Translating Classical Chinese Poetry into English*. (http://www.aasianst.org/absts/1999abst/china/c-28.htm)

【译文】The sound of the river reminded Father of an autumn night during his childhood, when the foreman of our family business, Arhat Liu, named after Buddhist saints, took him crabbing on the riverbank. On that gray-purple night a golden breeze followed the course of the river. The sapphire-blue sky was deep and boundless, green-tinted stars shone brightly in the sky: the ladle of Ursa Major (signifying death), the dustpan of Sagittarius (representing life); Octans, the glass well, missing of its tiles; the anxious Herd Boy (Altair), about to hang himself, the mournful Weaving Girl (Vega), about to drown herself in the river. Uncle Arhat had been overseeing the work of the family distillery for decades, and Father scrambled to keep up with him as he would his own grandfather.

本段翻译涉及不少中国文化方面的内容，译者大胆地采用了直译加注释的手法，如"北斗勺子星——北斗主死，南斗簸箕星——南斗司生"被译为 the ladle of Ursa Major (signifying death), the dustpan of Sagittarius (representing life); "焦灼的牛郎要上吊，忧愁的织女要跳河"被翻译为 the anxious Herd Boy (Altair), about to hang himself, the mournful Weaving Girl (Vega), about to drown herself in the river。这些原文读者都未必充分理解的内容，对于译文读者可能遇到的困难是可以想象的。不仅如此，汉语中景物描写与思想感情的内在联系，译文读者在多大程度上能够接受同样是个无法说清楚的问题。从这个意义上讲，翻译中的文化失真同样难以避免。

再看下面的例子：

【原文】共产党员一定要有朝气，一定要有坚强的革命意志，一定要有不怕困难和用百折不挠的意志去克服任何困难的精神，一定要克服<u>个人主义</u>、<u>本位主义</u>、<u>绝对平均主义</u>和<u>自由主义</u>，否则就不是一个名副其实的共产党员。

【译文】A Party member must be full of vigour and strong in revolutionary will, be endowed with the drive to defy all difficulties and to persevere in overcoming them, and be determined to rid himself of <u>individualism</u>, <u>departmentalism</u>, absolute <u>egalitarianism</u> and <u>liberalism</u>; otherwise, he is not a Party member in the real sense of the term.(中英双语在线 http://www.corpus4u.org/)

我们先来看英语中几个 isms 的意义：

individualism: belief in importance of individual: the belief that society exists for the benefit of individual people, who must not be constrained by government interventions or made subordinate to collective interests (*Encarta® World English Dictionary*)

departmentalism: tendency to consider only own department: the tendency of government departments to follow their own interests（*Encarta® World English Dictionary*）

egalitarianism: a belief in human equality especially with respect to social, political, and economic affairs （*Merriam-Webster Online Dictionary*）

liberalism: political theory stressing individualism: a political ideology with its beginnings in western Europe that rejects authoritarian government and defends freedom of speech, association, and religion, and the right to own property（*Encarta® World English Dictionary*）

除了 departmentalism 与汉语中的"本位主义"比较接近以外，其他的三个 isms 都与汉语中的意义相差甚远。以翻译作为桥梁的跨文化沟通难免存在文化失真，消除其中的障碍通常要经历一个长期的过程。本节所选择的翻译实例，或出自译界公认的高手，或引自最权威的双语库。文化失真的出现并非出在译者身上，而是由于两种语言中存在着的天然文化屏障，随着全球化的不断深入，问题将会逐步得到解决。当初有人认为汉语中的"龙"应该翻译成 Loong，避免同英语中那个凶神恶煞般的 dragon 区别开来。如今，词典已把 dragon 一词的两个义项区分得清清楚楚，人们在交流时也不会产生任何误解。

第四节 文化与修辞翻译实例

本节中，我们讨论一下翻译实践中文化与修辞如何翻译的问题。下面的段落选自英国《卫报》(The

Guardian）2004 年 5 月 10 日由拉里·埃利奥特（Larry Elliott）撰写的一篇题为 "That Old Greenspan Magic Seems To Be Fading" 的文章，文章中含有许多文化与修辞方面的内容。

That Old Greenspan Magic Seems To Be Fading [1]
格老爷子的魔力似乎正在消失

（1）汉语中"老爷子"是对老人的尊称，与这里的 That Old Greenspan 意思相仿。另外，用"格老爷子"指格林斯潘在中文报刊杂志中也很常见。

【原文】For the best part of 20 years, [2] Alan Greenspan has been a symbol of the stupidity of ageism. [3] He became chairman of the US Federal Reserve at 61, when plenty of workers have already been tossed on the scrapheap and many others are preparing to wind down for retirement. His golden years in charge of the US economy were when he was pushing 70 and he's still there aged 78. Greenspan is the doyen of central bankers, still talked about in almost reverential terms by his peers. The fact that the Fed chairman rarely gives interviews and makes public pronouncements that are to economics what Finnegans Wake is to literature only adds to the mystique. [4]

【译文】在过去 20 年的大部分时间里，艾伦·格林斯潘代表了一种形象，他不断证明了"人老不中用"的说法是多么愚蠢。他 61 岁时当选为美联储主席，而大批工人到了这个年龄早就遭到遗弃，另一些人则考虑结束自己的工作生涯，为退休做好准备。格林斯潘将近 70 岁的时候，才迎来了自己执掌美国经济的黄金岁月。如今他已 78 岁高龄，却依然稳居其位。他是央行银行家中的老资格，时至今日，同僚们一谈起他依然肃然起敬。这位美联储主席很少接受采访，也很少在公开场合发表自己的观点。他的这种作风更增添了自身的神秘感，就如同文学界《为芬尼根守灵》的神秘莫测一样，格林斯潘在经济学界也是个神秘莫测的人物。

（2）for the best part of 20 years 中的 best part 是指二十年中的大部分时间。从实际情况看，截止到本文发表时，格林斯潘任美联储主席也不到二十年。类似的例子：

For the best part of an hour he exposed what was really going on in the international motor industry.

They had been drinking for the best part of an hour but none were drunk.

That's not the children's mistake, that's ours, because we couldn't actually for the best part respond in a meaningful way.

（3）在 a symbol of the stupidity of ageism 中，ageism 的意思是"对老年人的偏见或歧视"，因此，the stupidity of ageism 的意思就是"对老年人的这种偏见或歧视是愚蠢的"。a symbol of the stupidity of ageism 的意思是说，格林斯潘代表了一种形象，他证明了那些对老年人的偏见或歧视是愚蠢的。

（4）Finnegans Wake（《为芬尼根守灵》）是爱尔兰作家詹姆斯·乔伊斯的作品，直到今天仍被许多人认为是一部无法令人完全解读的作品。该书像一座迷宫，给人以虚幻、飘渺的感觉，如同梦境一般。作者更著名的一部作品是《尤利西斯》。乔伊斯的这两部作品一直是西方评论界关注的焦点，乔伊斯也因此被尊为西方现代派的祖师，对后世创作影响巨大。本文作者用《为芬尼根守灵》的神秘来比喻格林斯潘的神秘。

【原文】It is, then, with some trepidation that the question has to be asked: [5] has Big Alan finally lost the plot? [6] At the start of last week, Greenspan presided over a meeting of the Fed which kept interest rates on hold at 1%, the level they have been pegged at for nearly a year. A statement accompanying the decision said the risks to inflation were balanced, which means the Fed thinks there is as much chance of the cost of living going up as going down. On Thursday, new joblessness claims in the US fell to their lowest level in getting on for four years, [7] and the picture of a recovering labour market was underlined [8] by Friday's non-farm payrolls [9] which showed an increase of 288,000, above what had been expected. The economy is expanding at an annual rate of 4.5%, surveys of both manufacturing and the service sector are strong, the housing market is booming, inflation has started to pick up.

【译文】虽然怀有敬畏之心，人们还是不禁要问：老谋深算的艾伦是否失算了？上周初，格林斯潘主持了一次美联储会议,决定将利率控制在 1% 的水平上,而这一水平已经保持了将近一年。随决定发布的一项声明指出,通货膨胀的风险处于平衡状态。这说明美联储认为,生活费用上涨或下降的几率大致相同。星期四公布的失业率已接近四年来的最低水平。劳动力市场正呈现出复苏景象,其原因是非农就业人数增加了 288,000 人,超过了人们的预期。美国经济以每年 4.5% 的速度增长。有关调查显示,制造业和服务业增长势头强劲,房产业日趋繁荣,通货膨胀已经开始显现。

（5）trepidation 有"战战兢兢,颤抖"的意思,这句话的意思是说,当人们向权威人士格林斯潘提出质疑的时候,心中不免忐忑不安,以至于颤抖起来。此处可理解为人们对格林斯潘怀有敬畏之心。

（6）to lose the plot 为英国俚语,意思是:be confused, to go off direction, whether with conversation or in one's activities, 有时也有 to go mad 之意。结合上下文可将其译为"失算"。本文的作者是英国人,故使用了该俚语。

（7）in getting on for four years 中,to get on for 为英语中的固定说法,意思是"接近,即将到来。"例如,She is getting on for sixty. 她年近 60 了。因此,本句话的意思是说"失业率已经接近四年来的最低水平。"

（8）underline 除了有 to draw a line under a word, to give extra weight to 和 to emphasize 之外,也有 to influence secretly 的意思。所以可将该句理解为:劳动力市场复苏的原因是非农就业人数的增加。

（9）non-farm payrolls 习惯上被译为"非农就业人数",而不采用"非农业薪金表"之类的说法。

【原文】Hardly surprisingly, Greenspan's call on inflation[10] is now coming under the microscope, even by those on the Keynesian left[11] who tend to favour expansionary macroeconomic policies. "Show me something, other than computers, where the price is falling," says Dean Baker of the Centre for Economic Policy Research in Washington. Baker is right. Clearly, risks to inflation are on the upside, and massively so. The economy has been injected with a cocktail of three growth-inducing drugs—negative real interest rates, a rising budget deficit and a falling currency. Oil prices have touched $40 a barrel and the labour market is tightening. It is hard to believe that Greenspan, a junkie[12] for economic data no matter how seemingly trivial, has not spotted all this. Rates in the US are far below a neutral level,[13] which would probably be around 5%, yet Greenspan is in no hurry to act.

【译文】在这样的背景下,格林斯潘处理通胀的方式受到百般挑剔也就不足为怪了。那些凯恩斯左派人士居然也加入了挑剔者的行列,而这些人平时却赞成扩张性宏观经济政策。华盛顿经济政策研究中心的迪安·贝克说:"除了计算机以外,难道还有别的东西在降价?"贝克是正确的。显而易见,通货膨胀的风险正呈上升趋势,而且上升幅度将会很大。美国经济已被注入了一副三合一增长剂,其中包括实际利率的降低、不断增长的预算赤字以及货币的贬值。石油价格已达每桶 40 美元,劳动力市场也在紧缩。无论这些数字显得多么微不足道,人们还是很难相信,像格林斯潘这样一位对经济数字如数家珍的老手,怎么可能对此视而不见?美国利率的中性水平大约在 5% 左右,而目前的利率则远远低于这一标准。然而,格林斯潘似乎并不急于采取任何行动。

（10）call 有 a special disposition to pursue a particular course 之意,也就是"部署,安排"的意思。Greenspan's call on inflation 是指格林斯潘将利率保持在 1% 水平上的这一安排。

（11）the Keynesian left：凯恩斯左派,亦称新剑桥学派。这一学派在理论上坚持最彻底的凯恩斯主义,叛离了以马歇尔为代表的传统理论的束缚。他们承认资本主义的现实是垄断竞争而不存在自由竞争；强调未来的不确定性对经济的影响；承认价格机制不能使市场均衡,从而使资本主义经济经常处于不平衡状态；承认资本主义经济增长促使利润增长,而随着利润的增长,收入在劳动和资本之间的分配更加不公。该学派理论上有两个突出的特点：一是在分析方法上采用历史观；二是特别注重收入分配问题。

（12）junkie 原指"有毒瘾者",也可指对某事"酷爱着迷的人"。例如,英语中就有 sports junkie, computer junkie, music junkie, shopping junkie 等说法。

（13）neutral level 应翻译为"中性水平",指对经济既无刺激作用,也无抑制作用的利率水平。

本章主要参考文献：

金惠康：《跨文化交际翻译》,中国对外翻译出版公司,2003年。

李定坤：《汉英辞格对比与翻译》，华中师范大学出版社，1994年。

Cecile Chu-Chin Sun: *Limits of Translation and Their Cultural Implications: The Case of Translating Classical Chinese Poetry into English.* (http://www.aasianst.org/absts/1999abst/china/c-28.htm)

翻译练习五

1. 将下面段落译成汉语：

（1）CHINA: A COLOSSUS WITH FEET OF CLAY: In remaking itself, China is also remaking the world. Yet its presence in the world economy remains, on many measures, far smaller than its 20 per cent share of the global population. Given its vast human potential, rapid growth in both its trade and its output is likely to continue for years.（http://www.ftchinese.com/story/001009207/ce）

（2）Angus Wilson is a social satirist with an itchy trigger finger. The novel is his shooting gallery, and the characters he sets up as targets not only have clay feet but clay minds and clay hearts as well. *Anglo-Saxon Attitudes* is his longest, cleverest and most annihilating display of literary marksmanship to date, and after it is all over, what hangs in the air is the acrid odor of an unrelenting misanthropy.

（http://www.time.com/time/magazine/article/0,9171,867232,00.html）

2. 将下面段落译成英语：

（1）我躺在汽车的心窝里，想起了那么一个晴朗温和的中午，那时的阳光非常美丽。我记得自己在外面高高兴兴地玩了半天，然后我回家了，在窗外看到父亲正在屋内整理一个红色的背包，我扑在窗口问："爸爸，你要出门？"

父亲转过身来温和地说："不，是让你出门。"

"让我出门？"

"是的，你已经十八了，你应该去认识一下外面的世界了。"

后来我就背起了那个漂亮的红背包，父亲在我脑后拍了一下，就像在马屁股上拍了一下。于是我欢快地冲出了家门，像一匹兴高采烈的马一样欢快地奔跑了起来。（余华《十八岁出门远行》）

（2）历经了近十年的爱情印证，我们所理解的爱不再是海誓山盟和大喜大悲，而是生活中的高山流水，是轻风细雨，是每日每日你归来的脚步，是我手下烫洗干净的衣裤和在外面采撷的一把野草是平淡又平淡的日日月月。

第六章

翻译中的数字表达

如果我们能够体会到这种平淡之中的幸福，能够在一粒沙中见世界，能够在锅碗瓢盆中品味出坦然，那么这就是生命中的一个大境界了。我们所期待的，不正是这样的一种德行？

爱情如是，人生亦如是，我们常常所自勉的淡泊明志，宁静致远，便在此罢了。

（程黛眉《梦里又飞花》）

英汉互译中的数字表达均需遵守有关规定，英美等国的出版物和我国的出版物均有约定俗成的表述方式，它们应成为译者在翻译时应遵守的普遍原则。翻译中的数字表达涉及的方面很广，如确数的表达、概数的表达、数字增减程度的表达、数量单位的表达、数字背后的文化内涵等等。本章所引数字表达实例大多来自翻译公司的真实材料和美国语料库（americancorpus.org），基本能够反映翻译市场在数字表达方面对译者的要求。

第一节 英汉出版物数字用法规定

一、英语出版物数字用法规定

（一）句首不用阿拉伯数字。

我们在阅读英语语篇时，很少发现句首使用阿拉伯数字，但中文却有这种句首使用阿拉伯数字的情况，译者常在不经意之间出现错误。

例1：

【原文】100 只鸭子死了，对他来说可是一笔不小的损失。

【初译】100 ducks are dead, which is really not a small lost for him.

【改译】One hundred ducks are dead, which is a significant loss for him.

例2：

【原文】有报道说 20% 的服装企业在经济危机中破产倒闭。

【初译】20% of garment enterprises are reported to go into bankruptcy in the economic crisis.

【改译】Twenty percent of garment manufacturers are reported to have gone bankrupt in the economic crisis.

（二）遇到日期、百分比、带单位的特殊数字，通常用阿拉伯数字。如果涉及的数目和单位是不定数时，可用单词表示。

例1：

【原文】发电机组计算时间以每天 24 小时，每年 300 天运行计算。

【初译】The calculation time of the generating unit is based on twenty-four hours each day, three hundred days each year.

【改译】For the convenience of calculation, the generating unit is assumed to be running 24 hours a day, 300 days a year.

例2：

【原文】外方将邀请中方五六名人员到境外实地考察和学习。

【初译】The foreign party will invite 5-6 persons from the Chinese party to carry out overseas field survey and study.

【改译】The foreign party will invite five or six people from the Chinese party for overseas field survey and study.

（三）1 至 9 用单词表示，10 以上的数目（包括 10）用阿拉伯数字（也有的以 100 为界限）。

例1：

【原文】蓄水池 10 米长、5 米宽。

【初译】The water tank is 10m long and 5m wide.

【改译】The water tank is ten meters by five.

例 2：

【原文】辅导方式：社区工作者每个月都要跟三四十名社区居民见面三四次，每次要辅导 25 到 30 分钟。

【初译】Tutorship: the community worker tutors thirty or forty residents three-four times per month, twenty-five-thirty minutes per time.

【改译】Tutorship: the community worker tutors 30–40 residents three or four times a month for 25–30 minutes each time.

（四）人数用阿拉伯数字表示显得更简洁明了，但不定数量、近似值用单词表示较恰当。

例 1：

【原文】2009 年，945 325 名游客参观了该博物馆。

【译文】In 2009, 945,325 visitors visited the museum.

例 2：

【原文】中国工商联房地产商会，会员包括开发企业、设计企业、建材商等，目前拥有会员 4500 多家，是中国规模最大的房地产行业组织。

【初译】China Real Estate Chamber of Commerce (CRECC), having more than 4500 members including real estate developers, design institutes as well as building material suppliers, is the largest organization in the Chinese real estate industry.

【改译】China Real Estate Chamber of Commerce (CRECC) is the largest organization in the Chinese real estate sector, with more than four thousand and five hundred members including real estate developers, design institutes and building material suppliers.

（五）在科技文章中，数字频繁出现，用阿拉伯数字比用单词陈述更有利。

【原文】树干高三十多米，在树干上钻一个直径 5 厘米的孔洞，二三小时内，就可流出一二十升金黄色的油状树液，成分十分接近柴油。

【初译】The tree is higher than thirty meters; when drilling a 5cm-diameter hole on its trunk, it will flow ten or twenty liters of golden oily sap in two or three hours, whose components are similar to those of diesel.

【改译】Once a 5cm-diameter hole is drilled in its trunk, this over-30m-high tree will flow 10–20 liters of golden oily sap in 2–3 hours. The composition of the sap is similar to that of diesel.

（六）遇到分数，可用带连字符号的单词表示。

【原文】该公司将年度利润的 3/10 投入研发当中。

【译文】The company spends three-tenths of its annual profit on R&D.

二、汉语出版物上数字用法的规定

阿拉伯数字笔画简单、结构科学、形象清晰、组数简短，所以被广泛应用。国家语言文字工作委员会专门起草了国家标准《出版物上数字用法的规定》(GB/T 15835—1995)，旨在对汉字数字和阿拉伯数字的书写系统明确分工，使中文出版物上数字的用法统一、规范。

根据《出版物上数字用法的规定》，我们根据翻译实践经验，总结相关规律如下：

（一）一般原则

1. 使用阿拉伯数字或是汉字数字，有时选择是唯一的。

（1）统计表中的数值，如正负整数、小数、百分比、分数、比例等，必须使用阿拉伯数字，如 48、302—125.03、34.05 %、63 %～68 %、1/4、1:500 等。

【原文】The nesting population of these birds has dropped by 80 percent since the 1960s, wildlife biologist John Ogden says.

【译文】野生生物学家约翰·奥格登认为，这些鸟儿的筑巢数量从 20 世纪 60 年代开始已经下降了 80%。

（2）定型的词、词组、成语、惯用语、缩略语或具有修辞色彩的词语中作为语素的数字，必须使用汉字,如一律、一方面、十滴水、二倍体、三叶虫、星期五、四氧化三铁、一〇五九(农药内吸磷)、八国联军、二〇九师、二万五千里长征、四书五经、五四运动、九三学社、十月十七日同盟、路易十六、十月革命、"八五"计划、五省一市、五局三胜制、二八年华、二十挂零、零点方案、零岁教育、白发三千丈、七上八下、不管三七二十一、相差十万八千里、第一书记、第二轻工业局、一机部三所、第三季度、第四方面军、十三届四中全会等。

【原文】In 2008, wind displaced about 34 million tons of carbon dioxide, equivalent to taking 5.8 million vehicles off the road.

【译文】2008年,通过利用风能,减少约3400万吨二氧化碳(CO_2)排放量,相当于路上减少了580万辆汽车。

2. 使用阿拉伯数字或是汉字数字。如物理量、非物理量、代码、代号中的数字,目前体例尚不统一。对这种情形,要求凡是可以使用阿拉伯数字而且又很得体的地方,特别是当所表示的数目比较精确时,均应使用阿拉伯数字。遇特殊情形,或者为避免歧解,可以灵活变通,但全篇体例应相对统一。

例1:

【原文】Obama is counting on revenue, estimated at $645.7 billion over a decade, to fund investments in renewable energy and other programs.

【译文】奥巴马目前通过政府财政收入来投资可再生能源及其他项目,预计十年将达到6457亿美元。

例2:

【原文】By building a dam instead of new coal plants to meet its growing demand for electricity, China will each year avoid spewing 100 million tons of carbon dioxide, 2 million tons of sulfur dioxide (the chemical agent of acid rain), 10,000 tons of carbon monoxide, 370,000 tons of nitrogen oxides, and huge amounts of fly ash — all serious atmospheric pollutants.

【译文】为了满足日益增长的电力需求,中国通过修建大坝发电站替代燃煤发电厂,每年将避免排放1亿吨二氧化碳,200万吨二氧化硫(酸雨中的化学成分),10 000吨一氧化碳,370 000吨氧化氮以及大量严重污染环境的粉尘。

(二)时间(世纪、年代、年、月、日、时刻)

1. 要求使用阿拉伯数字的情况

(1)公历世纪、年代、年、月、日。如公元前8世纪、20世纪80年代、公元前440年、公元7年、1994年10月1日等。注意:年份一般不用简写。如:1990年不应简作"九〇年"或"90年"。引文著录、行文注释、表格、索引、年表等,年月日的标记可按XXXX-XX-XX这种扩展格式来书写。如:1994年9月30日和1994年10月1日可分别写作1994-09-30和1994-10-01,仍读作1994年9月30日、1994年10月1日。年月日之间使用半字线"–"。当月和日是个位数时,在十位上加"0"。

【原文】Shopping malls began to spread in the 1990s in Turkey with the first malls built in Istanbul in 1987 and in Ankara in 1989.

【译文】继1987年伊斯坦布尔第一家大型购物中心建成、1989年安卡拉第一家大型购物中心建成后,大型购物中心于20世纪90年代开始在土耳其盛行起来。

(2)时、分、秒。如4时、15时40分(下午3点40分)、14时12分36秒,也可以采用04:00(4时)、15:40(15时40分)、14:12:36(14时12分36秒)这样的格式。

2. 要求使用汉字的情况

(1)中国干支纪年和夏历月日。如丙寅年十月十五日、腊月二十三日、正月初五、八月十五中秋节等。

【原文】It was the third day of the Spring Festival, Nan and four other young men were on duty at the office of the village militia.

【译文】这是大年初三,南跟其他四个年轻人在村民兵办公室值班。

(2)中国清代和清代以前的历史纪年、各民族的非公历纪年。这类纪年不应与公历月日混用,并应采用阿拉伯数字括注公历。如秦文公四十四年(公元前722年)、太平天国庚申十年九月二十四日（清咸丰十年九月二十日，公元1860年11月2日）、藏历阳木龙年八月二十六日（1964年10月1日）、日本庆应三年（1867年）。

【原文】In 1714 (the fifty-third year of the reign of Emperor Kangxi) the Qing government ordered the mapping of Taiwan to determine its size.

【译文】康熙五十三年（1714年），清政府派员测绘台湾地图，勘丈全境里数。

（3）含有月日简称表示事件、节日和其他意义的词组。如果涉及一月、十一月、十二月，应用间隔号"·"将表示月和日的数字隔开，并外加引号，避免歧义。涉及其他月份时，不用间隔号，是否使用引号，视事件的知名度而定。如"一·二八"事变（1月28日）、"一二·九"运动（12月9日）。

【原文】The White House was absolutely obsessed, worked 24/7 after September 11, to make sure terrorist attacks didn't happen.

【译文】在"九·一一"事件后，白宫惶惶不可终日，全天候执勤，确保恐怖主义袭击不再发生。

（4）近代英语文学作品译成汉语时，其中的年、月、日可用汉字表达，因为英语原文中的这类数字也是用单词而非阿拉伯数字表达的。例如，可将 the sixth moon of the year eighteen eighty five 翻译为"一八八五年六月"。这样处理是为了仿拟近代英语的质朴特色。

（三）物理量

物理量量值必须用阿拉伯数字，并正确使用法定计量单位。小学和初中教科书、非专业科技书刊的计量单位可使用中文符号。如 8736.80 km（8 736.80 千米）、600 g（600 克）、100 kg～150 kg（100 千克～150 千克）、12.5 m²（12.5 平方米）、外形尺寸是 400 mm×200 mm×300 mm（400 毫米×200 毫米×300 毫米）、34℃～39℃（34 摄氏度～39 摄氏度）、0.59 A（0.59 安[培]）等。

【原文】Tanta is the capital of the Nile Delta province Gharbiyya, located less than 100 km north of Cairo.

【译文】坦塔是尼罗河三角洲上嘎比亚省的首府城市，位于开罗北部不到100公里的地方。

（四）非物理量

1．一般情况下应使用阿拉伯数字。如 21.35 元、45.6 万元、270 美元、290 亿英镑、48 岁、11 个月、1 480 人、4.6 万册、600 幅 550 名等。

【原文】Entry Fee: 1 Section 25 USD or 15 Euros, 2 Sections 30 USD or 20 Euros.

【译文】门票：一个区域25美元或15欧元，两个区域30美元或20欧元。

2．整数一至十，如果不是出现在具有统计意义的一组数字中，可以用汉字，但要照顾到上下文，求得局部体例上的一致。如一个人、三本书、四种产品、六条意见、读了十遍、五个百分点。

【原文】He said, it's easy to have mercury levels five to six times the upper limit by eating lots of fish.

【译文】他说，大量吃鱼很容易使汞含量达到上限的五六倍。

（五）多位整数与小数

1．阿拉伯数字书写的多位整数和小数的分节

（1）专业性科技出版物的分节法：从小数点起，向左和向右每三位数字一组，组间空四分之一个汉字（二分之一个阿拉伯数字）的位置。如 2 748 456、3.141 592 65。

【原文】Partnering with local governments and others, the company has helped create 126,421 units of affordable housing around the state.

【译文】该公司与地方政府及其他部门合作，在全州范围内已经援助修建了 126 421 套经济适用房。

（2）非专业性科技出版物如排版留四分空有困难，可仍采用传统的以千分撇","分节的办法。小数部分不分节。四位以内的整数也可以不分节。如 2,748,456、3.1415926。

2．阿拉伯数字书写的纯小数必须写出小数点前定位的"0"。小数点是齐底线的黑圆点"."。如 0.46 不得写成 .46 和 0·46。注意，在法国、德国等一些欧洲国家中习惯用","来表示小数点，如 0.46 就写为 0,46，在翻译时要注意到这种表述习惯，不要感觉出现了逻辑性错误，而在这些国家中，也存在 .46 的表述，切不可将这个小数点视为句号，只要稍加观察，就会发现作为小数点的"."是紧接后面的数字，没有空格，但其前面有留有空格；用作句号的"."在前面不留空格，紧接单词，而其后则有一个空格。

3．尾数有多个"0"的整数数值的写法

（1）专业性科技出版物按照数值修约规则处理。

（2）非科技出版物中的数值一般可以"万"、"亿"作单位。如三亿四千五百万可写成345,000,000，也可写成 34,500 万或 3.45 亿，但一般不得写作 3 亿 4 千 5 百万。

4．数值巨大的精确数字，为了便于定位读数或移行，作为特例可以同时使用"亿、万"作单位。如我国 1982 年人口普查人数为 10 亿 817 万 5 288 人；1990 年人口普查人数为 11 亿 3 368 万 2 501 人。

5．一个用阿拉伯数字书写的数值应避免断开移行。

6．阿拉伯数字书写的数值在表示数值的范围时，使用浪纹式连接号"～"。如 150 千米～200 千米、-36℃～-8℃、2 500 元～3 000 元。

（六）概数和约数

1．相邻的两个数字并列连用表示概数，必须使用汉字，连用的两个数字之间不得用顿号"、"隔开。如二三米、一两个小时、三五天、三四个月、十三四吨、一二十个、四十五六岁、七八十种、二三百架次、一千七八百元、五六万套。

【原文】Five or six years ago, he'd fallen off his bike and banged up his left knee.

【译文】五六年前，他从自行车上摔下来，摔坏了左膝盖。

2．带有"几"字的数字表示约数，必须使用汉字。如几千年、十几天、一百几十次、几十万分之一。

【原文】Several obstacles prevented researchers from employing the types of research designs that can produce unambiguous results.

【译文】有多道屏障限制了研究人员，使他们无法采用不具模糊结果的研究设计类型。

3．用"多"、"余"、"左右"、"上下"、"约"等表示的约数一般用汉字。如果文中出现一组具有统计和比较意义的数字，其中既有精确数字，也有用"多"、"余"等表示的约数时，为保持局部体例上的一致，其约数也可以使用阿拉伯数字。

【例1】这个协会举行全国性评奖十余次，获奖作品有一千多件。协会吸收了约三千名会员，其中三分之二是有成就的中青年。另外，在三十个省、自治区、直辖市还设有分会。

【例2】该省从机动财力中拿出 1 900 万元，调拨钢材 3 000 多吨、水泥 2 万多吨、柴油 1 400 吨，用于农田水利建设。

（七）代号、代码和序号

部队番号、文件编号、证件号码和其他序号，用阿拉伯数字。序数词即使是多位数也不能分节。如 84062 部队、国家标准 GB 2312—80、国办发 [1987]9 号文件、总 3147 号、国内统一刊号 CN 11—1399、21/22 次特别快车、HP—3000 型电子计算机、93 号汽油、维生素 B_{12}。

（八）引文标注

引文标注中版次、卷次、页码，除古籍应与所据版本一致外，一般均使用阿拉伯数字。

【例1】列宁：《新生的中国》，见《列宁全集》，中文 2 版，第 22 卷，208 页，北京，人民出版社，1990。

【例2】刘少奇：《论共产党员的修养》，修订 2 版，76 页，北京，人民出版社，1962。

【例3】李四光："地壳构造与地壳运动"，载《中国科学》，1973（4），400～429 页。

【例4】许慎：《说文解字》，影印陈昌治本，126 页，北京，中华书局，1963。

【例5】许慎：《说文解字》，四部丛刊本，卷六上，九页。

第二节 确数的表达

英汉数量词表述有概数，也有确数。一般情况下，确数翻译应采取的方法是：保留数字，直接翻译。汉语的数字表述我们在上一节已经做了详细论述。由于对英语数字表达的总结不多，我们在本节特地选择如下有代表性、在翻译实践过程中容易出错的英语数字表达作为例子，并且整理了一些英文数字表达原则。

一、基数词在表示确切数字时,不能使用百、千、百万、十亿的复数形式;但是,当基数词表示不确切数字,如成百、成千上万,三三两两时,基数词则以复数形式出现。基数词表示人的不确切岁数或年代,用几十的复数形式表示。

【例1】Three hundred employees are working for the company.

【译文】该公司有三百名员工。

【例2】If I cared for thousands and thousands of dying people, I should be able to say what I want about anything.

【译文】如果我将成千上万即将死去的人挂在心上,我就会懂得我自身的任何需求。

【例3】He had invited dozens of foreign correspondents to lunch one day last fall and, after many questions about business trends, one journalist pressed him on how it felt to be worth so much in a country in which many people struggle to get by.

【译文】去年秋季的某一天,他邀请了数十名国外记者共进午餐。在问了几个关于经济趋势的问题后,有一个记者向他发难:在这么一个国家当中,许多人都得过且过,如何感到自己还有如此大的价值?

【例4】Sampson, a heavyset man in his sixties who is partial to gold chains and safari suits, began by describing himself as " the man who was ordained by Martin King."

【译文】萨普森六十多岁,长得结结实实,喜欢带金链子和穿旅行服。他一开口就把自己说成是"马丁·金委派来的人"。

二、序数词在使用时,通常前面要加定冠词the;但是如果序数词前出现不定冠词a或an时,则表示"再——","又——"。

【例1】Wall knew how to fight, and their arms snaked around each other, furiously twisting, as each sought advantage. Then the gun cracked, twice. And a third time. Jack shouted, an inarticulate cry. Wall fell to the floor, smoke rising from his chest. The gun hit the floor with a thud. David kicked it into the corner. (Amor Vincit Omnia, *Analog Science Fiction & Fact,* New York: Apr 2008)

【译文】华尔知道怎么打架,他们手臂交缠在一起,用力扭打起来,不让自己吃亏。然后,枪响了两声。紧接着又再响一声。杰克叫了起来,结结巴巴的。华尔倒在地上,胸口还冒着开枪后散发的烟气。枪砰的一声掉到地板上,戴维将枪踢到了墙角。

【例2】Not only do Canadians have no enforceable right to any particular medical service, they don't even have a right to a place in line when health care is rationed. The 100th person waiting for heart surgery is not "entitled" to the one hundredth surgery, for example.

【译文】加拿大人对于任何特殊医疗设施不但没有强制性权利,而且在医疗保健配额供应的时期,甚至没有排队的权利。比如,第100个等待心脏手术的病人就"无权"获得安排在第100次手术。

三、世纪可以用定冠词加序数词加世纪"century"表示,也可以用定冠词加百位进位加'或s表示。如the sixth(6th)century翻译为公元6世纪,the 1900s直接翻译为20世纪。这里,用百位数整数表示的世纪比这一百位阿拉伯数字本身多一个世纪。年代用定冠词及基数词表示的世纪加十位整数的复数形式构成。如in the 1950s(in the fifties of the twentieth century 或 in the nineteen fifties)直接翻译为"在20世纪50年代"。

【例1】I wore parachute pants in the 1980s, flannel in the 1990s and was unemployed in the 2000s.

【译文】上世纪80年代我穿着伞裤,90年代穿法兰绒;到21世纪,我失业了。

【例2】In response to the growth of the market economy in the nineteenth century, Ojibwe harvested berries for sale or found work picking berries for large regional produce enterprises in addition to harvesting them for subsistence.

【译文】19世纪市场经济快速发展,奥基布韦响应这一趋势,他采浆果不光是为了生计,还进行销售,并且将采浆果作为一份工作,向当地大型农产品企业供货。

四、分数是由基数词和序数词一起来表示的。基数词作分子,序数词作分母,除了分子是"1"

以外，其他情况下序数词都要用复数形式。如 3/4：three fourths 或 three quarters，1/3：one third 或 a third。当分数后面接名词时，如果分数表示的值大于 1，名词用复数；小于 1，名词用单数。如 1 1/2 hours 一个半小时（读作 one and a half hours）、4/5 meter 五分之四米。表示"n 次方"的说法：指数用序数词，底数用基数词。如 10 的 7 次方 the seventh power of ten（ten to the seventh power）。

【例 1】In terms of the more familiar powers of ten, an animal that is ten to the fourth (10,000) times larger than another uses only ten to the third (1000) times more energy and lives ten to the one (10) times as long.

【译文】按照十的 n 次方来对比，一种动物比另外一种动物大十的四次方倍（10,000），则消耗的能量则为十的三次方倍（1000），而存活的寿命则只有十的一次方倍（10）。

第三节 概数的表达

英汉概数表达方式同中有异，二者差别并没有超出词序范围。在对概数表达方式进行翻译处理时，对等译法是最常用的翻译方法。究其原因，主要是因为英汉中存在相对等或相类似的概数表达方式，且对等译法简单、直接，易于实施。变异译法、省略法作为辅助译法，需要译者结合语境具体灵活操作。

概数一般有两种表达方式：第一种为概数词 + 数词。如：英语中的"about twenty"、"six or so books"；汉语中的"六个多"、"三只左右"。第二种为相邻数词连用（norm）。如：英语中的"five or six persons"、"one or two lumps of sugar"；汉语中的"八九千"、"七八岁"。

本书从概数词 + 数词、相邻数词连用两方面，对英汉概数进行比较，并就相关翻译提出一些方法。

一、表示大约数目

大约数目指的是围绕特定数目、以及比特定数目或多或少的数目。汉语在数词前加"约"、"约计"、"大约"、："近"、"差不多"、"大概"等词，或在数词后加"左右"、"上下"等词表示。英语在数词前加 some, about, around, nearly, almost, approximately, roughly, more or less, in the neighborhood of, in proximty to 等词或词组，或在数词后加 or thereabout, or so, in the rough 等词组表示。

【例 1】An LV-branded handbag costs me 1000 USD or so.

【译文】一个 LV 手包大概花了我 1000 美元。

【例 2】Some 1,200 people are dying every day from malnutrition and relevant diseases.

【译文】每天约有 1 200 人死于营养不良和相关的疾病。

二、表示"少于"的数目

表示比特定数目少或小的数目，汉语在数词前加"少于"、"小于"、"低于"、"不到"、"不及"、"不足"等词，或在数词后加"以下"、"以内"、"以里"等词表示。英语在数词前加 fewer than、less than、under、below、within 等词或词组表示。

【例 1】Sugar-free pops still taste sweet and are mostly water, so they have fewer than 20 calories and no fat.

【译文】无糖汽水仍有甜味，主要成分是水，含不到 20 卡路里，不含任何脂肪。

【例 2】Each is a relatively new art form created within the last fifty years.

【译文】每一种都是相对较新的艺术形式，创立于过去五十年当中。

三、表示"差不多"的数目

差不多，是一种特殊的表示"少于"的数目的方法，接近特定数目或仅差一点。汉语在数词前加"近"、"将近"、"接近"、"几乎"、"差不多"、"差一点"、"差一点不到"等词表示。英语在数词前加 nearly, almost, toward, close on 等词或词组表示。

【例 1】Forests cover less than three-quarters of the land, with one-tenth glaciated and slightly more than one-fifth inhabited or cultivated.

【译文】这个地方差不多四分之三都是森林，十分之一是冰川，居住与耕地面积只有五分之一多一点。

【例 2】She smiled, getting on toward fifty and still concerned with male attention.

【译文】她笑了，将近五十岁的人了，依然注意吸引男人。

四、表示"多于"的数目

表示比特定数目多或大的数目，汉语在数词前加"多于"、"大于"、"高于"、"超过"、"挂零"、"零头"等词，或在数词后加"多"、"来"、"几"、"余"、"以上"等词表示。英语在数词前加 more than、over、above、upwards of 等词或词组表示，或用在数词后加 and more、odd、and odd 等词或词组表示。

【例 1】Programs that lasted more than 45 hours had a greater impact on both reading and mathematics than shorter programs, but only up to a point.

【译文】与课时较短的课程相比，超过 45 课时的课程对阅读与数学的影响更大，但也只高出一个点。

五、表示"介于"的数目

表示介于两个特定数目之间的数目，汉语用"到"、"至"等词连接两个数词，或用"介于……之间"表示。英语用 (from)…to；(anywhere) between…and… 表示。

【例 1】The number of Internet users in China has jumped from 2 million in 1998 to 9 million in 1999 and to 20 million in 2000.

【译文】在中国互联网用户数量从 1998 年的 200 万，增至到 1999 年的 900 万，再增至到 2000 年的 2000 万。

【例 2】Between one and two thirds of the population is dehydrated by about two to four cups of water at any given time.

【译文】有三分之一到三分之二的人在任何时间都会脱水两到四杯。

六、表示"相邻"的数目

连用两个相邻的数字，表示一个不确定数目。英语用 or 连接两个相邻数字来表示。注意"三三两两"是特殊的"相邻"的数目。表示"两个或两个以上"等，英语在数词后加 or more 表示。如 a) two or three 两三个；b) sixty or seventy 六七十；c) three thousand or four thousand 三四千；d) by twos and threes 三三两两；e) two or more 两个或两个以上。

【例 1】Snow falls thickly on the girls who sleep by twos and threes on mounds of torn-up ferns.

【译文】女孩们三两成群地睡在干草堆上，身上覆盖了一层厚厚的积雪。

【例 2】We're looking forward to having a good, constructive dialogue with our Israeli friends when they visit Washington in the next seven, seven or eight days.

【译文】我们的以色列朋友将在一周或七八天后来到华盛顿，我们期待与他们进行一场友好的建设性对话。

七、表示"数十"等数目

表示"数十"、"数百"、"数千"等不确定数目，英语在 ten / dozen / score / hundred/thousand / million / billion 等数词的复数形式后加 of 构成。例如：

a) tens of (20–99)；dozens of (24–99); scores of (40–99) 数十／几十／好几十

b) hundreds of (200–999)；several hundred 数百／数以百计／几百／好几百／成百

c) thousands of (2,000–9,999)；several thousand 数千／数以千计／几千／好几千／成千

d) tens of thousands of (20,000–99,999) 数万／数以万计／几万／好几万

e) hundreds of thousands of (200,000–999,999) 数十万／几十万／好几十万

f) millions of (2,000,000–9,999,999) 数百万／几百万／好几百万

g) tens of millions of (20,000,000–99,999,999) 数千万 / 几千万 / 好几千万

h) hundreds of millions of (200,000,000–999,999,999) 数亿 / 几亿 / 好几亿

i) 数十亿 / 几十亿 / 好几十亿 billions of (2,000,000,000–9,999,999,999)

上面所列不确定数目的表达是从严格意义上讲的，人们在实际交流时对它们的理解未必那样精确，例如，dozens of 虽说应当介于 24–99 之间，但将其理解为 100 左右也未尝不可。

八、数字的虚指义

在数字习语中，有些数字并不代表它本身具体数目，而是一种脱离了数字实指的文化意义。作者恰当地运用数字的虚指用法，一般都具有夸张、强调或比喻等修辞功能，可使文章语言凝练生动、生辉添色，达到言简意赅，渲染气氛的效果。因此，在翻译数字的虚指义时不能从字面上的意义去理解，而应该从文化意义上去领会。

【例 1】How many times do I have to tell you not to leave your homework till the eleventh hour?

【初译】我必须跟你说多少次，不要将家庭作业留到十一点钟再做？

【改译】跟你说了多少遍了，别把作业留到最后一刻再做。

原文中"the eleventh hour"不是第十一个小时，即十一点钟，而指在任何一种情况下的"最后一刻"或"危机时刻"。

【例 2】白发三千丈，缘愁似个长，不知明镜里，何处得秋霜。（李白《秋浦歌》）

【译文】The hoary hair is ten miles long,

Because the sorrows are as long.

In mirror, no one knows at all,

Where came on head the frost of fall?（Source Unknown）

在李白诗中，浪漫表现手法很多，这里"白发三千丈"是夸张的说法，这里的数字不能从字面上去理解。虽然翻译为 ten miles long，但译文读者也不会从字面上去理解。

第四节 数字增减程度的表达

一、表示增加、上升等

1. 英语中表示上升、增长、增长百分之多少等意思时，可用 increase, rise, grow 及 up 等词表示。例如：

【例 1】Statistics reveal that gang-related murders decreased by 40.9 percent, but rapes increased 8.1 percent and aggravated assaults were up by 9.1 percent.

【译文】统计数字显示，团伙谋杀案下降了 40.9%，但强奸案上升了 8.1%，而恶性袭击案件上升了 9.1%。

【例 2】The global economy in 2000 grew at its fastest pace in over a decade and a half.

【译文】2000 年全球经济增幅为过去十五年来之最。

【例 3】The city's job losses increased much more rapidly between 2000 and 2001 than they did between 1998 and 1999.

【译文】2000—2001 年该市失业率上升速度要比 1998—1999 年快很多。

2. 表示迅速、大幅度增加或上升时，可以使用 jump, leap, soar, shoot up 和 skyrocket 等词，其中 soar, shoot up 和 skyrocket 比 jump, leap 程度上更强。例如：

【例 1】Revenues grew by $10 billion from 1998 to 1999, and then jumped by another $60 billion to $100 billion in 2000.

【译文】1998 年到 1999 年，财政收入增幅为 100 亿美元，2000 年大幅上升到 600–1000 亿美元。

【例 2】Actual foreign direct investment rose by 24.2% to $4.58 billion in the first two months of this year while contracted FDI shot up by 47.1% in the same period.

【译文】今年前两个月，实际外商直接投资额上升了 24.2%，达到了 45.8 亿美元，同期合同外商直接投资额大幅上涨了 47.1%。

3. 表示 A 为 B 多少倍时，可以使用 A is n times as great/long/much as B、A is n times greater/longer/more than B、A is n times the size/length/amount of B，翻译为 A 的大小 / 长度 / 数量是 B 的 n 倍（或 A 比 B 大 / 长 / 多 n–1 倍）。当相比的对象 B 很明显时，than（as, of）B 常被省去。表示增加到 n 倍（或：增加 n–1 倍）时，可以使用 increase/raise/grow/go/step up/multiply to n times、increase/raise/grow/go/step up/multiply n times / n-fold、increase/raise/grow/go/step up/multiply by n times、increase by a factor of n，翻译为增加到 n 倍（或：增加 n–1 倍）。一般也常见 double（增加 1 倍）、treble（增加 2 倍）、quadruple（增加 3 倍）这样的表述，英语中还有一种用 again 而不用倍数词来比较倍数的方法。

【例 1】This book is three times as long as (three times longer than/three times the length of) that one.
【译文】这本书的篇幅是那本书的 3 倍（即长两倍）。
【例 2】The production of integrated circuits has been increased to three times as compared with last year.
【译文】集成电路的产量比去年增加了两倍。
【例 3】The output of chemical fertilizer has been raised five times as against 1986.
【译文】化肥产量比 1986 年增加了 4 倍。
【例 4】The efficiency of the machines has (been) more than trebled or quadrupled.
【译文】这些机器的效率已提高了 2 倍或 3 倍多。

二、表示维持在某种水平或程度

在英语语境中，maintain, stand at 和 remain at 表示保持在某种特定的水平或程度上；而 hover around 则表示保持在某种水平或程度上下。例如：

【例 1】I want Air Support up and to maintain at 1,500 feet.
【译文】我希望空中支援达到 1500 英尺并维持在这一高度。
【例 2】If oil remains at about $130 a barrel, it will dramatically alter the industry's economic operating model, some aviation analysts say.
【译文】部分航空分析师谈到，如果石油维持 130 美元一桶，将会极大改变航空业的经济运营模式。
【例 3】Political success in Iraq is tied closely to President Bush's own political standing. His overall approval ratings have hovered around 40 percent.
【译文】在伊拉克的政治成功与布什总统的政治立场密切相关。他总体支持率一直维持在 40% 上下。

三、表示减少和下降

1. 英语中表示减少、下降或下降百分之多少时，可以用 decrease, fall, down, drop, slide, slip, shrink, dip 以及 reduce 等词。例如：

【例 1】Waist size is especially a concern if your guy is over 30, when metabolism slows and testosterone levels decrease by about 1 percent each year.
【译文】年过三十，新陈代谢减缓，睾酮水平每年约下降 1%，腰围也成为一大烦恼。
【例 2】Italy's population is expected to shrink from 57 million today to 41 million by 2050.
【译文】到 2050 年，意大利人口预计将从现在的 5700 万人缩减到 4100 万人。

2. 英语中表示倍数减少时，可以用 A is n times as small/light/slow as B，以及 A is n times smaller/lighter/slower than B。这两种表达都翻译为 A 的大小 / 重量 / 速度是 B 的 1/n，或 A 比 B 小 / 轻 / 慢 (n–1) /n。当相比的对象 B 很明显时，than/as B 常被省去。表示减少到 1/n 或减少 (n–1)/n 时，一般可以用 decrease/reduce/slow down/shorten n times/n-fold，decrease//slow down/(be) shorten(-ed)/be reduced by n times，decrease/slow down/(be) shorten(-ed)/be reduced by a factor of n。经常发生混淆的是，decrease (by) 3 times 应译为"减少 2/3"，而不是"减少 3/4"。

【例1】Switching time of the new-type transistor has decreased 3 times.

【译文】新型晶体管的开关时间缩短了1/3（即缩短至2/3）。

【例2】When the voltage is stepped up by ten times, the strength of the current is stepped down by ten times.

【译文】电压升高9倍，电流强度便降低9/10（即90%）。

【例3】The costs of deep-water oil and gas development have fallen by a factor of three over the last 15 years, dramatically extending the frontier of commercial activity.

【译文】过去15年来，深海油气开采成本下降了三分之二，极大地扩大了商业化开采范围。

【例4】The principal advantage of the products is a two-fold reduction in weight.

【译文】这些产品的主要优点是重量减轻了1/2。

四、同比/环比的表达

在数字比较过程中，必须清楚同比与环比概念，否则增加或减少均没有可比性。在英汉翻译过程中，同比与环比的表述有很多种方式，我们一一进行分析翻译。

首先，先从概念上理解什么是同比，什么是环比。

同比发展速度：用以说明本期发展水平与去年同期发展水平对比而达到的相对发展速度。如，本期2月比去年2月，本期6月比去年6月等，使用这个指标，如某年、某季、某月与上年同期对比计算的发展速度，就是同比发展速度。数学公式为：同比发展速度＝本期值/上年同期值×100%。同比增长率：本期同比增长（下降）率(%) =［(本期值/上年同期值 –1）］× 100%。需要说明的是：（1）如果计算值为正值（+），则称增长率；如果计算值为负值（–），则称下降率。（2）如果本期指本日、本周、本月和本年，则上期相应指上日、上周、上月和上年。

环比发展速度：报告期水平与前一时期水平之比，表明现象逐期的发展速度。分为日环比、周环比、月环比和年环比，如计算一年内各月与前一个月对比，即2月比1月，3月比2月，4月比3月……12月比11月，说明逐月的发展程度。环比增长率数学公式：本期环比增长（下降）率(%) = ［(本期值/上期值) –1］× 100%。

比较同比与环比：同比周期是一年，环比周期则可以是日、周、月、年等。

1. 关于同比的英文，一般用year on year（YoY）。如同比增长率year-on-year growth rate。另外也常用growing XX% compared with the same period of the previous year、over the same period of the previous year、on a year-on-year basis、like for like。还有in the year to 或者 the 12-month 等周期为一年/12个月的时候，相互的比较也是同比情况。

【例1】Exports of traditional products like garments and accessories increased only 2.8 percent year on year.

【初译】出口传统产品例如服装或服装配件等，则仅仅比上年同期增长了2.8%。

【改译】服装及配饰等传统产品出口额同比增长仅为2.8%。

【例2】In the first half of the year, China's banking system pumped out 7.37tn yuan (US$1.08tn) in new loans, an increase of more than 28% year on year.

【译文】在今年上半年，中国的银行系统提供了7.37万亿元人民币（合1.08万亿美元）新贷款，同比增长超过28%。

【例3】Single-family starts numbered about 78,200 by the end of March, a drop of more than 50 percent compared with the same period last year.

【初译】截止3月底，单亲家庭开始数量约为78200户，比去年同期下降超过50%。

【改译】截止三月底，独栋房屋开工数量约为78200套，同比下降超过50%。

【例4】Total sales in December 2001 were up by 10.8%, with a like for like increase of 5.3%.

【译文】2001年12月销售额增长了10.8%，同比增长了5.3%。

2. 环比（Chain Index）的英文表述有多种多样，如 day on day, week on week, month on month, quarter on quarter。另外，也有其他表述方式，如：

【例1】不过一旦进入九月份，投资以及制造业活动均会开始**环比恢复**。

【译文】In the coming September, investment and manufacturing activities will begin to restore the chain.

【例2】In Singapore, industrial output rose by 24.3% in April alone. The 12-month rate of increase leapt to 51%.

【译文】新加坡四月份工业产出环比增长 24.3%，同比增长 51%。

【例3】Thailand's economy grew at an annualised rate of 16% in the three months to the end of March.

【译文】以年率计算，泰国今年第一季度经济环比增长 16%。

第五节　数量单位的表达

一、英语表达中一般不使用量词

汉语中数字和名词连用时，往往离不开量词起桥梁作用，否则表达时就会不通顺，不符合汉语的表达习惯。而英语数字和名词连用时无需加量词就可将数量表达得很清楚，这也是英语的表达习惯。一般而言，如果可数名词只论个数，不论及其他度量单位的话，都不使用量词，但一般翻译成汉语时都需要加量词。如：

【例1】An airplane took off one hour ago.

【译文】一架飞机在一小时前起飞了。

【例2】Over 14 years, he has gone through <u>106 proteins</u> and protein components–and <u>2,000 monkeys</u>.

【译文】十四年来，他研究了 <u>106 种蛋白质</u>与蛋白质成分——还有 <u>2 000 只猴子</u>。

【例3】It would cost $1 billion and Congressional backers said that it could spur the sale of up to <u>250,000 cars</u> and trucks.

【译文】国会支持者称，刺激销售量达到 <u>25 万辆汽车</u>与卡车，则需要投入 10 亿美元。

在上面三个例子中，英语原文并无量词也无须量词，但翻译成汉语时，若不加"架"、"种"、"只"、"辆"等，汉语语句就不通顺，不符合汉语表达习惯。

二、英语表达中使用量词的情况

1. 当可数名词需要使用其他度量单位时，一般需要用到量词。如 a bunch of flowers（一束鲜花）、a cluster of grapes（一串葡萄）。但英语中量词很有限，如 bunch、piece、pair、cluster、ton、liter、cup 等等，因此，很多不可数名词都使用同一量词来度量。虽然英语表达中使用同一量词，但翻译成汉语时应注意汉语的表达习惯加上正确的量词。如 a pot of soup 翻译为"一锅汤"，而 a pot of black tea 则翻译为"一壶红茶"。

【原文】Habitat destruction, agricultural chemicals, and other human influences are taking a heavy toll on the world's pollinators–a diverse group of <u>more than 100,000 species</u> of insects, birds, and mammals that live in tropical and temperate forests, deserts, and farm belts.

【译文】栖息地破坏、农业化学药品及其他人类影响的全球的传粉动物产生了重大影响——这些传粉动物生活在热带与温带森林、沙漠与农田当中，群体庞大而复杂，<u>超过 10 万种昆虫</u>、鸟类与哺乳动物。

2. 不可数名词没有表示复数的"-s"标志，因此前面不可有数字，只可以用数量词。例如我们可以说 There isn't much furniture in the office 但不能说 There are not many furnitures in the office。不可数名词借用单位词（unit word）来实现其数量大小，如：a piece of、a cup of、a drop of、a lump of、a handful of、a flash of、a blade of、a head of、a bar of、an ear of 等。如果数目是超过"一"，就以确实

数目取代"一",如 two pieces of、three cups of 和 five lumps of 等。

【例1】They took out two handfuls of dry grass and mixed it with the lit coals.
【译文】他们拿出两把干草,跟燃煤混在一起。
【例2】A flash of orange in the distance caught his attention.
【译文】远处一道橙色的光芒引起了他的注意。
【例3】They had six bars of chocolate and six pints of water.
【译文】他们有六条巧克力,还有六品脱水。

3. 有些名词如 scissors、trousers、spectacles、tongs、pliers 等,都以复数形式出现,如:The scissors are lying on the table. 剪刀在桌子上、The spectacles fit me nicely. 眼镜很适合我。如果要给这些名词表示单数"一"的意思,也需要借用单位词了,例如:Clement has just bought a pair of scissors. 克莱门特买了一把剪刀、The mechanic repaired the machine with a pair of pliers. 技工用一把钳子来修设备。

4. 现代英语注重简洁,合成形容词便应运而生,其中有一种是用来表示数目的,方法是:"数目 + 名词"。如:a five-year plan 五年计划、a ten-dollar bill 十美元纸币、a two-hour meeting 两小时会谈、a three-day conference 三天会议等。必须注意的是,这种合成形容词中的名词,只能以单数形式出现。如果用复数,就错了,如:a five-years plan, a ten-dollars bill, a two-hours meeting, a three-days conference,这类错误,虽然频率不是很高,但也要留意才好。

第六节 数字相关翻译

一、容易望文生义的数字表述

英语中有不少由数字组成的习语,容易出现望文生义错误,应该慎之又慎。例如:

原　文	望文生义	真实意义
One-horse town	只有一匹马的镇子	乡村小镇
to look after number one	争第一	为自己打算
Three score and ten	古稀之年	人的一生
four-letter words	四个字母组成的词	下流话
The two eyes of Greece	希腊的两只眼	雅典和斯巴达
The third degree	第三度	严刑逼供
five and dime	五块一	廉价物品商店
Twelve good men and true	十二个真正好男人	陪审团
The fifth wheel	第五只轮子	累赘

二、英汉数字词汇空缺现象

1. 汉语文化中的词汇空缺

英语中的许多数字词汇在汉语中没有相应的表达,仅仅看字面往往百思不得其解,译者必须进行查证。例如:

Five it！= 拒绝回答。
Give me five. = 击掌庆贺。
five dollar words = 复杂的字眼。
Catch 22 = 无所适从的尴尬局面。
one over the eight = 喝(酒)过量。
three sheets in the wind = 酩酊大醉。
to be at sixes and sevens = 乱七八糟。
to arrive at the eleventh hour = 高兴极了。

to be dressed up to the nines = 打扮得非常漂亮。

behind the eight ball = 处境危险，无可救药。

eleven plus examination = 英国 11 岁儿童参加的小学毕业升中学的考试。

2. 英语文化中的词汇空缺

汉语中有"张三"、"李四"、"王五"等称呼，英语中虽有 Tom, Dick or Harry 的说法，但它们毕竟与汉语中的说法有着本质的区别，在这方面两种语言中缺乏严格意义上的对等词语。不过，汉语中某些数字式固定用词作为译借词已经进入英语，如："四书"（the Four Books），"五经"（the Five Classics），"四人帮"（Gang of Four），"三国"（the Three Kingdoms），"一国两制"（one country, two systems）等。

汉语诗文里的数字词汇也很多，在翻译成英语时通常不能直译。看下面的例子：

【例 1】蝴蝶梦中家万里，杜鹃枝上月三更。（崔涂《旅怀》）

【译文】In a fond dream, I see my home thousands of miles afar, yet when I wake up was a cuckoo in my sight on a twig and the moon at midnight.

我国古代把夜晚分为五个时段，叫五夜或五更。而"三更"是 23 时到 1 时这段时间，因此翻译成"midnight"。

【例 2】人生有酒须当醉，一滴何曾到九泉。（高翥《清明日对酒》）

【译文】Enjoy your wine and get intoxicated as long as you have your days, not a single drop you could taste after your life in the graves.

"九泉"在汉语里指黄泉、阴间，因此译成了"after your life in the graves"。

【例 3】一封朝奏九重天，夕贬潮阳路八钱。（韩愈《自咏》）

【译文】To the Celestial Court a proposal was made, and I am banished eight thousand miles away.

"九重天"在我国古代喻指皇帝的宫殿，因此译成"Celestial Court"。（三个例子选自郭著章、傅惠玉：汉英对照《千家诗》，武汉大学出版社，2004 年。）

三、习语中数词的修辞特点

数词的功能可从两个方面考察：一是它的基本功能，一是它的修辞功能。数词的修辞功能在文学作品和日常语汇中比比皆是，包括比喻、夸张、委婉、含蓄等。对于数词修辞的恰当使用可增强语言的表现力，收到良好的修辞效果。

1. 比喻

比喻主要分为明喻和暗喻，数词习语主要用作暗喻，极少数用作明喻。例如：

【例 1】A hundred to one it will be a failure.

【译文】这事极可能失败。

"A hundred to one"字面意义是"一百与一之比"。由于"一百"与"一"（石头之于鸡蛋）相比占有绝对的优势，故而引申为"可能性极大"。

【例 2】Millions support their action.

【译文】广大人民群众支持他们的行动。

millions 本是"数百万"的意思，这里喻指"广大人民群众"。

【例 3】New York's Four Hundred can generally be counted on for good copy.

【译文】纽约的上流社会总能闹出点趣闻轶事。

Fourth Hundred 始自 1892 年，当时纽约名流 William Astor 夫人决定把参加她私人舞会的客人人数减少至四百，以后人们便把 (the) Fourth Hundred 比喻为"上流社会人士"。good copy 在这里的意思是"有趣的新闻"。

2. 夸张

用数词习语进行夸张，能使读者对所描述的事物留下深刻的印象。例如：

【例 1】A thousand words of hearsay are not worth a single glance at the reality.

【译文】百闻不如一见。

本句的意思是，上千次的道听途说不如对事实的一瞥，中文里称"百闻不如一见"。

【例2】Thanks a million.

【译文】非常感谢。

这里 a million 用于夸大感谢的程度，表达了说话人由衷的感激之情。

【例3】Her eyes were shining brilliantly, but her face lost its color within twenty seconds.

【译文】她的两眼闪光，晶莹明亮，可是她的脸在一霎那间突然变色。

这是个比喻与夸张相结合的例子。夸张和比喻有着密切的关系，夸张往往是通过比喻来实现。

本章主要参考文献：

国家标准《出版物上数字用法的规定》（GB/T 15835-1995）

郭著章、傅惠玉：汉英对照《千家诗》，武汉大学出版社，2004年。

明安云：《英汉数字的文化差异》，湖北大学学社，2002（5）。

周志培：《汉英对比与翻译中的转换》，华东理工大学出版社，2003年。

翻译练习六

1. 将下面段落译成汉语：

At the plants in Neuf Brisach and Singen, Specialty Sheet covers two products sectors with 2,100 employees and a total annual capacity of around 600,000 tonnes:

· APA (Aluminium Packaging Applications) produces some 430,000 tonnes per year for the packaging industry: can stock (can body and can end) for beverage cans and closure sheets, as well as food packaging and technical hot coil.

· ACS (Automotive and Customized Solutions) each year delivers around 170,000 tonnes of automobile sheet and surface-treated sheet for applications in architecture, lighting and solar energy.

The main customers of ACS are the French and German automobile industries, which are supplied with special sheet and strips for many different applications in the body, chassis and drive areas, as well as heat exchangers and high-gloss products, for example for headlight reflectors and decorative trim.

The plant at Neuf Brisach was founded 40 years ago by Pechiney as "Rhenalu". In 2003 it was taken over by Alcan. On an extensive site around 400,000 tonnes of aluminium strips and sheet are produced each year.

2. 将下面段落译成英语：

《四川宜宾市宜庆公路项目盈利计算规则》"三、宜庆路经济效益分析"中指出：前三年、第四至第五年、第六至第八年、车流量平均分别为12000辆/天、15000辆/天、21000辆/天，每辆运载6吨，收费60元/辆计算，年收入分别为2.592亿、3.24亿、4.536亿，分别扣减1.48816亿、2.0721亿、1.9988亿（包括折旧、公路维修费、管理费用、年利息、营业税、所得税，其中高县政府企业所得税留成部分分别为0.50544亿、0.3159亿、0亿），年税后利润分别为1.10384亿、1.1679亿、2.5372亿。前十年扣出两年建设期，前八年税后总利润为13.31892亿，减去抢险、维修等费用1.2亿，共计12.11892亿。

3. 将下面段落译成汉语：

Each county received equal representation in the state senate, just as each state had equal representation in the U.S. Senate. The new Georgia constitution designated the specific number of representatives each county would have in the state house of representatives. State senators served for three-year terms, house members for one year. Senators had to be at least twenty-eight years of age, and to have resided in the United States for not less than nine years, in Georgia for at least three years, and in the county from which they were elected for six months or more. Senators also were required to own at least two hundred and fifty acres of land or two hundred and fifty pounds or more of other property. House members had to be at least twenty-one years old, and to have resided in the United States for not less than seven years, in Georgia for at least two years, and in their county for three months.

第七章

专业知识与文本翻译

美国当代翻译理论家尤金·奈达（Eugene A. Nida）在《翻译理论与实践》（*The Theory and Practice of Translation*）一书中指出，一个称职的译者应具备五个方面的条件：（摘自许建中：《工商企业翻译实务》，中国对外翻译出版公司，2002年，第19页。）：

1. 必须熟悉原语。仅能理解原文信息的大意或能查字典是远远不够的，还必须能吃透语义的微细区别、词语的情感含义以及决定文章风味情调的各种文体特色。

2. 译者必须精通译入语。这一点比第一点更为重要。在翻译中，译者对原文信息可以通过查阅字典、注释和专业文献加以理解，而对于是否精通译入语的问题却没有别的东西可以替代。翻译中最常见而且最严重的错误，主要是因为不精通译入语而造成的。

3. 精通一门语言同具备专业知识并不是一回事。例如译者也许精通某种语言，而对核物理或化学却一窍不通。要翻译这些学科的技术资料，单凭一般的语言知识是不够的。也就是说，翻译者不仅要掌握原语和译入语，还必须充分了解所译题材。

4. 译者必须具备"移情"本领，即能体会原作者的意图。此外，译者还必须具备一些与原作者类似的文化背景；如果不具备，就应尽快地弥补这一缺陷。

5. 译者必须具备语言表达的才华和丰富的文学想象力。

奈达强调了译者必须对两门相关语言有扎实的知识，同时要具备相关行业的专业知识。译者是培养出来的，而不是天生的。他们当然必须对两门相关语言有扎实的知识，但职业训练也不可或缺。根据文本的性质，提供不同的训练。

《社会科学文本翻译指南》（Michael Henry Heim and Andrzej W. Tymowski: *Guidelines for the Translation of Social Science Texts*. American Council of Learned Societies, New York, 2006）中提到："不同的文本需要不同的译者。学术性的社科文本的翻译最好由从事学术研究的社科工作者承担，因为专业知识对翻译的成功至关重要。以一般大众为读者对象的政府和非政府组织的文本最好由专业译者翻译，他们最好有相关领域的经历或接受过相关领域的培训。"的确如此，一个理想的专业译者不仅应该熟知一般性的翻译技巧，还必须用相当长的时间来熟识相关领域的知识。译者在翻译实践中，对于完全陌生的领域，可以通过如下步骤逐步掌握专业知识，最终成为相关领域翻译的行家里手。

第一、通读全文找到相关知识点，通过在线搜索引擎、网络百科知识、行业语料库等方式查找背景知识。

第二、如果对于相关知识仍然不清楚，可向行家请教。如向名家博客发出提问，或通过"百度知道"等方式发布自己的疑问。

第三、翻译完成后，对于自己没有把握的内容，可放到目的语单语语料库进行检查。如你把"燃煤发电厂"翻译为 coal-fired power plant，可将其放到 americancorpus.org（美国语料库）进行检索，得到48条结果，在 google 检索得到约130万条结果，基本可以确信可用。再如，有一篇关于矿物质的文章，主要分析"膨润土"的构成，而"膨润土"在一般专业词典里查不到，此时可将"膨润土+mineral"在 google 上查询，第一页就发现了中国膨润土专委会的网站，点击进去后在网站名称与域名的英文都是 bentonite，因此可以选用。

对于专业性较强的翻译，语料库可起到不可或缺的作用。关于语料库翻译内容，请参阅第二章《语料库在翻译中的应用》。本章中选取了北京悦尔翻译公司翻译库中的一些内容，包括冶金、建筑、医药与经管四个方面，下面所讲内容是对译者切身感受的总结。

第一节　冶金行业中的专业知识

冶金翻译过程中涉及的知识点很多，碰到的专业词汇大多数都很常见，但意思跟常见意思又有很大区别。翻译过程中应该借助《英汉冶金大字典》等专业工具、辅之以语料库及网络搜索引擎检索，以达到改进译文质量的目的。看下面的实例：

Qatalum [1] Buys Complete Tapping [2] System from HMR
卡塔尔铝业公司从 HMR 公司购买整套出铝系统

（1） Qatalum=Qatar + Aluminium，翻译为"卡塔尔铝业公司"。这种构词法在公司名称中常见，如 Alcan=Aluminium Company of Canada（加拿大铝业公司）、Sinopec=China Petroleum & Chemical Corporation（中国石油化工集团）等。

（2） Tapping。在整篇文章中，翻译好这个词很关键，把这个词理解透，基本上下文翻译也就比较顺畅了。查阅《英汉冶金大字典》发现其意思为"攻螺丝；出铁、出钢"。结合文意，铝业公司购买出铁、出钢系统说不通，翻译时可以率先考虑换为"出铝"，将这两个词放入北大 CCL 语料库进行检索，得出 11 条结果，但都不是用作名词，语义都是"出 + 铝 XX"的表述。由于 CCL 语料库只收录了 4.77 亿字，字数有限，有些专业词汇与低频词汇不一定收录其中。鉴于此，将"出铝"放到 google 进行搜索，就会发现有 800 多万条相关记录，在专门的铝业技术文章中，屡屡提到"出铝"术语，因此，可用"出铝"这样字典所没有提供的表述。

【原文】HMR Hydeq AS [3] has been awarded a contract [4] to deliver a complete tapping system to the aluminium plant in Qatar. The contract includes twelve tapping vehicles [5] together with the crucible [6] cleaning and other stationary equipment to transport all liquid aluminium [7] in the smelter. Hydro, 50% owner of Qatalum, is a long-term customer to HMR, and HMR Hydeq's vehicles are used in all Hydro smelters.

【译文】HMR Hydeq 股份有限公司中标向卡塔尔一家铝厂供应一整套出铝系统。该中标合同包括十二辆出铝车，另外还有坩埚清洁及厂内运输液铝的其他固定设备。海德鲁公司（Hydro）拥有卡塔尔铝业公司（Qatalum）50% 股份，是 HMR 公司的长期客户，在所有冶炼厂中均采用 HMR Hydeq 出铝车。

（3） AS 在这里为大写，用作名词，具有实际意思，不是作为副词使用。其意思为"股份有限公司"。如果缺乏这点背景知识，AS 这个常见的英文单词就会被误用，甚至在翻译过程中误以为是打字错误。查阅张昌平主编《世界电子公司手册》（中国电子学会，1986 年第一版）发现欧洲国家对有限责任公司与股份有限公司的区分如下：

国别 \ 公司名称	有限责任公司在公司名称后标	股份有限公司在公司名称后标
德国	GmbH；如：Assmann GmbH	AG；如：Bayer AG
意大利	S.R.I.；如：Italiana Condutlori S.R.I.	S.P.A.；如：CADIA S.P.A.
丹麦	APS；如：+LYS APS	AS；如：Dencon AS
荷兰	BV；如：Enraf-Nonlus B.V.	NV 如：Oce. Van. Der Grinlen N.V.

（4） Award a contract 字面意思为授予合同；award 在这里是"中标后授予合同"的意思，因此，翻译为"中标"即可。

（5） Tapping vehicle 的翻译。根据标题中已将 tapping 翻译为"出铝"，我们需要对 vehicle 进行上下文分析，这里 vehicle 的作用是"transport all liquid aluminium"，因此翻译为"车"即可。将"出铝车"这个关键词语放到 google 检索，发现类似表述超过 400 万条，验证了这个术语的通用性，因此可用。

（6） crucible 的翻译。《英汉冶金大字典》只给出一个意思："坩埚"。坩埚是用极耐火的材料（如粘土、石墨、瓷土或较难熔化的金属）所制的器皿或熔化罐。结合上下文，发现意思完全与文中意义吻合。

（7） liquid aluminium：液铝、液态铝、熔融金属铝。

【原文】HMR Hydeq, situated in Ardal, Norway, designs and manufactures special purpose vehicles [8]. With customers all over the world, the company today has about 70 employees, including a growing engineering department which develops its own technology. HMR Hydeq started as a department of Hydro Aluminium and is today a part of [9] the HMR group, established in 1956 as a family company. HMR group comprises ten divisions [10], all of them supplying products to the processing industry.

【译文】HMR Hydeq 公司总部位于挪威 Ardal 地区，主要设计与制造各种特种用途车辆，客户遍及全球。该公司目前有近70名员工，其工程部越来越大，专门研发自有技术。HMR Hydeq公司一开始是海德鲁铝业公司的一个部门，今天已成为HMR集团（1956年成立的家族公司）的一员。HMR集团共有十个事业部，向加工行业提供各种产品。

（8）special purpose vehicle：特种用途车辆。

（9）a part of 的翻译。翻译时不能按照字面意思，不能翻译为"XXX集团的一部分"，英汉表述时语义存在差异，汉语应调整为"一员"，具体为某一家公司。

（10）division是一个有许多意义的常见词，其中"部门：政府或公司的一个部分，属一行政或功能单位"的义项与上下文比较接近，因此，我们似可把原文中相关部分翻译为"HMR集团共有十个部门"。但考虑到公司内部具体的市场部、财务部、人力资源部、技术部、生产部等都使用department一词，我们仍需对division的意义进行考察。大集团中生产不同产品的公司其实就是一个division，因此，我们可将其翻译为"事业部"，它在语义上大于具体部门。

【原文】With tapping vehicles from HMR Hydeq, one person can tap, weigh, transport, de-dross [11] and discharge the molten aluminium in a safe and efficient way. One vehicle with a capacity of 8.5 tonnes can move 250 tonnes of liquid metal in 24 hours. No splashing [12], no overloading, no metal loss: one machine and one operator only.

【译文】使用HMR Hydeq出铝车，一个人就可以安全、高效地完成出铝、过秤、运输、除渣及卸载液铝所有作业。一台出铝车容量为8.5吨，24小时内即可运输250吨液态金属。没有任何喷溅，没有任何超载，没有任何金属损失：只需要一台设备与一名操作员即可。

（11）de-dross：这是一个根据英文构词法（word forming）构造的构成词。De-为指示字干、介词和副词的词根，主要表示"除去、离去、剥离、向下"等意思。词干"dross"为（金属熔化时浮升至表面的）渣滓，因此de-dross可翻译为"除渣"。在汉译英过程中也有类似的情况，在碰到难于理解的专业术语时，可以考虑根据词干以及构词法来试着寻找对应的翻译。如"降水井"、"除尘"、"去矿物质处理"等，可分别翻译为"dewatering well"、"dedusting"以及"demineralising"。

（12）splashing：喷溅。

【原文】Safety first: Excellent safety features result from transporting the molten metal in a closed system, where it cannot splash during transport or discharging. An on-board [13] weighing system prevents overload, while a closed cab provides an excellent micro-environment and good visibility, and full hydraulic suspension [14] on all wheels ensures excellent working conditions for the operator. All operations are controlled from the cab by electrical buttons and joysticks. The keyboard and the monitor, which the driver uses to communicate with the vehicle, are situated ergonomically around the operator. The on-board weighing device can be linked up to the smelter's production planning system.

【译文】安全第一：通过封闭系统来运输熔融金属，运输或卸载过程中不会产生任何喷溅，其安全性能非常出色。机载称重系统防止车辆出现超载情况，而封闭驾驶室能够提供绝佳的微环境与良好的能见度，并且车轮上的全液压悬挂系统能够确保操作员获得一流的工作条件。所有作业都通过电动按钮与操纵杆从驾驶室内进行控制。键盘与监视器就位于操作员旁边，方便驾驶员与车辆进行沟通，完全符合人体工程学原理。机载称重设备可以与冶炼厂生产规划系统连接起来。

（13）on-board：《现代英汉字典》对"on board"的注解为"在船上，在公共交通工具内"。根据上下文，此处on board应为在车上，但翻译为"在车上的称重系统"不够专业，翻译时应尽量在汉语中找到意义对等的表述方式：机载称重系统。"on-board"翻译为"机载"。在翻译过程中，注意连字符"-"的妙用。在此处如不用连字符，"on board"就是一个介词短语，无法表示实意。通过连字符连接，就可以将介词短语、名动结构、形名结构等结合起来，在文中充当定语。如a state-of-the-art technology（一项先进的技术）、human-oriented policy（以人为本的政策）、environmentally-friendly measures（环保措施）、a world-class carmaker（世界一流的汽车制造商）等等。

（14）suspension：车辆的悬挂系统，就是指由车身与轮胎间的弹簧和避震器组成整个支持系统。悬挂系统应有的功能是支持车身，改善乘坐的感觉，不同的悬挂设置会使驾驶者有不同的驾驶感受。外表看似简单的悬挂系统综合多种作用力,决定着轿车的稳定性、舒适性和安全性,是现代轿车十分关键的部件之一。

【原文】Independent operation: The vehicle does not depend on ancillary equipment, like compressed air, cranes, tilting platform, nor on other operators on the floor. It can lift and fetch the crucible without external help, and has own compressor for tapping and discharging crucibles. The vehicle has a kneeling function [15], so it can tilt the crucibles in any direction to empty them efficiently. For such a large vehicle, its turning radius is small as it turns with one or more axles [16]. Construction with high quality steel, which HMR uses in all models, reduces the weight of the vehicle from 20 to 30% so that the vehicles can carry a heavier payload.

【译文】独立操作:出铝车无需依赖压缩空气、起重机、倾卸平台等辅助装置,也不需要其他操作员在地面上进行指挥。出铝车能够在没有外力情况下提升坩埚并进行移动,其自带压缩机能够对坩埚进行出铝与卸载操作。出铝车还具有下蹲功能,可以朝任何方向倾斜坩埚,从而高效进行卸载。对于这样一辆大型车,由于可以采用了一个或多个轮轴,其转弯半径很小。由于 HMR 使用优质钢来建造各种型号出铝车,使得出铝车重量降低 20%–30%,提高了运送的有效载荷。

(15) kneeling function:字面意思为"跪下功能",结合车辆的操作考虑,应该是降低高度,能够触及更低的物件,因此调整为"下蹲"。

(16) axle:轮轴,即由轮和轴组成、能绕共同轴线旋转的机械。轮轴是一种能够连续旋转的杠杆,支点就在轴心,轮轴在转动时轮与轴有着相同的转速。

【原文】Hot crucible cleaning prolongs lining lifetime: The HMR tapping vehicle has integrated ladle [17] cleaning and tube cleaning stations, which clean tubes inside and outside, and also pre-heat siphon tubes [18]. Together they form a complete closed tapping system, which reduces manpower needs, temperature loss, and oxidation compared to other systems–HMR has now many customers who are convinced of these benefits. At the HMR ladle cleaning station, the crucible can be cleaned while it is still hot, which reduces the total number of crucibles a smelter needs, and extends the lifetime of the crucibles. It is not unusual to prolong lifetime up to 18,000 hours for the crucible lining.

【译文】对坩埚进行热清洁可以延长内衬使用寿命:HMR 出铝车整合有铝包清洁站与管道清洁站,清洁管道内外部分,并且对虹吸管进行预热。与这些设备一起,构成了整套封闭出铝系统。与其他系统相比,HMR 系统大大降低了人员需求、温度损失与氧化程度——现在,HMR 客户众多,他们对这些优点心悦诚服。在 HMR 铝包清洁站中,趁热对坩埚进行清洁,一方面可降低冶炼厂所需坩埚数量,另一方面也延长来坩埚的使用寿命。坩埚内衬使用寿命高达 18 000 小时的并不罕见。

(17) ladle:《英汉冶金大字典》释义为"桶"。这个词在冶金行业中经常见到,本来的意思是"勺子",作为术语翻译为"钢包",指的是盛钢水的容器,用钢制成,内砌耐火砖,钢水由底部的口流出,进行浇铸,也叫"钢水包"。结合上下文,此处应将 ladle 翻译为"铝包"。

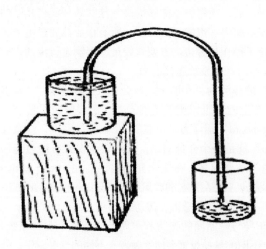

(18) siphon tube:虹吸管,指的是液体产生虹吸现象所用的管子。虹吸现象是指液体从比较高的地方通过一条拱起的弯管,先向上再向下流到比较低的地方去的现象,使用时管内必须先充满液体,见下图:

【原文】Green solution: The environment visibly gains from the enclosed system, since the exhaust [19] from the crucible during tapping is fed under the pot hooding. The enclosed system and the short cycle time together reduce the temperature drop in the metal, which again saves energy for re-melting in the cast house [20].

【译文】环保解决方案:通过密封系统获得的

环保效益非常明显,因为在出铝过程中从坩埚排出的废气又进入到坩埚防护罩下面。密封的系统及较短的循环时间一起作用,大大降低了金属的温降情况,为铸造车间进行再熔作业节约了能源。

(19) exhaust:废气。

(20) cast house:铸造车间。

第二节 建筑工程行业的专业知识

我们身边的建筑工程比比皆是,但人们对于相关的术语往往不熟悉,例如:汽吊、桥吊、龙门吊、电葫芦、塔吊等等,即使查阅专业词典找到了相应的英文,也不一定能够理解它们的意义并进行翻译。此时通过 google 或 baidu 图片搜索进行关键字检索,找到相关图片,许多问题也就容易解决了。上面的几个专业名词对应的英语分别为 autocrane, overhang crane, gantry crane, motor hoist 和 tower crane。对于建筑工程行业的专业知识,我们要从背景材料开始了解,借助搜索引擎、图片搜索、专业词典等来了解具体含义,然后再安排翻译。下面我们以相对陌生的海上采油平台加固措施为例,理解相关翻译技巧及专业知识。

Calling for reinforcements [1]

Bad weather or a shifting seabed calls strengthening of oil rigs [2] ' legs

采油平台加固解决方案

恶劣的天气与漂移的海底要求加固采油平台支柱

(1) 在英汉翻译过程中,汉语标题内容比较丰富,并且常见对偶句式;英文标题比较简单,言简意赅,翻译时须根据读者对象稍作调整。"Calling for reinforcements"字面意思是"需要各种加固",这样的表述在汉语中很少见,因此在翻译时可以进行一些调整,如可将其翻译为"采油平台加固解决方案",添加了"采油平台"后,使得原文意义在汉语中的表述更加明确和具体。

(2) 在翻译 oil rigs 时,首先找到一张 oil rigs 的示意图,然后根据图来分析相关部件的功能及术语表达。找图可通过 google 或者 baidu 的图片搜索引擎,输入关键词"oil rigs"之后,即可看到相关图片。我们下面提供的一张示意图显示,oil rigs 应该翻译为"采油平台"。

【原文】The hurricanes suffered by the US in 2005 have shown that very little can get in the way of the weather if it wants to knock over an oil platform. Similarly, the ever-changing geological nature of the ground at the bottom of the sea can make a platform unsteady on its legs [3].

【译文】2005 年,飓风席卷美国。这场灾害显示,如果恶劣天气要摧毁一座采油平台,人们几乎没有什么办法可以阻止。同样,由于海底地壳不断变动,采油平台支柱也会处于不稳定状态。

(3) legs:原意为"腿",这里可考虑译为"支架"、"支柱"、"支腿"等。这里选择了"支柱",因为插入海底的是钢管架。

【原文】Steel jackets [4] are becoming increasingly common in the reinforcement of rig legs, as is liquid grouting to secure them. The Ekofisk platform in the North Sea has seen the benefit and is still one of the largest projects for one of the companies dealing in this specialised sector. Scandinavian engineer Densit [5] has pumped thousands of tonnes of grout [6] between the piles and sleeves of platforms' legs around the world.

Oil Drilling System

【译文】在采油平台支柱加固方面,钢管架变得日益常见,而灌浆液也频频使用,确保加固钢管架的性能。北海 Ekofisk 平台是这一专业领域中最大的项目之一,已经领略到灌浆的优点。斯堪的纳维亚 Densit 工程公司在全球范围内,已经将数千吨灌浆注入到平台支柱与套管之间。

(4) steel jackets:钢管架,一般用于近海平台的搭建。

(5) Scandinavian engineer Densit:这三个单词的组合经常被误译

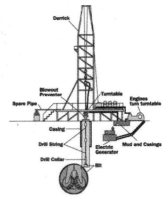

为"斯堪的纳维亚工程师 Densit",主要原因是 engineer 在词典里常仅给出"工程师"的义项,而没有"工程公司"的义项。如果 Densit 是工程师,他一个人不可能"将数千吨灌浆注入到平台支柱与套管之间"。经过查证 Densit 是一家工程公司,该公司拥有专利产品 Ducorit 高强度灌浆材料。在工程建设材料的翻译中,类似于 engineer 指"工程公司"的情况还有许多,如将 designer 翻译为"设计单位",supervisor 翻译为"监理单位",builder 翻译为"施工单位"等等。另外,类似于 Densit 的公司名称没有在科技翻译过程中,对于在中文没有对应官方说法的,保留英文原文即可。目前,许多公司为了实施其国际化战略,在全球范围内统一其 logo 与名称,越来越多地只使用英语一种语言来表述其名称,如 Honda、Toyota、Nokia、LG 等。但需要一提的是,国内出版物对于英文人名、地名、公司名称的表述要求,仍然需要使用汉语音译方式来表达。

(6) grout:灌浆。指为防渗或加固向建筑物地基、大体积混凝土和土石建筑物内部灌注某种浆液的工作。通常使用水泥、黏土、沥青、硅酸钠等浆液。灌浆也用于油田井喷抢险。

【原文】In June 2005 Densit carried out grouting of two wells at Shell's Champion field [7] in Brunei with its patented Ducorit high-strength grout. The grouting had two purposes: one was to stop the ongoing corrosion of the outer casing [8], the other purpose was to strengthen sections of the outer casing, which under heavy corrosion attack that had reduced its structural capacity.

【译文】2005 年 6 月,Densit 公司在壳牌公司文莱 Champion 油田,利用其专利产品 Ducorit 高强度灌浆完成了两个油井的灌浆工作。灌浆具有两大目的:第一、让外壳免受腐蚀;第二、对于腐蚀严重、结构性能受到影响的外壳部分进行加固。

(7) well:油井;field:油田。

(8) casing:外壳。通过参阅上文示意图可了解其具体所指。

【原文】Prior to the grouting operation in Brunei the wells were inspected using special camera equipment. The objective of the conductor [9] inspection was to determine and assess the accessibility of the annulus between the outer casing and the conductor—information that was used in the planning of the grouting operation. The mixing spread and the grout pumps were erected [10] on the deck of a workboat from which the grouting work was carried out. During the grouting operation, the workboat was anchored up next to the platform and access to the platform was established through the use of a temporary steel gangway [11].

【译文】在文莱进行灌浆操作之前,使用专用摄影设备对油井进行检查。导管检查的目的在于测量与评估外壳与导管之间环形空间的通畅性——这一信息将用于计划灌浆操作。在作业船上安装搅拌设备与灌浆泵,在船上进行灌浆作业。在灌浆操作过程中,作业船锚定在平台附近,通过临时钢舷梯上下采油平台。

(9) conductor:导管。

(10) erect:安装。Erect 本意为"树立、直立",但此处可翻译为"安装"。Equipment erection and debugging 指的是"设备安装与调试"。

(11) gangway:舷梯。指的是舷门所设以供旅客(工作人员)上下船的活动扶梯。

【原文】The workboat was also used for wire line work [12] and the trial proved that the grouting work and wire line work or other well services are conveniently carried out at the same time. A grout hose with a steel outlet [13] was lowered down to target depth of about 15 to 20m below sea level, which is the level where the corrosion ends due to the lack of oxygen supply. Crucially the grouting work was carried out no impact on the producing wells.

【译文】作业船还用于开展钻油工作。试验证明,灌浆工作、钻油工作及其他油井服务可以同期进行。灌浆软管(带钢制出浆口)下放到海平面以下 15 到 20 米目标深度之中;在这一深度以下,由于缺乏氧源,不会发生腐蚀。至关重要的是,灌浆工作对油井正常开采没有任何影响。

(12) wire line work 字面意思为"管线工作"或"线路工作",这跟石油开采、作业船都没有太大关系。通过查找《英汉 512 专利大字典》发现,wire line 具有"深井开凿"之意,从而确定其为"钻油"。

（13）A grout hose with a steel outlet. 这个短语中包含一个介词短语 with a steel outlet，如翻译为"带钢出浆口的灌浆软管"则显得很啰嗦，可在"灌浆软"之后使用括号来注释相关内容，以确保行文的流畅。

【原文】The material used in the Ducorit Reinforcement Method is purely mineral and contains no constituents not ordinarily included in concrete and mortar formulations. The strength characteristics exhibited by Ducorit exceed those of conventional materials by a factor of five to 10 [14]. Mixing and pumping require high-performance equipment of standard types.

【译文】在Ducorit加固法中使用的材料只是矿物质材料，在混凝土与灰浆配方中一般没有的成分也不会包括在这些材料当中。Ducorit展示出的强度特性超过传统材料5–10倍。其搅拌与抽吸则需要高性能的标准型设备。

（14）A exceeds B by a factor of five to 10：factor 在这里不能翻译为系数，而是倍数，即 A 超过 B 5–10 倍。这里 five to 10 没有写为 five to ten，可参阅本书第六章相关部分了解其中的原因。

【原文】Grouting as a form of reinforcement is likely to grow in popularity as platforms age and safety becomes even more of a concern. Already it has found another application in offshore wind turbines, especially popular in northern Europe. The foundation of offshore wind turbines is often a monopile [15] drilled or hammered into the seabed. In order to establish a stronger bond between the monopile and turbine tower, a Ducorit-grouted [16] connection between the monopile and transition piece can be used.

【译文】随着采油平台使用寿命与安全问题日益受到关注，灌浆加固方式很可能会在采油平台当中盛行起来。在北欧颇为流行的海上风力发电涡轮机上，灌浆已经发现了另外一大用途。海上风力发电涡轮机的根基经常是一根单体柱，直接钻入或铆入海底。为了确保单体柱与涡轮塔之间连接稳固，可以使用Ducorit灌浆来连接单体柱与过渡件。

（15）monopile：单体柱。前缀"mono-"表示"单一"的意思，如 monoatomic（单原子的），monoaxial（单轴的），monopoly（垄断）等等。

（16）Ducorit-grouted 属于名动加过去分词结构，用作定语，意为"使用Ducorit材料进行灌浆的"。类似的结构还有 a Beijing-based company，a student-led conference，a rapper-turned actor，a heart-felt story 等等。

第三节 医药行业的专业知识

在医药行业中，涉及的化学物质名称较多。据统计，目前超过1800万种化学物质都具有独立的拉丁语名称，确保一物一名。翻译这些化学物质名称时，必须参考网络搜索引擎、专业词典、相关数据库（如CAS）等相关资料方可确保准确。医药翻译对译者的医学知识要求很高，译文质量优劣关系到人身安全。不过只要认真了解相关知识、翻译时借助大量参考资料、向懂行者虚心求教，加上译者应有的审慎态度，一般译者顺利完成这类翻译还是可能的。下面，我们以一篇专业性较强的医药文章为例，探讨医药翻译中的一些问题。

Technology Tackles Resistance [1] Products in the Pipeline [2] are Showing Success in Beating Drug Resistance
技术攻克耐药性
试制产品在攻克耐药性问题上显露成效

（1）resistance 通常的意义为"抵抗、阻力"等，这里的意义为"耐药性"。翻译过程中往往需要事先通读全文，才能够了解常见单词的具体含义。一般情况下，标题翻译可以留到全文翻译结束之后。耐药性指的是病原微生物对抗生素等药物产生的耐受和抵抗能力。耐药性的产生使正常剂量的药物不再发挥应有的杀菌效果，甚至使药物完全无效，从而给疾病的治疗造成困难，并容易使疾病蔓延。人们一般认为耐药性的产生是微生物基因突变造成的，耐药性变异一旦产生即可传给后代，同时转移给原来没有耐药性的敏感菌，使耐药性细菌逐步增加。

（2）in the pipeline：字面意思是"在管道中"。查阅《简明英汉字典》，得到五个义项：(a) 在准备中；(b) 在完成中；(c) 在进行中；(d) (货物)运输中；(e) 即将送递。结合上下文，应该选择（b）、（c）义项，将 Products in the pipeline 翻译为"试制产品"。

【原文】New drugs are demonstrating significant breakthroughs in the treatment of drug-resistant bacteria [3]. Many life-threatening diseases are now resistant to the antibiotics developed to combat them; reengineered antibiotics and a new class of protein inhibitors aim to redress the balance.

【译文】新药在处理耐药性细菌方面正显露出重大突破。现在，许多威胁生命的疾病对现有抗生素产生了耐药性；各种再造抗生素与一类新型蛋白质抑制剂目标重新调整平衡。

（3）drug-resistant bacteria 为合成词，将其理解透彻也就把握住了全文。如翻译为"对药物具有抵抗力的细菌"不能确保表述是否专业，应该查找相应的背景资料，最终才能翻译为业内行话"耐药性细菌"。放到 google 与 baidu 去检索，"耐药性细菌"关键词结果超过 40 万条，可用。需要注意的是，国内也常见"抗药细菌"的说法，与"耐药性细菌"意思完全一致，翻译中要确保上下文的一致，所以仍然采用"耐药性细菌"的说法。

【原文】Phase III clinical trials data on the first of a new class of glycylcycline [4] antibiotics, presented at the Interscience Conference on Antimicrobial Agents and Chemotherapy [5] in Washington DC, US demonstrated considerable clinical efficacy. US pharma firm Wyeth hopes that Tigecycline [6], its new "superantibiotic", will stem [7] the rising tide of multidrug-resistant bacteria including Methicillin Resistant Staphylococcus Aureus (MRSA) [8].

【译文】在美国华盛顿召开的抗微生物药物与化疗跨学科大会（ICAAC）介绍了第一款新型甘氨酰四环素类抗生素的三期临床试验数据。美国惠氏医药公司希望新型"超级抗生素"——替加环素能够抑制耐甲氧西林金黄色葡萄球菌（MRSA）等多种耐药性细菌的蔓延狂潮。

（4）glycylcycline：甘氨酰四环素类抗生素。化学元素符号都采用拉丁文表示，即使是母语为英语的人对拉丁文也不甚熟悉，并且作为化学元素的拉丁文名称一般都比较长，在拼写过程中经常出错，而一般人很难发现其中错误。国内关于化学物质英文名称词典不多，并且更新也不及时。遇到此类情况类可利用搜索引擎中查找，然后再进行验证。美国化学文摘社于 1965 年建立了庞大的 CAS 化学物质登记系统，利用化学物质结构图一致性的特点，对其分子结构图进行算术运算，并经一系列差错检测后，使每个化合物达到一物一名，具有独一无二的 CAS 化学物质登记号。截止 1998 年 10 月，CAS 登记号已经登记的化合物总数超过了 1800 万个。

（5）Interscience Conference on Antimicrobial Agents and Chemotherapy：对于这类国际大会，一般都有正式的官方译法。因此可通过网络搜索引擎进行关键字检索，一般为"完整英文或英文缩写 + 语义明确的中文（如"大会"）"。ICAAC 的中文表述为"抗微生物药物与化疗跨学科大会"，切不可想当然自己胡乱翻译。

（6）Tigecycline：替加环素；分析同（4）。

（7）stem 有"滋生、阻止"之意；根据上下文，选择"阻止"之意。

（8）Methicillin Resistant Staphylococcus Aureus (MRSA)：专有名词，必须通过网络检索或者词典验证，最终翻译为"耐甲氧西林金黄色葡萄球菌（MRSA）"。

【原文】Dr Evan Loh, vice president of cardiovascular and infectious disease at Wyeth, said: "Tigecycline is a structurally distinct and re-engineered tetracycline. A modification at the ninth position of the core structure enables the drug to bind to bacteria at the 30S ribosomal subunit with significantly increased affinity [9] compared with any prior generation tetracycline. By this means it is able to combat typical bacterial resistance mechanisms such as efflux pumps and ribosomal protection [10]. The structural modification also improves pharmacokinetics, making the drug more effective at penetrating tissues.

【译文】惠氏公司负责心血管和传染性疾病的副总裁 Evan Loh 博士说："替加环素是一种结构独

特、重新改造的四环素。与之前历代四环素相比，其核心结构第九位进行了改良，与细菌 30S 核糖体相结合的亲和力大大增强。通过这种方式，将能有效战胜外排机制和核糖体保护机制等典型细菌耐药性机制。结构改良也改进了药物代谢动力，使得药物可以更有效地渗透进入组织。

（9）affinity：亲和力，指的是两种以上（含两种）的物质结合成化合物时相互作用之力。

（10）efflux pumps and ribosomal protection：外排机制和核糖体保护机制。重点是 efflux pump 翻译为"外排"。是有些物质在细胞膜内被一层膜所包围，形成小泡，小泡逐渐移到细胞表面，小泡膜与细胞膜融合在一起，并且向细胞外张开，使内含物质排除细胞外，这种现象叫做外排作用。细胞可以通过外排作用向外分泌物质。

【原文】"In-vitro [11] and pivotal clinical studies with data from almost 3000 patients in 40 countries demonstrated a very broad spectrum of activity with excellent clinical efficacy," Dr Loh said. "It is effective as a monotherapy against both gram negative and positive bacteria [12], anaerobes, atypical organisms and many multidrug-resistant pathogens including those carrying extended spectrum beta lactamases [13] and acinetobacter [14]."

【译文】"在 40 个国家的近 3000 名患者活体外临床研究与关键临床研究表明，该药物用途广泛，具有极好的临床效力。" Loh 博士如是说："作为防治革兰氏阳性和阴性菌、厌氧菌、非典型病原体与多种多重耐药病原体（包括携带超广谱 β-内酰胺酶与不动杆菌的病原体）的单药治疗方式，其效果卓著。"

（11）in-vitro：拉丁语，意为"在活体外部、在人造环境内"。"in vitro fertilization"指的是体外受精、试管内受精。与之相对应的"in vivo"意为在"活体内"，心理学中"in vivo desensitization"为"体内脱敏"。

（12）gram negative and positive bacteria：革兰氏阳性和阴性菌。革兰氏染色法用龙胆紫（亦称结晶紫）来染病菌，所有细菌都染成了紫色，然后再涂以革兰氏碘液，来加强染料与菌体的结合，再用 95% 的酒精来脱色 20～30 秒钟，有些细菌不被脱色，仍保留紫色，有些细菌被脱色变成无色。最后再用复红或沙黄复染 1 分钟，结果已被脱色的细菌被染成红色，未脱色的细菌仍然保持紫色，不着色。这样，凡被染成紫色的细菌称为革兰氏阳性菌，染成红色的称为革兰氏阴性菌。大多数化脓性球菌都属于革兰氏阳性菌，它们能产生外毒素使人致病，而大多数肠道菌多属于革兰氏阴性菌，它们产生内毒素，靠内毒素使人致病。常见的革兰氏阳性菌有：葡萄球菌、链球菌、肺炎双球菌、炭疽杆菌、白喉杆菌、破伤风杆菌等；常见的革兰氏阴性菌有痢疾杆菌、伤寒杆菌、大肠杆菌、变形杆菌、绿脓杆菌、百日咳杆菌、霍乱弧菌及脑膜炎双球菌等。在治疗上，大多数革兰氏阳性菌都对青霉素敏感；而革兰氏阴性菌则对青霉素不敏感，而对链霉素、氯霉素等敏感。所以首先区分病原菌是革兰氏阳性菌还是阴性菌，在选择抗生素方面意义重大。

（13）extended spectrum beta lactamases：超广谱 β-内酰胺酶（ESBLs）。如果临床出现产 ESBLs 菌株，则对第三代头孢菌素（它们是头孢噻肟、头孢他定、头孢哌酮、头孢曲松等）耐药，及对单环酰胺类抗生素（氨曲南）耐药。目前大肠埃希氏菌（大肠杆菌）、肺炎克雷伯氏菌是最常见的产 ESBLs 菌株的细菌。其次，阴沟肠杆菌、粘质沙雷氏菌、弗劳地枸橼酸菌以及铜绿假单孢菌，也可出现产 ESBLs 菌株的细菌。对付产 ESBLs 菌株，目前最有效的抗生素为碳青霉烯类（泰能），另外头孢西丁及含酶抑制剂的复合剂、氨基糖甙类也有一定的疗效。

（14）acinetobacter：不动杆菌。不动杆菌广泛分布于外界环境，主要分布在水和土壤中，亦常存在于人的皮肤、呼吸道、消化道和泌尿生殖道中。不动杆菌均为条件致病菌，可引起中耳炎、脑膜炎、烧伤感染、败血症和泌尿系感染。

【原文】The phase III trials, required to further establish safety and efficacy data by testing on a wider patient base, evaluated Tigecycline in complicated intra-abdominal infections and complicated skin and skin structure infections. Further trials are still in progress in community and hospital-acquired pneumonia [15].

【译文】三期试验要求在更多患者试验的基础上，进一步确立安全性、功效性数据，并评估替加环素对复杂的腹内感染与皮肤、皮肤组织感染的疗效。针对社区与医院获得性肺炎所进行的深入试验仍在进行当中。

（15）community and hospital-acquired pneumonia：社区与医院获得性肺炎。社区获得性肺炎是指在

医院外罹患的感染性肺实质炎症，包括具有明确潜伏期的病原体感染而入院后平均潜伏期内发病的肺炎。医院获得性肺炎是指患者入院时不存在，也不处于感染潜伏期内，而于入院 48 小时后在医院内发生的肺炎。细菌是医院获得性肺炎最常见的病原，占 90% 以上，真菌、病毒及其他病原体较少见。

【原文】However, the drug's promising activity [16] against the growing number of resistant pathogens is what is likely to generate the most interest in the product. These include vancomycin-resistant enterobacter, MRSA, acinetobacter, and organisms carrying extended spectrum beta lactamase.

【译文】然而，该药物治疗耐药性病原体的积极前景，可使人们对该产品产生极大兴趣。这些病原体包括耐药性肠道杆菌、耐甲氧西林金黄色葡萄球菌（MRSA）、不动杆菌以及携带超广谱 β-内酰胺酶的病原体。

（16）promising activity：积极前景。注意，promising 在这里不是许诺的意思，而是"有前途的、有希望的"。

【原文】Another company at the Interscience meeting demonstrated a different approach to tackling bacterial infection. Researchers from Paratek Pharmaceuticals in Boston, US have identified drugs based on small organic molecules called "multiple adaptational response" (MAR) [17] protein inhibitors. The drugs target transcription factors, the molecular switches which turn on and off bacterial mechanisms leading to infection and, ultimately, antibiotic resistance.

【译文】在跨学科会议上，另一家公司展示了另外一种处理细菌感染的不同方法。美国波士顿 Paratek 医药公司研究人员已经发现了基于有机小分子的药物，称为"多重适应性反应"（MAR）蛋白质抑制剂。该药物的目标是转录因子——分子开关，能够控制引起感染、并最终产生抗生素耐药性的细菌机制。

（17）"multiple adaptational response"（MAR）：多重适应性反应。适应性反应指的是机体受到低剂量环境因子预刺激后，对后续高剂量的刺激产生耐受的现象。

【原文】Paratek's Michael Alekshun said: "MAR is present in nearly all clinically important bacteria. Using the crystal structures of two MAR proteins, Paratek has developed compounds to inhibit the binding of MAR proteins to DNA targets in several bacterial strains [18]. The proof of principle has now been established in a mouse model."

【译文】Paratek 医药公司 Michael Alekshun 说："多重适应性反应（MAR）几乎存在于所有具有临床意义的细菌当中。通过使用两个 MAR 蛋白质的晶体结构，Paratek 医药公司已经研发出多种化合物，在多个菌株当中抑制 MAR 蛋白质吸附到 DNA 目标。这一原理现已通过小白鼠试验得到验证。"

（18）bacterial strain：菌株，表示任何由一个独立分离的单细胞（或单个病毒粒子）繁殖而成的纯种群体及其后代。因此，一种微生物的每一个不同来源的纯培养物均可称为该菌种的一个菌株。菌株实际上是某一微生物达到"遗传性纯"的标志，一旦菌株发生变异，均应标上新的菌株名称。

第四节 经管文章中的专业知识

经济管理类文章中的术语比较常见，为大多数人所熟知。因此，在翻译过程中，进行词义区分最为关键。掌握了相关经管文章的写作套路，如常用指示代词指代上文提到的事物、使用连字符构造新词等，翻译起来才比较得心应手。

Collaboration essential to success [1]
企业成功离不开协作

（1）标题中 essential to success 为后置定语修饰 collaboration，另外，全篇内容也是讲如何通过合作达到成功。因此，可将标题翻译为"企业成功离不开协作"。

【原文】Most organisations are struggling to establish effective collaboration and teamwork across all of their departments, which results in higher employee turnover [2], according to management consultancy Hay Group [3].

【译文】根据管理咨询公司合益集团的研究，大多数组织在建立部门之间有效协作及提升团队精神方面步履维艰，因而导致了较高的员工流动。

（2）turnover：容易误译为"营业额"，该词在这里指"员工流动"。

（3）Hay Group：公司名称翻译一般应采用官方正式译名，如不存在官方译名，可保留原英文名称。

【原文】In research based on data [4] covering 1.2 million employees from more than 400 companies worldwide, Hay Group found that just over half of all employees felt there was an atmosphere that encouraged cooperation and the sharing of ideas [5] across their company while less than half said the various parts of their company worked well together.

【译文】研究数据来自全球 400 多家公司的 120 万名员工。合益集团的研究发现，只有略高于一半的员工感到公司内部具有鼓励协作、交流思想的氛围；不到一半的员工认为公司不同部门之间一起工作良好。

（4）In research based on data：在以数据为基础的研究当中。在翻译成汉语时，可按照原文的意义进行翻译，不必完全按照英语的句法结构翻译，本书第四章中对此有详尽论述。

（5）cooperation and the sharing of ideas：A and B of ideas 同是 encourage 的宾语，这里 of ideas 只修饰 B 不修饰 A，它们之间的关系可从语义上加以判断。

【原文】Hay said it found that the senior management team in many companies was not a team, but rather a group of functional and business unit heads [6] with little inclination or incentive [7] to cooperate. Only a third of the companies researched responded favourably when asked about the level of communication between departments within their organisation.

【译文】合益集团称，发现许多公司管理高层不是一个团队，而是一些职能部门和业务部门的头头，他们不想与他人合作，也没有与他人合作的动力。当问及组织内部各部门之间的沟通水平时，只有三分之一的受调查公司做出了满意的回答。

（6）functional and business unit heads 指职能部门和业务部门的领导。

（7）incentive：《美国传统字典》的释义为（a）Something, such as the fear of punishment or the expectation of reward, that induces action or motivates effort;（b）Serving to induce or motivate. 根据上下文，此处 incentive 的第二个义项"诱使或激励"才是正确的意义选择。

【原文】The consultancy noted that in today's business environment, where organisations are often team-based and complex, the management of roles and relationships between individuals and business functions is essential.

【译文】合益集团指出，当今商业环境中各组织之间的关系复杂，组织之间又往往以团队划界。因此，对于个人作用及其个人之间的关系、不同业务部门职能及其之间的关系进行管理，是必不可少的。

本句中的 The consultancy 指代"合益集团"。理解本句需对句子结构进行分析，在以 that 引导的宾语从句中，主句的主语是 the management，谓语部分是 is essential；而 in today's business environment 为壮语成分，where organisations are often team-based and complex 则用来修饰 business environment。

【原文】"A lack of cross-functional teamwork [8] creates lower levels of productivity and growth and makes it much more difficult for organisations to operate efficiently or achieve their strategic objectives," commented Mark Royal, senior consultant with Hay's Insight division [9]. "What's more, by making it more difficult for individuals to carry out their responsibilities, employees are frustrated in their current positions and job turnover is much higher."

【译文】"对于各个组织而言，缺乏跨职能团队协作会降低生产力水平，阻止企业发展，运营效率低下，难于实现战略目标。"合益集团研究事业部资深顾问 Mark Royal 评论说，"况且，由于个人履行职责变得更加困难，员工对其现任职务感到沮丧，员工流动会更高。"

（8）cross-functional teamwork：跨职能团队协作。跨职能团队由不同职能部门的员工组成，他们走到一起是为了完成某项任务。通过不同部门员工之间的合作，可以激发新观点的产生，解决面临的问题，协调复杂的项目。

（9）Insight division：可译为"研究事业部"。Insight 的意思是：ideas about the true nature of something。要了解事物的本质特征必须进行认真研究，这样才能把工作做好。大公司的 Insight division 就从事这方面的工作。

【原文】In separate research Hay found that the most admired companies (10) are generally the ones that distinguish themselves from others by fostering cultures that support collaboration by encouraging teamwork at the top through executive performance measures (11) and by holding executives accountable as a team for strategy implementation.

【译文】在分项研究中合益集团发现，最受尊敬的公司通常以培育自身文化而变得与众不同，这种文化通过以下方式支持协作：通过管理绩效措施鼓励高层树立团队意识，赋予作为战略实施团队的管理人员一定的责任。

（10）most admired company：最受尊敬公司。财富500强对"最受尊敬公司"排名的评价标准是：国际化程度、创新能力、员工智慧、社会责任、管理质量、服务质量。

（11）executive performance measures：管理绩效措施。

【原文】top of this list (12) –which covered only US companies–was computer firm Dell, which knocked retailer Wal-Mart to fourth from its previous number one position. The other most admired brands in the top five (13) included General Electric, Starbucks and Southwest Airlines.

【译文】在美国最受尊敬公司榜单上，戴尔电脑公司位列榜首，打败了零售企业沃尔玛公司，使其由原先第一位下降到第四位。最受尊敬公司的前五名还包括通用电气、星巴克及西南航空。

（12）this list：这里指代最受尊敬公司榜单。

（13）top five：前五名。类似的用法还有 Global Top 500 Enterprises：全球五百强企业。

翻译练习七

1. 将下面段落译成汉语：

Highlights of the new coil coating line

The production capacity of the new line is approx. 60,000 tonnes per year, which is a high volume considering the thin gauge of the strip being coated. In order to process aluminium coils for packaging products as well as for architectural products in different alloys (1xxx, 3xxx, 5xxx and 8xxx series), the line is designed to handle a wide range of strip thicknesses from 0.15 through 0.8 mm. The width of the sheet is from 1,050 through 2,050 mm. With speeds of up to 250 m per minute the line rivals other high speed coating plants for can-end stock operating in the western hemisphere.

The wide range of strip dimensions makes particularly strict demands on the flexibility of the plant. A novel feature of the Samara plant in this context is the incorporation of a swivelling edge trimming shear in a can-end line which enables flying strip width variation from coil to coil while the strip is passing through.

In view of the strip flatness required, the line is equipped with the latest generation of "Levelflex" stretch-bend-levelling machinery. This high-tech equipment ensures perfect flatness of the strip irrespective of the quality of the incoming coils.

The strip coating equipment recently developed by BWG is attracting particular attention. Besides fully automatic adjustment of the coating rolls, there is a "swivelling back-up roll" for which BWG has filed a patent application. This enables coating to be carried out as usual towards the drum or, optionally, towards the tension of the strip. The latter option is particularly beneficial for strip thicknesses of less than 0.3 mm: for example, it avoids undesired coating on the reverse side when the strip width is changed or when the strips are not running true. Regarding the use of water-soluble coatings, this feature proved to be beneficial for the Samara operations from the very beginning.

Curing downstream of both coaters is performed in floating-type furnaces, utilising the "lay-on-air" technology developed by BWG VITS Metal Treatment. The furnace downstream of the finish coater is with 86m between the rolls one of the longest of its kind. It is designed for highest energy efficiency. During regular operation the energy content of 1,100 kg of solvents per hour that Samara applies is utilised for an "autothermic" operation mode. In this mode the complete line operates almost without the use of primary gas once the process has been started. The energy content of the solvents is sufficient to operate the regenerative thermal oxidisers (RTO), to reduce chimney stack temperature down to 150°C and to prepare hot water for the cleaning process.

The line is fully computerised and equipped with all the necessary tools to provide safe operating conditions both for the operators and the environment. For example, a combined extract-and-input ventilation system located in a coating cabin completely changes the air 60 times per hour.

The complete coating line was developed and supplied by BWG from Duisburg, Germany, and is the latest technology of its kind. BWG has obtained expertise in plant and machinery for ferrous and non-ferrous metals over a period of many years. The company began developing its present standards in 2000, but it supplied high speed can stock lines to the then VAW (now Hydro) in Germany and to Alcoa in the UK back in the 1980s. A new coater concept was jointly developed by BWG and ThyssenKrupp Steel when converting Thyssen's "EBA2" electrolytic galvanising line into a thin-film coating plant for the production of high-grade automotive sheet. With this know-how BWG was able to increase its involvement in the aluminium industry: the success story began with a contract from Alcoa Architectural Products in Merxheim, France. This plant is designed to coat aluminium strips 2 metres wide, mainly for use in the architectural field.

第八章

法律与合同文本翻译

据报道，由于日本对《波茨坦公告》的回复存在翻译错误，最终导致美向日投下两颗原子弹。相关报道如下（摘自互动百科，http://w.hudong.com/a0b196dec18142319549aefa0e6bcf39.html）：

1945年7月26日，美、中、英三国签署《波茨坦公告》，敦促日本无条件投降，并且给予日本投降和结束战争的某些承诺。这是日本避免彻底毁灭的最后机会。

7月27日，日本内阁举行会议讨论是否接受《波茨坦公告》。内阁有主战和主降派，会议没有结论。由于苏联没有签署《波茨坦公告》，日本要求苏联斡旋，想与盟军进行和谈，正在等待苏联的答复和盟国正式的最后通牒。

7月28日下午，首相铃木贯太郎召开记者招待会。以中文翻译而言，铃木在会上的讲话有多个版本。当时，日本官方通讯社——同盟通讯社发表铃木声明的英文译本是："I consider the Joint Proclamation a rehash of the Declaration at the Cairo Conference. As for the Government, it does not find any important value in it, and there is no other recourse but to ignore it entirely, and resolutely fight for the successful conclusion of the war."

将上述英文翻译成为中文：我认为联合公告只是重复开罗会议声明。对于（日本）政府来说，看不到重大意义，而且已经没有其他选择，只能完全将它忽略，并且为了成功地结束战争而坚定地战斗。

可以看到日本首相明确地拒绝了《波茨坦公告》，决心要与盟军决一死战。日本拒绝《波茨坦公告》之后，美国于8月6日向广岛投下原子弹令10万人丧生。8月9日，美军再以原子弹轰击长崎市。

美国总统杜鲁门回忆此事时说："在下达了准备使用原子弹的命令之后，我向陆军首长指示，只要没有日本可能接受最后公告的消息，投弹的命令就有效。"

那就是说，如果日本不拒绝《波茨坦公告》，美国就不会向日本投掷原子弹。根据战后文献和裕仁天皇及铃木首相的发言，日本没有拒绝《波茨坦公告》，只是暂时不予置评，等待苏联的回复。

节录自铃木首相在战后所写的文章："《波茨坦公告》是日本投降的最后机会，但是高叫'一亿玉碎'的军部不接受此公告，结果我决定暂不表态。……然而，国内舆论和军部的强硬派还是认为，应对公告加以彻底反击，以鼓舞士气。……为此，我只好在7月28日的内阁记者会上作出声明，大意是该公告不值得重视。这使我后来感到非常遗憾。"

有些人说铃木首相一语误国，没有明确地表示暂时不评论此事。也有人认为铃木当时确实是拒绝了《波茨坦公告》，只是日后日本遭到原子弹袭击才倒过来说。也有人说是翻译的人译错了，令日本遭到原子弹袭击的悲惨下场。

查看铃木当年回应《波茨坦公告》的日本原文，原载于昭和二十年(1945年)7月29日《每日新闻》："共同聲明はカイロ會談の燒直しと思ふ、政府としては重大な価値あるものとは認めず黙殺し、斷固戰争完遂に邁進する。"

将上述日文翻译成中文：我认为联合公告只是重复开罗会议声明。对于（日本）政府来说，看不到重大意义，不作回应并且坚定地迈向战争终结。

这段声明和日本官方通讯社——同盟通讯社的英文译本内容有很大差别。同盟通讯社说的"而且已经没有其他选择，只能完全将它忽略，并且为了成功地结束战争而坚定地战斗"是无中生有。铃木的声明中没有用"没有其他选择"、"完全将它忽略"和"坚定地战斗"等字眼。在铃木的声明中，"黙殺"一词只能译成"不作回应"，不能说是"ignore it entirely(完全将它忽略)"。令人更加摸不着头脑的事情发生在美国，日本的同盟通讯社将"黙殺"错译为"ignore it entirely(完全将它忽略)"，美国的路透社和美联社将"ignore it entirely"误报为"reject(拒绝)"。

日本战时首相铃木说"不回应"《波茨坦公告》，日本同盟通讯社将铃木的话说成"完全忽略"《波茨坦公告》，美国的路透社和美联社将铃木的话说成"拒绝"《波茨坦公告》。美国战时总统和军方首长看到的文本是美国的路透社和美联社发出的版本。结果，日本就是在政客、译者和编辑的疏忽之下，吃了两颗原子弹才无条件投降。

当时，美国总统罗斯福收到的铃木发言文本，不是日本官方通讯社同盟通讯社的英文译本，而是美国通讯社的英文重写版本。笔者不明白为何要重写如此重要的声明，用原文不就好了吗？

英文重写版本如下："I consider the *Joint Proclamation* a rehash of the *Declaration at the Cairo Conference*.

As for the Government, it does not attach any important value to it at all. The only thing to do is to reject it. We will do nothing but press on to the bitter end to bring about a successful completion of the war."

将这一重写英文翻译成为中文：我认为联合公告只是重复开罗会议声明。对于（日本）政府来说，完全没有附带任何重大意义。我们只能拒绝它。我们能做的事情只有为了成功地终结战争而战斗到最后一刻。

战后，日本人埋怨铃木首相没有明确地说对《波茨坦公告》"暂不置评"，却用了意义含糊不清的"默杀"。"默杀"这个词没有对应的英文单词，即使在日文也可以解作"不置评"或者"拒绝"。关乎国家存亡的声明，不应该说得模棱两可。

铃木是位日本政客，日本政客说话一定是模棱两可，这是惯例，不应该将责任放在铃木身上。同盟通讯社的翻译者在不清楚铃木首相声明的原意情况下，选择错误的译文，把"完全忽略"《波茨坦公告》的话硬塞进铃木的口中。美国的路透社和美联社编辑又将"拒绝"《波茨坦公告》的话硬塞进铃木的口中。这种误会与两国的民族特性又有没有关系呢？！这是个值得深思的问题。

结果，历史因铃木吃的"两只死猫"而变成日本吃的"两颗原子弹"。

上面的报道给人们的启示是，不准确的翻译轻则攸关个人利益，重则伤及国家民族。与文学翻译相比，非文学翻译对于准确的要求要高出许多，特别是法律翻译，任何一个小错误都有可能引发大麻烦，因此法律翻译把"准确"视为"灵魂"，译者对原文意义不能随意增加、减少或曲解。

第一节 法律文本翻译的难点

一、法律体系制约属性

法律是一种国家现象，由于不同国家法律体系不同，因此许多法律概念也有着不同的分类规则、法律渊源及社会经济原则。正是这些不同构成了法律体系的制约属性，给法律文本译者带来了很多障碍。法律体系制约属性首先反映在人们对事物、事物之间的关系、人们的行为等方面的看法不同。看下面一段原文和译文：

【原文】In Britain all criminal trials are held in open count because the criminal law presumes the innocence of the accused until he has been proved guilty beyond reasonable doubt. The prosecution and the defense get equal treatment. No accused person has to answer the question of the police before trial. He is not compelled to give evidence in count. Every accused person has the right to employ a legal adviser to conduct his defense. If he can not afford to pay, he may be granted aid at public expense. In criminal trial by jury, the judge passes sentence, but the jury decided the issue of guilt or innocence. The jury composed of 12 or ordinary people. If the verdict of the jury can not be unanimous, it must be a majority.

【译文】在英国，所有的刑事审判都在法院公开进行。因为刑法认为，在消除合理怀疑证明被告有罪之前，他是无辜的。原告与被告同样平等，审判时被告不必回答警察的问题，不许强迫被告提供证据。每位被告都有权雇佣律师为其辩护。如果他不能支付律师费，可以用公用费用提供帮助。在由陪审团进行的刑事审判中，法官判刑，但陪审团决定是否有罪。陪审团一般由12人组成。如果陪审团不能做出一致判决，也必须是多数决定。

（http://wenku.baidu.com/view/f674b251f01dc281e53af0ab.html）

上文中"在消除合理怀疑证明被告有罪之前，他是无辜的。"就是所谓"无罪推定原则"。无罪推定是指任何人，在法院没有以确实、充分的证据证明其有罪以前，不得认为其有罪或者应推定其无罪。我国1996年新修订的刑事诉讼法第12条规定，"未经人民法院依法判决，对任何人都不得确定有罪"。我国的刑事诉讼法由此确立了无罪推定原则的合理内核，但我国在刑事诉讼中尚未引进沉默权，因此，还不能说我国已经全面地确立了无罪推定原则。法律界对我国引进沉默权的问题多有争论，持反对意见者认为，应当稳步建立我国的沉默权制度，任何事情不能脱离中国的实际太远，否则就会走向其本意的反面。我国传统法律文化中，几乎没有无罪推定原则的概念，这从县太爷的口头禅中可见一斑:"大胆刁民,竟敢狡辩,到了大堂之上还不如实招来,来呀!大刑伺候!"中国监狱大墙上的八个大字——"坦白从宽,抗拒从严",显然是对"有罪推定原则"的绝妙注解。然而要改变这一切,绝非一朝一夕之事。

译者对法律体系制约属性缺乏敏感度或没有必要的法律知识,很容易在不经意间犯下错误。看下面一段引文:

1995年王守东在纽约成立了一家经营中草药的公司,中文写着"北京中医院",然而英文名叫"World Health Inc."(应该翻译为"世界健康公司"),主要从事中草药和保健品的买卖。2000年夏,王守东等人因涉嫌无照非法行医遭到警方逮捕。由于在美国,中医原本无法可依,也就不可能有行医执照。中医看病只能叫咨询,开处方也是把中草药当作营养补品,建议病人服用。中医并没有给病人进行打针、输液、化验等西医诊疗,因此构不成违法。美国警方在"北京中医院"也没有查到任何与西医有关的证据,因此,如果因为王守东用中医方法对病人进行治疗属于无照行医,那么就等于承认中医与西医具有同等的地位,但这又完全不符合现有的美国法律。2年多后,该案结案时法院判王守东需要为在广告中给请来的中国专家冠以专科医生的名称承担法律责任,但他可以继续从事中医药工作。(吴莲英,蒋基昌:"试论中医的法律地位对中医英译选词的影响",《中华中西医杂志》,2007年2月)

中国传统医学西方人知之甚少,而我们的翻译人员又对西方国家的医药法律法规不甚了解,因此导致了上述案件的发生。广义上讲汉语中"医生"就是"治病的人",而英语中doctor则有着严格的定义:(1) a person licensed to practice medicine;(2) a person who has awarded a doctor's degree, the highest degree that can be offered by a university. 美国人的思维是,那些中国专家既不是经过注册行医的人,又不是大学里获得博士学位的人,你为什么冠以他们"医生"的头衔?所以你要承担法律责任。这无疑是法律体系制约属性带来的翻译问题。

再看我国《民法通则》第七十五条的英译:

【原文】公民的个人财产,包括公民的合法收入、房屋、储蓄、生活用品、文物、图书资料、林木、牲畜和其他法律允许公民所有的生产资料及其他合法财产。

【译文】A citizen's <u>personal property</u> shall include his lawfully earned income, housing, savings, articles for daily use, objects d'art, books, reference materials, trees, livestock, as well as means of production the law permits <u>a citizen to possess</u> and other lawful property.(国务院法制局译本)

陈忠诚先生曾就本段译文提出两点批评,一是shall在这里用法不规范,应将shall去掉,再将后面的include加上s;二是a citizen to possess意为"公民占有","公民所有"应该翻译为a citizen to own(陈忠诚:《民法通则》AAA译本评析 北京:法律出版社,2008.7 pp91-92)。一个比陈先生指出的更为严重的问题是,personal property并不等于汉语中所说的"个人财产"。看下面一段对personal property解释的文字:

A type of property which, in it's most general definition, can include any asset other than real estate. The distinguishing factor between personal property and real estate is that personal property is movable. That is, the asset is not fixed permanently to one location as with real property such as land or buildings. Examples of personal property include vehicles, furniture, boats, collectibles, etc.(From http://www.investopedia.com/)

由此可见personal property实际上指的是"动产",并不包括房屋在内。因此,在英语中personal property includes ...housing... 的说法是自相矛盾的。汉语中"公民的个人财产"可翻译为the private property of a citizen 或者the lawful property of a citizen。

另外一个例子来自我国2001年《婚姻法》第二十五条,看下面的原文和译文:

【原文】非婚生子女享有与婚生子女同等的权利,任何人不得加以危害和歧视。不直接抚养非婚生子女的生父或生母,应当负担子女的生活费和教育费。直至子女能独立生活为止。

【译文】A <u>natural child</u> shall have the equal rights of a legitimate child, and shall not be harmed or discriminated against by any person. The natural father or mother that does not directly upbring his or her natural child shall undertake the expenses for the living and education of the natural child until the child is able to live an independent life.

（http://www.lihunnet.com/MarriageLaw.htm）

上段译文中的 A natural child 是否等于汉语中的"非婚生子女"？看下面的解释：

NATURAL CHILDREN. In the phraseology of the English or American law, natural children are children born out of wedlock, or bastards, and are distinguished from legitimate children; but in the language of the civil law, natural are distinguished from adoptive children, that is, they are the children of the parents spoken of, by natural procreation. (John Bouvier: *A law dictionary*, adapted to the Constitution and laws of the United States, Lawbook Exchange 2004, p189）

在英美法系中 natural children 主要指"非婚生子女"，而在大陆法系中则指"亲生子女"，是相对于养子女而言的。实际上 natural children 泛指亲生子女，可以是婚生的，也可以是非婚生的。再看加纳对 a natural child 的解释：

A natural child is a EUPHEMISM for bastard, illegitimate child, or nonmarital child. But the phrase is nearly meaningless, all children being natural. (Bryan A. Garner: *Garner's Modern American Usage*, Oxford University Press, 2003. p543.）

加纳认为，所谓 a natural child 只不过是"杂种"的委婉语，其实这种说法几乎没有意义，因为所有孩子都是自然生产的（natural）。

由此可见，将"非婚生子女"翻译成 a natural child 并不合适，首先它是英美法系中的概念，我国现行法律体系极具大陆法系特点，一般被认为属于大陆法系国家。在大陆法系中 a natural child 泛指亲生子女，可以是婚生的，也可以是非婚生的。另外，a natural childd 在英美法系中为"杂种"的委婉语，用在正式的法律文本中也不合适。其实，"非婚生子女"即使在英美法系国家也大多表述为 a child born out of wedlock 或者 a child born outside of marriage。

二、对等词语的翻译

法标准术语：	plaintiff（原告），defendant（被告），recidivism（累犯），bigamy（重婚罪），homicide（杀人者），affray（在公共场所斗殴罪）等。
借用术语：	sadism（性虐待狂），abortion（堕胎），artistic work（艺术作品），continental shelf（大陆架），monogamy（一夫一妻制）等。
拉丁语：	actus reus (犯罪行为)，mens rea (犯意)，aliba (不在犯罪现场)，caveat emptor (买方自慎之)，bona fide (善意)等。
法语：	loi fondamentale（根本法），questionnaire（调查表），saisie（查封、扣押），voir dire（预先审查），writ de mesne（中间令状）等。
具有专门法律意义的普通词：	action（诉讼），consideration（对价，约因），minor（未成年），major（成年），party（当事人），instrument（法律文件），find（裁决）等。

译者必须懂得相关的法律知识才能理解这些词语的内涵，当然也要熟悉它们在汉语中的对等说法。对于初学法律翻译的人士来说，最好的办法就是能够找到一些法律著作的双语文本，逐步学习法律知识并熟悉其中的对等说法。在翻译中遇到自己不熟悉的内容时，一定要查证以免出现错误。看下面的例子：

【原文】 As for the nonpolitical occupations of the <u>justices</u>, all 108 had legal training and all had practiced law at some stage in their careers. Only 22 percent had state or federal judicial experience immediately prior to their appointments, although more than half had <u>served on the bench</u> at some time before their nomination to the Supreme Court. As with their colleagues in the lower federal judiciary, the justices were much more likely to have been politically active than the average American, and virtually all shared many of the ideological and political orientations of their appointing president.

（www.uscourts.gov/bankruptcycourts/.../chapter7.html）

【译文一】 对于审判员非政治性职业生涯而言，所有 108 名审判员均参加过法律培训，并且在各自职业生涯的某个阶段均从事法律工作。虽然半数以上高院法官在提名进入高院之前在某段时间内均担任过法官职务，但只有 22% 在任职之前在州或联邦具有司法经验。跟下级联邦司法系统审判员一样，高院审判员要比普通美国人在政坛上更为活跃，事实上，他们采用了现职总统许多意识形态与政治取向。（学生译文）

【译文二】 至于具有非政治性的法官职业，108 位法官全都受过法律训练，并在自己的职涯中从事过法律工作。虽然半数以上在被提名最高法院法官之前都曾担任过法官职务，但只有 22% 就任前曾担任过州或联邦的司法职务。这些法官和下级联邦司法体系的同僚一样，他们在政治上的活跃程度比一般美国人要高，与任命他们的总统拥有许多相同的意识形态和政治取向。

上段原文中有不易理解的词和短语各一个，它们是 justices 和 on the bench，经查阅它们的意义分别为：

1. justices: Judges. Officers appointed by a competent authority to administer justice. They are so called, because, in ancient times the Latin word for judge was justicia. This term is in common parlance used to designate justices of the peace.

（http://www.lawyerintl.com/law-dictionary）

2. on the bench: presiding as a judge in a court; substituted from a sports event, or waiting to be brought on as a substitute (en.wiktionary.org/wiki/on_the_bench)

由此我们可以认为，justices 的意思是"法官"，on the bench 指的是"法官职务"。这两个译法在谈论美国法律制度的汉语文本中也得到了证实。在学生提交的作业中，有人将"severed on the bench"翻译成"在台上任职"，这显然是没有认真查证而造成的错误。上面译文一中 on the bench 的译法是正确的，但译文的第一句和最后一句与原文意义略有出入。诸如此类约定俗成的译法还有许多，看下面一段：

【原文】The U.S. court system, as part of the federal system of government, is characterized by dual hierarchies: there are both state and federal courts. Each state has its own system of courts, composed of civil and criminal trial courts（民事和刑事初审法院）, sometimes intermediate courts of appeal（中级上诉法院）, and a state supreme court（州最高法院）. The federal court system consists of a series of trial courts (district courts)（初审法院（称为地方法院）serving relatively small geographic regions, circuit courts（巡回法院）of appeal that hear appeals from many district courts in a particular geographic region and the Supreme Court of the United States（联邦最高法院）. The two court systems are to some extent overlapping in that certain kinds of disputes (such as a claim that a state law is in violation of the Constitution) may be initiated in either system. They are also to some extent hierarchical, the federal system stands above the state system. Litigants who lose their cases in the state supreme court（州最高法院）may appeal their cases to the Supreme Court of the United States. (http://songleilegalenglish.fyfz.cn/art/210492.htm)

【译文】美国法院体系是政府联邦体系的组成部分，它以两级结构为特点：包括州法院和联邦法院。每个州都有自己的法院体系，由民事和刑事初审法院组成，有时还包括（中级）上诉法院和州最高法院。联邦法院体系则包括：一系列面向相对较小的地区的初审法院（称为地方法院），巡回法院——审理众多位于特定地区的地方法院的上诉案件，和联邦最高法院。由于一些争议事项（比如声称州的某一法律违宪）可以诉诸两个法院体系的任何一个，因此这两个体系在某种程度上是重叠的。然而在某种程度上，这两个体系又是垂直的，联邦法院体系位于州法院体系之上。在州最高法院败诉的当事人可以上诉至联邦最高法院。（宋雷译）

在英汉法律语篇翻译中，也有不少对等说法不一致的情况，看下面一段：

Trials in the United States are based around the adversarial system. This concept simply means that all proceedings are a competition between the two sides – prosecutor and defendant in a criminal case, plaintiff and defendant in a civil suit. In the adversary system, the parties are responsible for initiating the proceedings, conducting the investigations, and presenting the evidence in court. Adversary proceedings are designed to allow each side to question the other's witnesses (called "cross-examination") and to respond to the other's arguments. The rationale for the adversary system is that it is thought to be the best way to ascertain the truth.

上文中 adversarial system 在汉语就有多种译法，如"对抗制"、"抗辩制"、"辩论制度"等；cross-examination 的译法也有"盘问"、"盘诘"、"反复讯问"和"交叉讯问"等说法。对于 adversarial system 的不同译法尚不至于因词害意，但 cross-examination 的译法当中一般认为只有"交叉讯问"是正确的，其他的说法均不够准确。对于此类现象译者也应当给予充分的重视，对于自己没有把握的译法必须进行查证。

在汉英法律语篇翻译中，一些特定法律概念的英译也给译者带来极大困难。这是因为法律汉语植根于中国法律概念系统，因而许多词语在英语中没有现成的说法。例如："差额选举"、"等额选举"、"统筹安排"、"厉行节约"、"量入为出"、"定罪量刑"、"供认不讳"等，它们均为法律汉语中的固化概念，翻译时只能采用意译、解释性翻译、创造新词语等方法。（杜金榜："中国法律法规英译的问题和解决"，《中国翻译》，2004 (3)，第 72—76 页。）笔者发现一些类似的固定表达也缺少权威性的英译，例如"滥用职权"就有 to abuse one's power, one's abuse of power and authority, to misuse one's authorities, to misconduct official duties 等说法；"徇私舞弊"也有 to commit malpractices for selfish ends, to engage in malpractices for selfish ends, to practise favouritism or embezzlement, to engage in malpractice for personal gains 等说法；"玩忽职守"的说法包括 to commit dereliction of duty, to neglect one's duties, to be derelict in one's duties 等等。对于这些悬而未决的问题，需要各方面专家共同探讨，最终找到比较好的解决方案。

三、同义和近义词的翻译

法律英语中存在着大量同义和近义词语，而法律汉语中相应的词语则比较少。例如，法律汉语中"原告"和"被告"没有太多其他词语可以替代，而法律英语中则不然，仅在《汉英法律词典》中，"原告"就有 actor, accusant, accuser, complaint, claimant, indicter, libellant, plaintiff, plaintiff accuser 等 10 种说法，而"被告"也有 defendant, fugiens, indictee, libellee, respondent, the accused, the accused party, accused person, charged party 等 9 种说法。面对这样的情况，译者在英译汉时遇到的困难还不算很大，但在汉译英时译者则必须搞清楚，同一个汉语词语相对应的多个英语词语之间的细微差别，否则就有可能在翻译时出错，下面就是一些相关的错误译例：

【例1】

【原文】以造谣、诽谤或者其他方式煽动颠覆国家政权、推翻社会主义制度的，处五年以下有期徒刑、拘役、管制或者剥夺政治权利；首要分子或者罪行重大的，处五年以上有期徒刑。（选自《中华人民共和国刑法》第一百零五条）

【译文】Whoever incites others by spreading rumors or slanders or any other means to subvert the State power or overthrow the socialist system shall be sentenced to fixed-term imprisonment of not more than five years, criminal detention, public surveillance or deprivation of political rights; and the ringleaders and the others who commit major crimes shall be sentenced to fixed-term imprisonment of not less than five years.

（http://cq.netsh.com）

原文中的"诽谤"一词被翻译为 slanders 不妥。slander 通常指"口头诽谤"，英语中另外一词 libel 指"文字诽谤"。根据原文语境我们可以判断出，"诽谤"这里显然指多种形式的诽谤，至少应该包括口头诽谤和文字诽谤。这里可以考虑使用 defamation 一词，该词涵盖 slander 和 libel 两方面意义。

【例2】

【原文】公司登记机关对需要认定的营业执照，可以临时扣留，扣留期限不得超过 10 天。（选自《中华人民共和国公司登记管理条例》第五十五条）

【译文】The company registration authority may temporarily distrain the business license which needs confirmation, and the time limit of distrainment shall not exceed 10 days. （http://www.law-lib.com）

《中华人民共和国公司登记管理条例》第五十四条中提到："任何单位和个人不得伪造、涂改、出租、出借、转让营业执照"。因此，原文二中的所谓"需要认定的营业执照"是指公司登记机关需要对"营业执照"的真伪进行鉴定，而 confirmation 的意思是 additional proof that something that was believed (some fact or hypothesis or theory) is correct. (*Cambridge Advanced Learner's Dictionary*)。也就是说，当人们对业已存在的事实、假设或理论做进一步确认的时候，才使用 to confirm 或 confirmation，可将译文中的 the business license which needs confirmation 修改为 the business license the authenticity of which has to be verified。英语中 to verify the authenticity of something 是个很常用的说法，介词 of 后面的宾语可以是 certificate，social security number，signature，identity card 等等。

【例3】

【原文】商标局应当自收到有关案件材料之日起六个月内作出认定，并将认定结果通知案件发生地的省（自治区、直辖市）工商行政管理部门，抄送当事人所在地的省（自治区、直辖市）工商行政管理部门。（选自中华人民共和国国家工商行政管理总局令《驰名商标认定和保护规定》第八条）

【译文】The trademark office shall make a decision about the relevant materials of a case, shall inform the administrative department of the province (autonomous region, municipality directly under the Central Government) where this case occurred of the decision, and send a copy of the decision to the administrative department of the province (autonomous region, municipality directly under the Central Government) where the involving parties are located.

（http://www.sh360.net/law/law12/3040.html）

原文中所谓"作出认定"是指商标局对他人是否擅自使用了与驰名商标注册人（当事人）相同或者近似的商标，从而是否对商标注册人造成了损害的认定。而商标局作出此认定的依据，是当事人提交的有关案件材料。从逻辑上说，"认定"不是关于对"有关案件材料"本身的认定，而是在分析了这些材料的基础上，对驰名商标注册人是否被损害所作出的认定。因此，译文中 make a decision about the relevant materials of a case 的译法不妥。另外用 make a decision 翻译"作出认定"也不妥当，应该使用 to determine 或者 to make（issue）a determination 来表示。综上所述，可将原文中"商标局应当自收到有关案件材料之日起六个月内作出认定"部分翻译为：Within a period of six months from the date of receiving the relevant materials of a case, the trademark office shall make a determination in respect of those materials.

四、法律翻译的风格把握

法律汉语具有表达直接和简洁的特点，与普通汉语相差不大，而法律英语则与普通英语相去甚远。一般人们认为，中国现有法律法规的翻译风格更贴近普通英语而不是法律英语。对此笔者有些不同看法。首先法律英语风格本身存在问题。看下面简明英语专家理查德·威迪克（Richard C. Wydick）的一段话：

We lawyers do not write plain English. We use eight words to say what could be said in two. We use arcane phrases to express commonplace ideas. Seeking to be precise, we become redundant. Seeking to be cautious, we become verbose. Our sentences twist on, phrase within clause within clause, glazing the eyes and numbing the minds of our readers. The result is a writing style that has, according to one critic, four outstanding characteristics. It is (1) wordy, (2) unclear, (3) pompous, and (4) dull. （Richard C. Wydick:*Plain English for Lawyers*, Carolina Academic Press 2005, p3）

为了更好地理解这段文字，我们把它翻译成汉语：

我们做律师的不使用简明英语，我们用八个词表达本可用两个词表达的内容，我们用古旧的、高深莫测的短语表达最普通的思想。我们追求精确却导致了文字的繁琐，我们小心翼翼却产生了冗词赘句。我们的句子佶屈聱牙，短语套入从句，从句中再套从句，这些使我们的读者眼花缭乱、心智麻木。按照一位批评家的说法，由此形成的文体风格具有如下四个显著特点：一、冗长繁琐；二、模糊不清；三、故弄玄虚；四、枯燥乏味。

理查德·威迪克的话并非无中生有，看下面的两个例子：

【例1】

A failure on the part of a person to observe any provision of the Highway Code shall not of itself render that person liable to criminal prosecution of any kind, but any such failure may in any proceedings (whether civil or criminal and including proceedings for an offence under the Traffic Acts, the Public Passenger Vehicles Act 1981 or sections 18 to 23 of the Transport Act 1985) be relied upon by any party to the proceedings as tending to establish or negative any liability which is in question in those proceedings.

上面的例子可谓冗长繁琐、枯燥乏味，大有故弄玄虚之嫌。作者其实没有必要将并不复杂的意义用复杂而又费解的语言加以表述。马丁·卡茨（Martin Cutts）认为，上面例子划线部分完全可以简洁地表述为：Disobeying the Highway Code is not a criminal offence.（Martin Cutts: *How to make laws easier to read and understand*, from www.clearest.co.uk）

【例2】

If the law of any country in which this policy operates requires us to settle a claim which, if this law had not existed we would not be obliged to pay, we reserve the right to recover such payments from you or from the person who incurred the liability.

上面的例子选自英国诺维奇联合保险公司（Norwich Union）的汽车保险单，其费解程度足以使法律专业人士不知所云。实际上此条款是为保护公司的利益而定，意思是说：如被保险车辆在英国以外的国家（特指欧共体的一些国家）发生赔偿事故，按照该国法律本公司应予以赔偿，但此赔偿并不属于本保险单的承保范围，此时本公司有权要求投保人或事故责任人承担相关费用。本条款的问题在于，any country in which this policy operates 并没有将相关的背景交待清楚，而且 if this law had not existed 的具体所指也令人费解。事实上，上面的意思完全可以用清晰、明确的语言加以表述：

If a claim arises in a country outside the United Kingdom, and the claim is not covered under the terms of this policy but we have to pay it because the law of that country requires us to do so, we may recover the payment from the person whose act or omission gave rise to the claim. （Nick Lear: "Plain English in a motor insurance policy", *Clarity*, No.44, December 1999）

由此可见，意义的明确表述未必需要复杂的句式或高深莫测的词汇。许多简明英语专家指出，实际上以简洁的语言往往更能够清晰地表达出复杂的意义。这样看来，我国法律法规的翻译风格更贴近普通英语并不是一件坏事，我们的问题似乎不是翻译风格的问题，而是语言表述的问题。看下面美国证券交易委员会（U.S. Securities and Exchange Commission）1998年颁布的《简明英语手册》（*A Plain English Handbook*）中对法律英语写作风格的要求：

(i) Short sentences;
(ii) Definite, concrete, everyday words;
(iii) Active voice;
(iv) Tabular presentation or bullet lists for complex material, whenever possible;
(v) No legal jargon or highly technical business terms; and
(vi) No multiple negatives.

对照上述要求，我们看一个法律汉英翻译的实例。原文出自《持有〈上海市居住证〉人员申办本市常住户口试行办法》（二〇〇九年二月十二日）中的第十四条。下面是汉语原文和英译文：

【原文】第十四条（法律责任）

行政机关工作人员应当依法履行职责，在执行本办法过程中徇私舞弊、滥用职权、索贿受贿的，由其所在单位或者监察机关给予行政处分；构成犯罪的，依法追究其刑事责任。

持证人员和单位应当书面承诺所提供证明材料的真实性，严禁弄虚作假。一旦发现虚假或者伪造，取消其再申请的资格，并记入社会征信体系。对骗取本市常住户口的，及时注销。构成犯罪的，依法追究其刑事责任。

【译文】Article 14 (Legal Liabilities)

The working personnel of administrative organs shall perform their duties according to law, and shall be given administrative punishments by their units or supervisory organs in case they bend the law for personal gain or engage in fraud, abuse their power or solicit or accept bribes; if the act constitutes a crime, the wrongdoer shall be prosecuted for criminal liability according to law.

The permit holders and their units shall vouch in writing for the authenticity of the certification materials provided, and are strictly prohibited from practicing fraud. Once fraud or falsification is found, their qualification for reapplication shall be canceled and such behavior shall be recorded into the social credit information system. The permanent residence registration obtained through deception shall be written off in a timely manner. If the act constitutes a crime, the wrongdoer shall be prosecuted for criminal liability according to law.（http://www.chinalaw.gov.cn/article/）

从风格要求的层面看，上面的译文至少有如下问题：
绝大多数句子使用了被动语态；
vouch for 和 in case 等用法古旧，不属于常用词语的范畴；
译文中 working personnel 和 administrative punishments 的说法翻译界有争议；
"构成犯罪的，依法追究其刑事责任"的翻译不妥；
绝大多数 shall 的使用属于误用或滥用。

按照英语的表达习惯，"构成犯罪的，依法追究其刑事责任"可翻译为 A person whose act constitutes a crime is subject to criminal liability according to law.，这样既符合英语的习惯表达，又避免了被动语态的使用。由于 shall 的使用常有歧义，目前澳大利亚和加拿大的法律文本几乎不再使用 shall，英美等国正式出台的许多法律法规也不再使用 shall。上面译文不过一百多个单词，其中却使用了八个 shall。

第二节　法律文本的句子翻译

在法律英语中，长句除了主谓结构之外，还存在许多从句、同位语、补充短语等修饰成分，其主从关系由各种连接词衔接。长句经常采用类属后置、同类排除、语境定义、常识判断等指导原则。

一、类属后置

类属后置是在罗列事物时，先举出具体事物最后列出这些事物的类，以免遗漏。常见的表达方式有 such as，like，covering，including but not limited to 等。这类翻译关键词明确，找准了关键词，就能比较容易进行翻译。

【例1】

【原文】Each State Party to the present Covenant undertakes to respect and to ensure to all individuals within its territory and subject to its jurisdiction the rights recognized in the present Covenant, without distinction of any kind, <u>such as</u> race, colour, sex, language, religion, political or other opinion, national or social origin, property, birth or other status. (Clause 1, Article 2, *International Covenant on Civil and Political Rights*)

【译文】本公约每一缔约国承担尊重和保证在其领土内和受其管辖的一切个人享有本公约所承认的权利，不分种族、肤色、性别、语言、宗教、政治或其他见解、国籍或社会出身、财产、出生或其他<u>身分等任何区别</u>。（官方译文）

原文中 such as 补充说明 distinction of any kind，属于类属后置现象。在英汉翻译过程中，可以将英文后置内容前置，在句子后面加上"等"，再补充上相应类属。

【例2】

【原文】"Confidential Information" means and includes all information <u>relating to the disclosing party</u> [1] <u>including but not limited to information, knowledge or data</u> [2] of an intellectual, technical, scientific, financial, cost, pricing, commercial or marketing nature [3] <u>which is not in the public domain</u> [4] and <u>in which the disclosing party has a business, proprietary or ownership interest or has a legal duty to protect, whether</u>

or not received from a third party in whatever form <u>(5)</u>, <u>including but not limited to technical data/know-how, drawings, photographs,</u> <u>(6)</u> specifications, standards, manuals, reports, formulae, algorithms, processes, information, lists, trade secrets, computer programs, computer software, computer databases, computer software documentation, quotations and price lists, research products, inventions, development, processes, engineering techniques, strategies, customers (<u>including</u> <u>(7)</u> any Personal Information and/or other nonpublic personal information about such customers and any list, description or other grouping of customers that is derived using any such Personal Information and/or other nonpublic personal information), internal procedures, employees, business opportunity <u>which the disclosing party considers to be confidential</u> <u>(8)</u> and <u>which is identified by the disclosing party as confidential</u> <u>(9)</u>, or <u>which might fairly be considered to be of a confidential nature</u> <u>(10)</u> and <u>which may be furnished by either party during the period of this Agreement</u> <u>(11)</u>. (翻译公司材料)

【译文】机密资料指所有与披露方相关的信息，包括但不限于具有知识产权、科技、财务、成本、定价、商业或销售性质的信息、知识或数据，这些资料都没有在公开领域发布，并且披露方对此具有商业、专利或所有权等权益，或具有保护这些信息的法律责任，不管这些信息是以何种方式从第三方获得，这些保密信息包括但不限于在本协议过程中由任何一方提供、且被披露方视为机密或合理认为具有保密性质的技术数据、诀窍、图纸、照片、规格、标准、手册、报告、配方、算法、工序、信息、清单、商业秘密、计算机程序、软件、数据库、软件文件、报价、价格表、研究产品、发明、研发、工艺、工程技术、策略、客户（包括与这些客户相关的个人资料与/或非公开的个人资料，以及任何从使用这些个人资料或非公开个人资料所得到的任何清单、介绍材料及客户细分情况）、内部流程、雇员、商机。（翻译公司译文）

这个例子是在合同文件中真实出现的例子，类属后置现象非常丰富，一环紧扣一环。翻译时必须搞清楚句子的成分和结构。整句话的主结构是"'Confidential Information' means and includes all information"；（1）为 all information 的后置定语；（2）为 all information 的类属后置；（3）为（2）的后置定语；（4）与（5）为 all information 的定语从句；（6）为 all information 的同位语，属于类属后置；（7）整个括号内的内容为 customers 的类属后置，起补充说明作用；（8）至（11）为四个定语从句，均修饰（6）相关内容，其中（9）和（10）之间用 or 连接，表示同一类属。区分清楚句子结构后，将类属后置部分适当处理，便可以合理组织中文翻译。

二、同类排除

同类排除是类属后置的例外情况，即如果类属词语跟随前面罗列的事物，具有排除性即不包括任何未列出的事物。常见句式结构为 unless, excluding, be not included 等。

【例1】

【原文】Section. 6. This article shall be inoperative unless it shall have been ratified as an amendment to the Constitution by the legislatures of three-fourths of the several States within seven years from the date of its submission.（*The Constitution of the United States*: Amendment XX）

【译文】第六款：本条如在国会送达各州之日起7年内，未经3/4之州议会批准为宪法修正案，将不发生效力。（《美国宪法修正案》二十）（官方译文）

原文中 unless 后面内容为排除例外，前面的主句内容生效。

【例2】

【原文】All taxes (excluding any income tax payable on the income of the CONSULTANT) by whatsoever name called and imposed by whichever authority in any jurisdiction shall be exclusively payable by the COMPANY.（翻译公司材料）

【译文】公司应负责支付所有以任何名义征收或任何政府部门在管辖区域内征收的税款（不包括咨询方的应缴所得税）。（翻译公司译文）

括号内部分为应被排除的信息，即 All taxes 当中不包括这些信息。

三、语境定义

语境定义是指词语所出现的语境可以起到对词语定义的作用。经常使用的词汇有 mean，be referred to as，for the purposes of the contract (law)，with a view to、in the context of 等。

【例1】

【原文】"SERVICES" shall mean the designing, developing and/or maintenance of software services and products, rendering of information technology and information technology enabled services rendered from the various Delivery Centers of the Consultant situated outside the territorial limits of People's Republic of China and shall include all other services performed in connection with the CONTRACT.（翻译公司材料）

【译文】"服务"系指在中华人民共和国领土范围外的众多咨询方交付中心所提供的一系列服务，包括软件服务和软件产品的设计、发展和维护，以及信息技术和信息技术相关服务的提供；此外，还应包括合同中规定的其他服务。（翻译公司译文）

一般合同与标准规范都需要对相关词汇进行定义，确保一些多义词在文中只具有相同的意义。Mean 与 be referred to 常用于合同的定义条款当中。

【例2】

【原文】Nothing in this Agreement shall affect the right to serve process in any other manner permitted by law or the right to bring proceedings in any other jurisdiction for the purposes of the enforcement or execution of any judgement or other settlement in any other courts.（翻译公司材料）

【译文】在本协议中，没有任何规定影响到以法律允许的任何方式服务工艺的权利或由于执行或实施任何其他法院的任何判决或其他处理而以任何其他司法方式提请诉讼的权利。（翻译公司译文）

【分析】for the purposes of 对于 any other jurisdiction 进行了限定，确保文意准确表述，不存在任何遗漏或不完善。

四、常识判断

常识判断是指：只要不与文本其他地方发生冲突，词语可按照普通意义去理解。

【例1】

【原文】The meetings of the Commission shall normally be held at the Headquarters of the United Nations or at the United Nations Office at Geneva. However, they may be held at such other convenient places as the Commission may determine in consultation with the Secretary-General of the United Nations and the States Parties concerned.（Clause 42.4, *International Covenant on Civil and Political Rights*）

【译文】和委会会议通常应在联合国总部或联合国驻日内瓦办事处举行，但亦得在和委会同联合国秘书长及各有关缔约国磋商后决定的其他方便地点举行。（《公民权利和政治权利国际公约》四十二条四款）（官方译文）

原文中 the Commission 指代上文提到的 Conciliation Commission，翻译时一般应明确指代对象，故翻译为"和委会"。

【例2】

【原文】In all criminal prosecutions, the accused shall enjoy the right to a speedy and public trial, by an impartial jury of the State and district wherein the crime shall have been committed, which district shall have been previously ascertained by law, and to be informed of the nature and cause of the accusation; to be confronted with the witnesses against him; to have compulsory process for obtaining witnesses in his favor, and to have the Assistance of Counsel for his defence.（*The Constitution of the United States:* Amendment VI）

【译文】在一切刑事诉讼中，被告应享受下列权利：由犯罪行为发生地的州和地区的公正陪审团予以迅速和公开的审判，该地区应事先已由法律确定；获知控告的性质和原因；同原告证人对质；以强制程序取得有利于自己的证据；并取得律师帮助为其辩护。（《美国宪法修正案》六）（官方译文）

按照常识判断进行翻译即可。

第三节 合同文本翻译

一、合同文本翻译基本要求

第一、合同文本翻译必须准确。英文合同为了准确、严密、清楚地表达，多以程式化语言的面貌出现，包括众多复杂长句和并列短语，这些给译者的理解会带来许多困难。因此，准确理解原文便成了译者的第一道难关，为了确保译文的准确，译者必须深刻理解原文意义。

第二、合同文本翻译必须严谨。英文合同句法结构复杂，译者必须清楚地理解各种分句和主句之间的关系，如果把握不好其中的逻辑关系，不能用严谨的目的语加以表述，就难免会出现误译或歧义。严谨还体现在对法律词语的翻译方面，英文合同中许多词语都具有严格的法律含义，译者必须在目的语中找到与之相匹配的对等说法。

第三、合同翻译需要文体的统一和规范。合同语言不仅遣词造句规范，风格也很正式，译者的译文也应该保持这样的风格。文学作品翻译对文采、韵味之类的要求并不适用于合同翻译，任何文学性发挥都被认为是不适当的。

二、合同文本翻译步骤

1. 翻译前通观全局，熟悉相关表述

译者在拿到一份合同时，必须先通读全文，了解原文的结构以及词语在具体上下文中的含义。要着重领会合同双方的利益划分，对于不清楚的内容需要查阅有关资料，对于不清楚的语言问题需要查证，切不可一拿到文本就提笔翻译。

2. 对重要词语仔细推敲，严格分析复杂句式结构

合同文本中的词语是构成合同最基本的单位，对合同中的重要词语意义要反复推敲，以便透彻理解原文。对于原文句法结构及其逻辑关系的分析也十分重要，翻译时如有必要可打散原文结构，按目的语习惯重新调整句式，以使译文具有可读性。

3. 理清条文层次，逐条进行翻译

合同文本一般包括定义条款、基本条款、一般条款和结尾条款。翻译时一定要理清层次，抓住重点，对合同条款内部结构、各条款之间关系要仔细琢磨、吃透其内涵。最后逐条进行翻译。

4. 润色修订，仔细修改

润色修订是翻译过程中不可缺少的步骤。在校改合同翻译文本时，要着眼于译文的严谨性和准确性。译者在交稿之前要逐词、逐句、逐段仔细修改。

三、合同翻译实例

MUTUAL CONFIDENTIALITY AGREEMENT

共同保密协议

THIS AGREEMENT is made on the _____day of_____2010 between Party A, having its office at _____ ("PARTY A") AND Party B, having its registered office address at ("Party B").

【译文】本协议于2010年_____月_____日签订，签订双方为甲方，注册办公地址为_____（简称为"甲方"）和乙方，注册办公地址为_____（简称为"乙方"）。

本节为合同开篇，属于程式化语言，找到双语对应的表述套用即可。

For purposes of this Agreement [1], the party that owns and/or [2] discloses confidential information is hereinafter referred to as [3] the "Disclosing Party" and the party that receives and/or accesses confidential information hereunder is hereinafter referred to as "Recipient."

【初译】鉴于本协议内容⁽¹⁾，拥有或⁽²⁾披露保密信息的一方以下简称为"披露方"。接收或⁽³⁾可以接触保密信息的一方以下简称为"接收方"。

【改译】在本协议中，拥有与/或披露保密信息的一方以下简称为"披露方"。接收与/或可以接触保密信息的一方以下简称为"接收方"。

（1）合同语言，【初译】属于想当然的翻译，【改译】进行了调整，考虑了英汉合同表述差异问题。
（2）合同语言严谨，需将并列与选择情况均表述清楚。【初译】只选择了表述"选择性"的汉语表达。
（3）程式化语言。

1. Purpose. The parties ⁽⁴⁾ hereto wish to explore a business opportunity of mutual interest ⁽⁵⁾ and in that either party may receive confidential information of the other party for the following purposes: _____.

【初译】目的。相关当事人希望本着相互利益开拓商机，为了能够_____一方可能收到另一方保密信息。

【改译】目的。协议双方希望本着双方互利原则开拓商机，为了如下目的_____一方可能收到对方的保密信息。

（4）Parties 在英文中是复数形式，没有具体指多少方。但在汉语合同中，需要明确提到甲方、乙方时称为"双方"，单独提到甲方或乙方时称为"一方"。【初译】翻译为"相关当事人"属于措辞不严谨。

（5）【初译】没有使用合同术语。

2. Definition. "Confidential Information" means any information, technical data, or know-how ⁽⁶⁾ (including, but not limited to, information relating to research, products, software, services, development, inventions, processes ⁽⁷⁾, engineering ⁽⁸⁾, marketing, techniques, customers, pricing ⁽⁹⁾, internal procedures, business and marketing plans or strategies, finances ⁽¹⁰⁾, employees and business opportunities) disclosed by the Disclosing Party to Recipient either directly or indirectly in any form whatsoever including, but not limited to, in writing, in machine readable or other tangible form, orally or visually (subsequently reduced to writing ⁽¹¹⁾) (i) that has been marked as confidential ⁽¹²⁾; (ii) whose confidential nature has been made known by Disclosing Party, orally or in writing, to Recipient; or (iii) that due to its character and nature, a reasonable person under like circumstances would treat as confidential.

【初译】定义。"保密信息"是指披露方向接收方直接、间接或以任何形式披露的任何信息，如技术数据、专有技术⁽⁶⁾（包括但不限于与研究、产品、软件、服务、研发、发明、加工⁽⁷⁾、施工⁽⁸⁾、营销、技术、客户、价格⁽⁹⁾、内部流程、商业或营销策划与战略、金融⁽¹⁰⁾、雇员和商业机会），包括但不限于书面形式，机器可读取数据，其他可触及形式，口头或可视形式（可以形成文本⁽¹¹⁾）(i) 标记为机密资料⁽¹²⁾; (ii) 披露方以口或书面形式告知接收方为机密资料；或 (iii) 由于资料的特点和性质，任何理性的人在向此情况下会将其视为保密资料。

【改译】定义。"保密信息"是指披露方向接收方直接、间接或以任何形式披露的任何信息、技术数据或专有技术⁽⁶⁾（包括但不限于与研究、产品、软件、服务、研发、发明、工艺⁽⁷⁾、设计⁽⁸⁾、营销、技术、客户、定价⁽⁹⁾、内部流程、商业或营销方案与战略、财务⁽¹⁰⁾、雇员和商业机会相关的信息）。披露方式包括但不限于书面形式、机器可读或其他有形形式、口头形式或可视形式（后续可形成书面形式⁽¹¹⁾）。上述信息、技术数据或专有技术：(i) 标记为保密信息⁽¹²⁾; (ii) 披露方以口或书面形式告知接收方为保密信息；或 (iii) 由于资料特点与性质，任何理性人在相关情况下均会视为保密的信息。

英语原文为一句话，其中包含各种复杂成分，如限定性补充成分"or know-how (including, but not limited to..."以及"in any form whatsoever including, but not limited to..."等等。【初译】按照英文句式结构一句话表述下来，读来不好理解也不易分清其中的逻辑关系。【改译】考虑到了英汉句法结构差异以及目的语读者的阅读习惯，把不同修饰成分进行了划分，将其中的一些翻译为独立的句子。【改译】在保持译文表述严谨的基础上，将原文翻译为三个独立的句子。【初译】中（6）~（12）均存在不同程度的误译问题。

3. Exclusions. Confidential Information does not include information, which: (i) is in Recipient's

possession at the time of disclosure; (ii) before or after it has been disclosed to Recipient, becomes part of the public knowledge or literature, not as a result of <u>any action or inaction</u> [13] of Recipient; (iii) is approved for release by written authorization of the Disclosing Party; (iv) is disclosed to Recipient by a third party not in violation of any obligation of confidentiality; or (v) is <u>independently developed</u> [14] by Recipient without reference to Confidential Information of the Disclosing Party.

【初译】非保密信息。如下信息不属于保密信息：(i) 保密信息披露之时，接收方已得知；(ii) 保密信息披露给接收方之前或之后，该信息在接收方未<u>采取任何行动</u>[13] 的前提下成为公众知识、<u>文学的一部分</u>；(iii) 披露方书面授权允许披露；(iv) 第三方不违反任何保密义务的前提下，向接收方披露；或 (v) 接受方不参照披露方所属保密信息的情况下，<u>独立发现信息</u>[14]。

【改译】例外情况。如下信息不属于保密信息：(i) 保密信息披露之时，接收方已得知；(ii) 保密信息披露给接收方之前或之后，该信息不因接收方<u>作为或不作为</u>[13] 而成为公开知识、<u>文献的一部分</u>；(iii) 披露方书面授权允许披露；(iv) 第三方不违反任何保密义务的前提下，向接收方披露；或 (v) 接受方不参照披露方所属保密信息的情况下，<u>独立开发获得相关信息</u>[14]。

本节内容是对上节 "保密信息" 例外情况的补充，两者结合确保合同涵盖了预见及未预见的各个方面。

(13)【初译】将 "action or inaction" 翻译为 "采取任何行动"，漏掉了 "inaction"；【改译】调整了句子顺序，改为 "作为或不作为"。

(14)【初译】改变了原文的意思，【改译】重新调整回来。

4. Use Limitations. Recipient agrees not to use the <u>Confidential Information</u> [15] for its own use or for any purposes except for the purpose expressly set forth above. Recipient <u>agrees not</u> [16] to copy, alter, modify, disassemble, <u>reverse engineer or decompile</u> [17] any of the materials unless permitted in writing by the Disclosing Party.

【初译】使用限制。接受方同意不把<u>信息</u>[15] 为个人所用，或用于上述规定目的之外。接收方<u>保证</u>[16]，在披露方未允许的情况下，不会复制、改变、修改、分解、<u>反求破解或反编译</u>[17] 任何资料。

【改译】使用限制。接受方同意不会把<u>保密信息</u>[15] 为自己所用，也不会应用于<u>上述目的之外的其他用途</u>。接收方<u>同意</u>[16]，未经披露方许可，不会复制、改变、修改、拆分、<u>仿制或改编</u>[17] 任何材料。

(15)【初译】将 "confidential information" 直接翻译为 "信息"，漏译了修饰词 confidential (保密的)

(16)【初译】不假思索地将 "agrees not" 翻译成了 "保证……不"；英语中 "agree" 一词与汉语中的 "保证" 语义上存在一定差别。

(17)【初译】中的 "反求破解或反编译" 令人费解。看一下词典对两词的解释：to reverse engineer = to study or analyze (a device, as a microchip for computers) in order to learn details of design, construction, and operation, perhaps to produce a copy or an improved version.（通过对计算机硬件设备或系统的分析，进行仿制的过程。）; to decompile = to take machine or source code for a computer program and convert it to a higher-level programming language so that it can be read by a human.（将计算机低级语言转化为高级语言以使人读懂的过程。）根据上面定义我们可将两词分别翻译为 "仿制" 和 "改编"。

5. Non-Disclosure. Recipient agrees not to disclose the Confidential Information to any third parties or to any of its employees except those employees who have a need to know the Confidential Information for accomplishing the stated purposes described herein and where such employees shall be made aware that the information is confidential and shall be under a written contractual restriction on nondisclosure and proper treatment of Confidential Information that is no less restrictive than the terms of this Agreement. Notwithstanding the foregoing, Recipient may disclose the Disclosing Party's Confidential Information to the extent required by a valid order by a court or other governmental body or by pursuant to an applicable law or <u>regulation</u> [18]; provided, however, that Recipient will use <u>all reasonable efforts</u> [19] to notify Disclosing Party of the obligation to make such disclosure in advance of the disclosure so that Disclosing Party will have a reasonable opportunity to object to such disclosure. Recipient <u>agrees</u> [20] that it shall treat the Confidential Information

with the same degree of care as it accords to its own confidential information of a similar nature [21]; provided that in no event shall Recipient exercise less than reasonable care [22] to protect the Confidential Information. Recipient agrees to advise the Disclosing Party in writing of any misappropriation or misuse by any person of such Confidential Information of which Recipient may become aware.

【初译】不透露。接收方同意不会把保密信息披露给第三方或己方员工。但是，如果员工需要知晓保密信息完成上述目标，接收方可以将信息披露给员工。员工必须意识到该信息为保密信息，必须签订书面合同，不泄露信息，妥善处理信息。保密严格程度不亚于本协议。尽管前述事项规定，如果法院发布有效法令，或根据有关法律规定[18]，接收方可能会披露保密信息。但是，接收方应在披露之前竭尽全力[19]通知披露方，披露方可以有机会，反对此类披露。接收方保证[20]，按照保护所属保密信息的程度或相似性质[21]，保护保密信息；且接收方应一直全力[22]保护保密信息。接收方保证，如果自己意识到出现滥用或误用保密信息的情况，将书面通知披露方。

【改译】不透露。接收方同意不会把信息披露给第三方或己方员工，那些需知晓保密信息完成所述目标的员工除外。掌握保密信息的员工应意识到该信息为保密信息，并应受书面契约限制，不泄露且妥善处理保密严格程度不亚于本协议的保密信息。尽管有上述规定，但如果法院或其它政府部门发布有效命令，或根据适用法律法规的要求[18]，接收方可披露对方的保密信息，但前提是接收方在披露前采取所有合理措施[19]通知披露方，使其具有合理机会拒绝相关披露。接收方同意[20]，应按照保护其类似性质自有保密信息的保护程度来对待保密信息[21]，前提是接收方在任何情况下均采取合理措施[22]保护保密信息。接收方同意，如果自己意识到出现滥用或误用保密信息的情况，将书面通知对方。

（18）程式化语言。【初译】使用了"尽管"，这是一个转折词，但接下来行文却没有使用"但"这一转折词，直接使用了"如果"，语义不严谨。【改译】将【初译】漏掉的内容都补充完整。

（19）【初译】对"all reasonable efforts"的翻译使得英汉语义表述程度偏差太大，不对等。

（20）分析见上文。

（21）理解错误。

（22）同（19）。

6. Third Party Information. Neither party shall communicate any information to the other in violation of the proprietary rights of any third party.

【初译】第三方信息。任何一方不得在侵犯任何第三方所有权的情况下，与另一方交流任何信息。

【改译】第三方信息。任何一方与对方交流任何信息均不应侵犯任何第三方所有权。

7. Return of Materials. Any materials or documents of Disclosing Party which are furnished to Recipient, and all copies thereof, at the earlier of Disclosing Party's request for return of the materials, or the termination of the business relationship between the Disclosing Party and Recipient, at the Disclosing Party's option, will either be: (i) promptly returned to the Disclosing Party; or (ii) destroyed by Recipient (with Recipient providing written certification of such destruction).

【初译】材料送还。对于任何披露方递送给接收方的材料或文件以及复印件，如果披露方要求送还或披露方与接收方商业关系终止，根据披露方的选择，材料可以：(i) 立即返还披露方；或 (ii) 接收方销毁（接收方提供销毁的有关证明文件）。

【改译】材料送还。对于披露方递送给接收方的任何材料或文件以及相关复印件，如果披露方与接收方商业关系终止，或披露方要求送还（以先到者为准），根据披露方的选择，相关材料与文件可以：(i) 立即返还披露方；或 (ii) 接收方销毁（接收方提供销毁的书面证明文件）。

8. No License. The Confidential Information shall remain the sole property of the Disclosing Party. No license is granted to Recipient under any patents, copyrights, mask work rights or other proprietary rights by the disclosure of any information hereunder, nor is any warranty made as to such information.

【初译】非授权。保密信息仍专属于披露方。如下披露任何信息涉及的，任何专利、版权、掩模作品权或其他所有权均未授予接收方，也未就此信息做出任何保证。

【改译】非授权。保密信息仍属于披露方的专有财产。没有向接收方授权通过信息披露方式获取任何专利、版权、屏蔽作品权或其它所有权,也未对披露信息做出任何保证。

9. Remedies. Recipient understands and agrees that the Disclosing Party is providing the Confidential Information to Recipient in reliance upon this Agreement, and Recipient will be fully responsible to the Disclosing Party for any damages or harm caused to the Disclosing Party by a breach of this Agreement by Recipient or any of its officers, directors, employees or consultants. Recipient acknowledges and agrees that a breach of any of its promises or agreements contained herein will result in irreparable injury to the Disclosing Party for which there will be no adequate remedy at law, and the Disclosing Party shall be entitled to apply for equitable relief, including injunction and specific performance, in the event of any breach or threatened breach or intended breach of this Agreement by Recipient. Such remedies, however, shall not be deemed to be the exclusive remedies for any breach of the Agreement but shall be in addition to all other remedies available at law or in equity.

【初译】补救。接收方知晓并同意,披露方根据本协议向接收方披露信息。如果接收方或其官员、主管、员工或咨询公司违反本协议,对披露方造成任何损失或损害,接收方同意负全责。接收方接受并同意,如果违反本协议任何许诺或协定,导致对披露方不可挽回的伤害,且根据法律补救不足,披露方有权申请衡平法上的救济,包括禁令、具体履行、任何接受方违反、威胁违反或有意违反本协议。然而,该补救不应视为对于违反该合同的完全补救,应视为依法补救或依衡平法补救之外的额外补救。

【改译】补救。接收方知晓并同意,披露方根据本协议规定向接收方披露保密信息;如果接收方或其管理人员、主管、员工或顾问违反本协议,对披露方造成任何损失或损害,接收方同意负全责。接收方接受并同意,如果违反本协议规定的任何承诺或协定,在接收方违反、被胁违反或有意违反本协议情况下,导致对披露方不可挽回的损失,且根据法律补救不足,披露方有权申请平等救济,包括法律禁令、具体履约。然而,该补救不应视为对于违反该合同的完全补救,应视为依法补救或依衡平法补救之外的额外补救。

10. Attorneys' Fees, Jurisdiction/Venue. In the event of any litigation or other legal proceedings between the parties, the prevailing party shall be entitled to reasonable attorneys' fees and all costs of proceedings incurred in enforcing this Agreement. The Courts in Beijing, China shall have exclusive jurisdiction to try and dispose of any proceedings arising out of this Agreement. The laws of China shall govern the validity, interpretation and performance of this Agreement.

【初译】律师费、司法管辖和司法辖区。如果双方之间产生诉讼,胜诉一方应负责律师费用,以及在执行本协议过程中产生的所有法律事务费用。中国北京法院拥有对本协议法律事务的专属管辖权。中国法律为本协议准据法,管辖本协议的有效期、解释和执行。

【改译】律师费、司法管辖和司法辖区。如果双方之间产生诉讼或其他司法程序,败诉方负责支付在执行本协议过程中产生的合理律师费及所有诉讼费用。中国北京法院拥有对本协议诉讼的专属管辖权。本协议效力、解释与履行均适用中国法律。

11. Termination & Survival. This Agreement will become effective as of the date first mentioned herein above and will continue to be in force for a period of one (1) year thereafter. Recipient's obligations under this Agreement with respect to Confidential Information it has received shall continue for a period of two (2) years after such disclosure.

【初译】协议终止与存续。本协议于上述首次提到之日开始生效,并持续一年有效。接收方对本协议下规定的保密信息承担两年的保密责任,从披露之日起。

【改译】协议终止与存续。本协议于上文首次提到的日期开始生效,有效期为一(1)年。接收方对所收到的保密信息根据本协议所承担的责任期限为披露后两(2)年。

IN WITNESS WHEREOF, each of the parties hereto have caused this Agreement to be executed by a duly authorized representative of such party as of the date first above written.

【初译】以资证明,双方同意由授权代表于上述生效日期执行本协议。

【改译】以资证明，双方由授权代表于第一段所述日期签署本协议。

本章主要参考文献：

陈忠诚：《民法通则》，AAA 译本评析法律出版社，2008。

杜金榜："中国法律法规英译的问题和解决"，《中国翻译》，2004 (3)。

A Plain English Handbook（www.sec.gov/pdf/handbook.pdf）

Richard C. Wydick: *Plain English for Lawyers*, Carolina Academic Press, 2005.

翻译练习八

1. 将下面段落译成汉语：

FORCE MAJEURE

Each party shall be excused from any failure to perform its obligations hereunder to the extent that such failure is due to any cause beyond its control, including without, limitation, to any acts to God, civil or military authorities, civil disturbance, war, strikes, fires, other catastrophes, or other 'force majeure' events beyond the reasonable control of the parties, within the scope of this Agreement.

Each party shall be entitled to rely on a "Foree Majeure" event in order to excuse non-performance provided it notifies the other party promptly of the event and takes all reasonable steps to mitigate the effect of the event. If the event shall continue for more that 30 days, then either party shall be entitled to terminate this Agreement by serving notice in writing, with immediate effect.

Upon conclusion of a "Force Majeure" event the parties shall reasonably endeavor to agree upon the necessary modification to each Work Order.（翻译公司材料）

2. 将下面段落译成英语：

20 世纪 70 年代末，中国共产党总结历史经验，特别是汲取"文化大革命"的惨痛教训，作出把国家工作中心转移到社会主义现代化建设上来的重大决策，实行改革开放政策，并明确了一定要靠法制治理国家的原则。为了保障人民民主，必须加强社会主义法制，使民主制度化、法律化，使这种制度和法律具有稳定性、连续性和权威性，使之不因领导人的改变而改变，不因领导人的看法和注意力的改变而改变，做到有法可依，有法必依，执法必严，违法必究，成为改革开放新时期法治建设的基本理念。在发展社会主义民主、健全社会主义法制的基本方针指引下，现行宪法以及《刑法》、《刑事诉讼法》、《民事诉讼法》、《民法通则》、《行政诉讼法》等一批基本法律出台，中国的法治建设进入了全新发展阶段。

20 世纪 90 年代，中国开始全面推进社会主义市场经济建设，由此进一步奠定了法治建设的经济基础，也对法治建设提出了更高的要求。1997 年召开的中国共产党第十五次全国代表大会，将"依法治国"确立为治国基本方略，将"建设社会主义法治国家"确定为社会主义现代化的重要目标，并提出了建设中国特色社会主义法律体系的重大任务。1999 年，将"中华人民共和国实行依法治国，建设社会主义法治国家"载入宪法。中国的法治建设揭开了新篇章。

进入 21 世纪，中国的法治建设继续向前推进。2002 年召开的中国共产党第十六次全国代表大会，将社会主义民主更加完善，社会主义法制更加完备，依法治国基本方略得到全面落实，作为全面建设小康社会的重要目标。2004 年，将"国家尊重和保障人权"载入宪法。2007 年召开的中国共产党第十七次全国代表大会，明确提出全面落实依法治国基本方略，加快建设社会主义法治国家，并对加强社会主义法治建设作出了全面部署。（节选自《中国的法治建设》白皮书）

3. 将下面段落译成英语：

ABC 公司信息技术保密协议书

保密

我同意在我服务于 ABC 期间不直接或间接地对没有被授权的单位和个人，包括 ABC 内部没有被授权员工泄露 ABC 财产信息。

ABC 以外的信息资料

我明白 ABC 已经收到并将继续收到 ABC 以外第三方的与 ABC 业务相关信息资料，我保证在我服务于 ABC 期间或离开 ABC 以后，我将不对任何单位和个人泄露这些信息，在没有得到 ABC 授权的情况下，我将不使用第三方的信息资料来从事其他任何相关的活动，我同意 ABC 以外的信息资料在该协议执行期间内属于保密信息资料的一部门。

资料归还

在任何一种情况下，ABC 向我要求，或我因各种原因结束在 ABC 的任职，我将立刻将使用过以及正在使用的全部 ABC 文件和 ABC 信息资料（无论是正式领取或非正式领取，在服务于 ABC 期间因工作关系获得的信息资料）归还上级负责人或 ABC 档案室，这些资料包括 ABC 全部纸张文件，工作记事薄，领取的磁盘，数据信息，参考资料，图案，会议记录，正式文件，软件，工具和工具书和任何其他属于 ABC 的没有提及的物品和信息资料。

对其他商标的保密

我理解 ABC 实行严格的公司保密制度的目的是为了保证对公司内部或其他企业单位的的权利不受到侵犯，我对该制度严格遵守的同时并有信心维护和执行 ABC 对财产权利的制度。我保证在我服务于 ABC 期间或离开 ABC 以后我将不对任何单位和个人泄露这些信息。

条款违约

如我服务于 ABC 期间因为我不遵守以上条款，该协议书有终止我服务于 ABC 的权利。如因我违约并对 ABC 造成直接经济损失，我同意全力协助 ABC 就挽回对技术专利和产品版权损失等属于 ABC 知识产权内的辅助工作，我同意承担挽回直接经济损失的全部费用和时间。

裁决

我同意如因为我对该协议书违约而造成了 ABC 直接或间接的经济损失，ABC 有权对我的行为诉讼于法律。

律师费用

我同意如因为我对该协议书违约而造成的 ABC 诉讼于法律，全部律师费用由我承担。（翻译公司材料）

第九章

翻译实战

翻译理论的学习，欣赏翻译大师的译作，一定数量的文学翻译实践，同各方人士的经验交流，所有这一切并不意味着你能够应对真实的翻译市场。翻译实战能力的提高离不开在市场中的摸爬滚打。译者通过翻译市场的锻炼，可以发现自身知识缺陷并进行弥补。翻译是一个无止境的过程。对于有志于翻译领域发展的人士，在学习翻译技术的过程中，也应该掌握市场上需要翻译什么样的材料，市场评价相关翻译质量的标准是什么，怎么样做一个让市场满意的译者。

本章的实战文章选自北京元培世纪翻译有限公司与北京悦尔翻译公司提供的真实翻译材料以及一些已得到市场认可的译文，其中对涉及保密信息部分已经进行了筛除。

我们选取了多个不同行业的文章，旨在让大家通过实战练习，真正掌握社会对翻译从业人员的要求与期待，从而在翻译学习过程中也能够更有针对性地查缺补漏，有针对性地学习到在社会工作中应该立即掌握的知识。

实战一：IT 文章中译英

【原文】

21 世纪上半叶信息科学技术的发展趋势

未来的几十年内，信息技术将继续以惊人的速度发展，进一步扩大影响力和渗透力，革命性地改变人类的经济发展形态和生活方式，将对学习娱乐、政府企业管理和文化传播等许多方面产生极其深远的影响。计算机与通信网络将在速度、容量、带宽、方便性、可靠性、安全性等方面不断取得新的进展，在取得原理性的科学突破之后将出现颠覆性的技术换代。

进入 21 世纪，信息科学与技术的发展将出现如下的新特点和新的发展趋势：

1. 信息科学技术的发展将更加关注全民普及、可持续发展、社会和谐及产业生态的开放性：

在重视信息领域核心和关键技术突破的同时，将更加关注信息技术的应用价值，关注信息技术的渗透性和技术的广泛普及，特别是关注缩小数字鸿沟和惠及全民，注重降低信息化的成本，提高信息产品的易用性、耐用性和安全性。如果我们能够做到这些，21 世纪很可能会出现一些专家预计的"信息科技应用的寒武纪大爆发"。

伴随着知识经济时代的到来，人们在重视技术的市场竞争能力及经济效益的同时，将更加重视信息技术对生态和环境影响，探索对有限自然资源和无限知识资源的分享、共享，追求可持续的发展。

在继续关注科学与技术紧密结合的同时，将更加重视信息科学与社会科学的结合、信息技术与人文艺术的结合，更加重视信息技术研究的伦理道德，关注信息技术对社会正反两方面的影响。

在继续发展工程技术的规模效益的同时，将更加重视信息技术的多样性和开放性。今后半个世纪中，信息领域将致力于形成一个开放、合作、共享的产业生态圈，突破现有市场和知识产权的框框，产生新的更大的市场、新的主流技术和新的知识产权形态。

2. 信息科学与技术将融入各种应用领域，成为交叉汇聚科学的纽带：

信息技术在 10 年以后，将会逐渐融合在其它技术领域中。未来我国在信息领域的发展，必须从跨领域的技术创新入手，而不应该只是维持信息技术的垂直升级，或者只向所谓的关键信息技术方向发展。

在重视技术作为生产力决定性因素的同时，将更加重视新的科学探索，特别是与纳米、生命、认知科学的交叉研究，实现汇聚发展。以信息技术特别是计算机仿真技术为纽带，将形成一系列新的科学，如信息生物学、社会信息学（社会计算）、纳米智能科学等。

未来半个世纪内，基于认知机理的智能信息处理在理论与方法上的突破，可能带动信息科学与技术的突破性发展。脑科学、认知科学与人工智能的密切结合，将解决认知科学和信息科学中的重大基础理论问题，使信息科学进入以模拟人脑（包括人脑反向工程）为特征的新时代。

【参考译文】

IST Development Trends in the First Half of the 21st Century

In the coming decades, information science and technology (IST) will continually develop at a noticeable speed. IST will further extend its influence and penetration, revolutionarily change our economic growth and lifestyle, and deeply affect study, entertainment, governmental management, corporate management, cultural communication and so on. Computer and telecommunication networks are going to have new developments in terms of speed, capacity, bandwidth, convenience, reliability and security. The great scientific breakthroughs will be followed by a revolutionary technical upgrade.

After entry into the 21st century, IST shows the following new features and development trends:

1. IST development will place more importance on society-wide popularization, sustainable development, social harmony and industrial openness:

In addition to the breakthroughs for core and key technologies in the information field, we shall pay much more attention to the value of applications, the permeability of information technology (IT), the popularization of relevant technologies, especially focus on shortening the digital development gap, making IST benefit the public, minimizing informationization cost, and improving information products' user-friendliness, durability and safety. If we can accomplish these objectives, the predicted Cambrian Explosion of IST will potentially occur in the 21st century.

With the coming of the knowledge economy age, the public attaches more importance to the effects of IST on ecosystem and environment, exploring how to share the limited natural resources of the earth and the unlimited knowledge resources of human beings, in addition to the competitive forces and economic benefits of technologies.

In addition to the combination of both science and technology, people will attach more importance to the combination of information science and social science, the combination of IT and arts, particularly the ethics and morality of IST studying, the positive and negative effects of IST on society.

People will attach more importance to the diversity and openness of IST, as the scale economy of engineering technologies is continually developed. In the next 50 years, the information field will be committed to form an open, cooperative and well-shared industrial circle, breaking through the framework for both the existing market and the intellectual property rights and generating a larger market, new mainstream technology and new intellectual property rights.

2. IST will be integrated with various application fields, being a link for the interdisciplinary technologies

In the next ten years, IST will be gradually integrated into other technical fields. As for the future development of IST, China must start from the technical innovation of the interdisciplinary technologies, other than singly maintain the vertical upgrade of the IT, or develop towards the so-called key information technologies.

In addition to the existing technologies, new sciences shall be laid stress on, particularly the interdisciplinary research on nano-technology, life and cognitive science, so as to realize an integral development. Some new sciences such as information biology, social science (social computing) and nano-intelligent science will be based on IT, especially through computer simulation.

In the next half a century, due to the breakthrough of cognitive-based intelligent information processing theory and methodology, it's potential to lead IST breakthroughs. The close combination of brain science, cognitive science and artificial intelligence will solve the great theoretic problems in cognitive science and IST, and bring IST into a new age with the characteristics of brain simulation (including brain reverse engineering).

实战二：机电文章中译英

【原文】

三. 安装手册

3.1 记录仪安装说明：

本智能温度记录仪为便携式移动设备，在开始记录安装使用之前，请确定记录仪各参数配置已经成功完成。在现场安装使用过程中，应该注意以下几点：

1) 记录仪在安装使用前，必须保证其要连接的接口与部件是连通的；

2) 记录仪最好安装或放置在比较显眼，易于安装和维护的地方，并注意固定，防止跌落，否则可能导致伤人或损坏；

3) 记录仪应安装在距离楼层地面 1.5 米以上，保证天线垂直向上（天线底部带磁铁，可吸附上冷链设备的顶部），并接收到信号。记录仪、电源变压器等物品不能处于冷链设备散热部件的上方或固定散热部件本身。禁止在潮湿环境中使用。禁止在带腐蚀性或易燃易爆的化学气体的环境中使用；

4) 记录仪正常工作状态，电源线、传感器、RS232 通信线、GSM 天线不易绷得太紧，应该使这四根线自然下垂，不应受到拉力的作用。过长的电源线、传感器、RS232 通信线、GSM 天线要用扎线带进行捆扎并固定到合适位置，以免将人绊倒。

5) 记录仪安装或放置要牢固、可靠，以免松动、滑落，以致损坏记录仪；

6) 电源变压器尽可能固定在冷链设备的合适位置，在长期震动或搬运冷链设备的过程中不能脱落和晃动；将电源插头插接到记录仪之前，必须测量电源变压器的输出电压是否在额定的范围内；

7) 传感器的安装要求：

a) 有些型号的冷链设备有预留的测试孔，在安装传感器时要求通过这个孔将传感器伸入冷链设备内部；

b) 传感器探头要固定在冷链设备内部，但不要将传感器探头直接贴在设备内部的金属上。要求固定传感器探头时，要有绝热衬底。另外，传感器探头不要固定在临时器件上，比如隔离板、物品框等；

c) 传感器引线在冷链设备内部不能折叠、打结。引线和探头要放置在容易取放的位置。在低温（如 −80℃）冷链设备中，传感器容易断裂，在安装时要特别注意内部走线整齐。

d) 传感器过长的引线要留在冷链设备的外部，并要用扎线带进行捆扎，并固定在冷链设备的合适位置；如有些设备需要更长的传感器引线，必须事先根据符合现场需求另外定做，不允许在现场加接引线。

【参考译文】

3. Installation Guide

3.1 Installation Instructions for the Recorder

This intelligent temperature recorder is a portable one. Please make sure that all the recorder parameters have been successfully set up before installing and using the recorder. Pay attention to the following items during installation and use:

1) Before installing and using the recorder, confirm the interfaces and connecting components are well connected;

2) It is advisable that the recorder is installed in an obvious place where is easy for installation and maintenance and well fixed to prevent it from falling down and to avoid personal injury or damage;

3) The recorder shall be installed at least 1.5m above the ground. Make sure that the antenna is vertical up (the antenna is equipped with magnet at the bottom and can be attached to the top of upper cold chain equipment) and receives signals. Both the recorder and power transformer must not be located above or fixed to the heat-radiating components of cold chain equipment. It is prohibited to use the recorder in humid, corrosive, flammable or explosive environment;

4) Under normal conditions, the recorder's power cord, sensor, RS232 communication line and GSM antenna shall not be over-tensioned but naturally droop under no tensile force. If these four lines are excessively long, them bind them and fix them in a place to prevent people from being stumbled.

5) The recorder must be installed or placed firmly and reliably to avoid any damage due to looseness and falling down;

6) Fix the power transformer at a proper position on the cold chain equipment so that it will neither drop down nor shake after long-time vibration or in the process of handling the cold chain equipment. Before connecting the power plug to the recorder, be sure to measure and confirm the output voltage of power transformer is within the rated range;

7) Requirements for the installation of sensor:

a) A test hole is reserved on some models of the cold chain equipment. When installing the sensor, it is required to insert the sensor into the equipment through the hole;

b) Fix the sensor probe in the cold chain equipment, but do not attach it directly to the metal surface inside the equipment. Heat-insulated substrate is necessary when it is required to fix the sensor probe. In addition, do not fix the sensor probe to a temporary component, e.g. separator, item frame, etc.;

c) The sensor's lead wire cannot be folded or kinked inside the cold chain equipment. The lead wire and probe shall be placed in an accessible position. The sensor in low-temperature (e.g. −80 ℃) cold chain equipment is liable to break, so pay special attention to orderly internal wiring at the time of installation;

d) The sensor's redundant lead wire shall be out of the cold chain equipment, bound with a binding wire and fixed at a proper position on the cold chain equipment. If any equipment needs a longer lead wire, it must be customized in advance as required by the installation site. It is not allowed to extend the lead wire on site.

实战三：电视解说词中译英

【原文】

《水韵昆山》

（CCTV-2 电视解说词）

缠绵婉转 清雅悠远的昆曲
是中国古代雅文化的代表
被称为"百戏之师"
六百年前它正诞生在中国的昆山

水 是昆山的灵魂
因为水 这片土地显得格外灵动秀美
昆山境内河网纵横 湖泊众多
是江南典型的"鱼米之乡"

清可鉴人的湖面 保存完好的生态
使阳澄湖闻名遐迩

在七十多种淡水产品中
又以阳澄湖大闸蟹最负盛名

傀儡湖与阳澄湖比邻

元明两代
许多艺术家常常泛舟湖上
拍曲和唱

被联合国教科文组织确认为
"人类口头与非物质遗产"的昆曲
正是发端于这碧波荡漾的傀儡湖畔

阳澄湖 傀儡湖和淀山湖
组成昆山境内的三大湖泊
昆山的水域面积达到全市总面积的 30%

整个城市沁润在一片碧绿之中

周庄是这碧水中的一颗明珠
被称为中国第一水乡古镇
宋代建镇
已有 900 多年的历史

古镇锦溪 四面环水
镇内湖荡密布 古桥联袂

千灯依水而建
物华天宝 人文荟萃

周庄 锦溪 千灯等水乡古镇
串成一串项链
装点在昆山的碧水之间
昆山的经济实力位居全国百强县之首
水 给这座新兴的工商业之城
带来了生生不息的活力

水 给了昆山生命的源泉
也赋予了昆山独特的气质
今天 由于善待水
昆山人的生活将更加美好

【参考译文】

Kunshan–a Waterside City

The lingering Kunqu Opera
a typical traditional Chinese culture
is reputed as the originator of the Chinese operas
and was generated in Kunshan over 600 years ago
Water is the soul of Kunshan

With water, this land shows even more graceful
With closely-intensive rivers and lakes
Kunshan typically is an abundant place in the South China

The clear water and well-protected biologic system
makes Yangcheng Lake well known

Among more than 70 fresh-water products
Yangcheng Lake Crab enjoys the greatest reputation

Kuilei Lake, neighboring to Yangcheng Lake
in the Yuan Dynasty and the Ming Dynasty
was a popular destination for the artists
who were often found drifting about and singing in boats

Kunqu Opera initially came to existence by this lake,
and later was recognized as
"Oral and Intangible Heritage of Humanity" by UNESCO

Yangcheng Lake, Kuilei Lake and Dianshan Lake
are three largest lakes in the domain of Kunshan
And the water-covered area accounts for 30% of Kunshan's gross area

The city is laid among a vast green land

And Zhouzhuang is a pearl in the green water
And is known as the first ancient waterside town in China
This town was established in the Song Dynasty,
more than 900 years ago

The ancient town Jinxi is surrounded by streams
with ancient bridges connecting blocks to blocks

The ancient town Qiandeng was established by the water
and is now known for its prosperity and civilization
The ancient water towns: Zhouzhuang, Qiandeng and Jinxi
seem as a string of the pearls
inlaid among the clear streams and green mountains
Kunshan's economic strength tops all the counties countrywide
The water streams make this rising commercial city
be full of energies
Water provides a life spring for Kunshan,
and endue Kunshan a unique characteristic
due to the well treatment of water
Kunshan people benefit a lot for their better life!

实战四:工程文章英译中

【原文】

Commissioning

A Commissioning Programme describes all essential activities of the preparation and implementation of the functional tests before relocating the excavator to the jobsite.

The commissioning activities to be carried out at the jobsite will be described in a separate programme and submitted on schedule.

The commissioning shall be in accordance with the requirements of the contract.

Assistance by the Client will be possible on the basis of agreements.

In the commissioning phase functional tests shall be performed in the responsibility of the Contractor. The functional tests shall include all settings, adjustments, tests and functional demonstrations to check the functionality of the components / equipment units and of the entire equipment.

At the beginning of the commissioning the Contractor shall state that the equipment is in a condition suitable for starting the functional tests, the previous design of the equipment complied with the contract and project and the requirements of labour protection were observed.

During the commissioning client- and object-specific regulations shall be observed and implemented to ensure the safety of persons, prevent accidents at work and avoid damage to the equipment.

Before carrying out and after completing the commissioning activities, safety precautions shall be implemented and checked so that faulty operation and danger to persons and property will be excluded.

After the daily completion of commissioning activities / functional tests the equipment shall be left in disconnected condition. The switching state shall be documented.

Complex commissioning activities / functional tests shall be coordinated with the client before starting work. Changes of the switching state shall be carried out in coordination with the client.

The functional tests shall start after completing the erection of the spreader and tripper car on the erection yard and shall be subdivided into component and functional group tests altogether including all settings, adjustments, tests and functional demonstrations to ensure the functionality of the components / equipment units and of the entire equipment for relocating the spreader and tripper car and for starting trial operation.

【参考译文】

试运行

试运行方案介绍在将挖土机转移到工作现场前进行功能测试准备与实施的主要活动。

工作现场的试运行活动在独立方案中介绍,并按时提交。

试运行应依照合同要求进行。

在客户同意的基础上,可以由客户提供援助。

在试运行阶段,功能测试应该由承包商负责。功能测试应该包括所有设置、调整、测试与功能演示,检查部件/装置及设备整体的功能。

在试运行开始时,承包商必须说明设备处于适合进行功能测试的状态,先前设备设计符合合同和项目规定,运行过程遵守劳动安全规定。

试运行过程中,应该遵守与执行客户与测试的具体规定,保证人员安全,防止现场事故,避免损坏设备。

在试运行前后,应采取并检查各项安全措施,排除错误操作,避免人物损坏。

完成一天的试运行活动/功能测试之后,设备应处于断电状态。开关状态应该进行记录备案。

对于复杂的试运行/功能测试，应该在开工前与客户进行协调。在客户的配合下，调整开关状态。在安装现场完成排土机和自卸车安装之后，才开始进行功能测试。测试应该细分为零部件测试、功能组测试，包括所有设置、调整、测试、功能演示，确保零部件/设备组件与整套设备功能正常，从而进行排土机与自卸车移机，以及开始进行试产。

实战五：食品文章英译中

【原文】

SHORT SUMMARY

A new foodstuff YASO™

A new foodstuff has been developed by the Hungarian company Fitorex Ltd. The product being world wide patented was first launched in Hungary in 2008 under the name YASO™.

What is YASO™ ?

It is known, that soy cannot be more popular in the feeding (public catering, home kitchens, restaurants) due to some of its disadvantageous properties. These are the unpleasant taste, distension and the inconvenient kitchen technique.

The sprouted soy bean (not the sprout alone!) has been known for more than thousand years and consumed in the Far East because of its high protein content. Fitorex, making use of this experience, was the first on the world to develop the biological transformation of the soy bean by a special, short time sprouting on an industrial scale. The new foodstuff produced by the technology of Fitorex :

- keeps all the valuable constituents of the soy
- it does not have properties which are unpleasant to the customers, i.e. the taste of YASO is pleasant, neutral
- it does not cause distension (it does not contain stachiose), optional quantities can be consumed
- It does not need any preparatory step in the kitchen, it is instantly apt for cooking.

YASO is a new foodstuff of plant origin of excellent quality, better than the soy, with high protein and fibre content, the composition of which is the same as of the meat.

The further advantages of YASO:

- it is cheap (its price is half of the meat)
- it can be easily used (like minced meat)
- iit is easy to digest
- it does not contain any artificial additives, preservatives, flavour intensifiers or colouring agents.
- it is cholesterol free
- persons suffering from flour and lactose sensitivity can also consume it
- YASO is produced from GMO-free soy seeds and does not contain any antibiotic
- Since YASO is a cheap but excellent source of full proteins, it can be used in schools, hospitals, public catering, army, etc.

YASO in Hungary

YASO has successfully been used by Sodexo since November 2008 in and around Budapest. Our main partners are Gastroyal (the biggest catering on the Hungarian market, it delivers to all parts of the country), Bakonygaszt (it has 18 kitchens). It is foreseen that P-Dusmann will soon also be our partner, which takes the major part of the hospital catering.

Fitorex is ready to work out and completely accomplish a project providing for the use of YASO in different countries.

【参考译文】

摘 要

新食品 YASO™

匈牙利 Fitorex 有限公司开发出了一款新食品。该食品获得全球专利,于 2008 年率先以 YASO™ 商标投入匈牙利市场。

什么是 YASO™?

众所周知,由于黄豆具有一定的缺陷性,如气味不好、食后容易放屁、烹饪麻烦等,所以不能够广泛用于各种饮食当中(大众餐饮、家庭厨房与酒店饭馆等)。

长芽的黄豆(不只是豆芽)自身蛋白质含量非常高,在远东地区已经食用了一千多年了。Fitorex 公司利用这一经验,在世界上率先通过一项特殊、短期催芽技术来实现黄豆生物转化,实现大规模生产。Fitorex 公司通过这一技术生产出来的新食品具有如下特点:

- 保持黄豆所有营养成分
- 不再存在让顾客讨厌的缺陷性,即 YASO 口感好,无杂味
- 不会导致放屁(不含水苏糖),吃多吃少随意
- 在厨房中不需要任何准备,可以立即进行烹饪

YASO 是一种来源于植物的新食品,质量上乘,远胜于黄豆,高蛋白、高纤维含量,成分与肉类相似。

YASO 其它优点:

- 价格便宜(价格是肉类的一半)
- 易于食用(口感像碎肉)
- 易于消化
- 不含任何人造添加剂、防腐剂、增香剂或着色剂
- 不含胆固醇
- 面粉、乳糖过敏者也可以食用
- YASO 由非转基因黄豆制作而成,不含任何抗生素
- YASO 价格便宜,是绝佳的全蛋白来源,可以用于学校、医院、大众餐饮、军队等

YASO 在匈牙利

从 2008 年 11 月起,Sodexo 公司已经在布达佩斯市内外成功使用 YASO。我们主要合作伙伴包括 Gastroyal 公司(匈牙利市场最大餐饮公司,遍及全国各地)与 Bakonygaszt 公司(有 18 家厨房)。预计负责大部分医院餐饮业务的 P-Dusmann 公司也将很快成为我们的合作伙伴。

Fitorex 准备计划并全力实施这一项目,向各个国家提供 YASO 产品。

实战六:招标文件英译中

【原文】

Instructions to Bidders

1. Scope of Bid

1.1 In connection with the Invitation for Bids indicated in the Bid Data Sheet (DBS), the Public body, as indicated in the BDS, issues these Bidding documents for the procurement of Works as specified in Section VI, Works Requirements. The name, identification, and number of lots (contracts) of the Open Advertised Bidding (OAB) are provided in the BDS.

1.2 Regarding large or complex contracts, no public body shall, without the prior approval of the Board, referred to in Section 2 of these ITB, advertise, invite, solicit, call for bids, or award such contracts. No Bidder shall sign a large or complex contract with a Public body, unless the award and draft contract have been approved by the Board.

1.3 Throughout these Bidding Documents:

(a) The term "in writing" means communicated in written form and delivered against receipt;

(b) except where the context requires otherwise, words indicating the singular also include the plural and words indicating the plural also include the singular; and

(c) "day" means calendar day.

2. Public entities Related to Bidding Documents and to challenge and appeal

2.1 The public bodies related to these bidding procedures and bidding documents are:

(d) The Procurement Policy Office, which serves as an independent procurement policy making and monitoring body, in charge of issuing standard bidding documents;

(e) The Central Procurement Board (Board), in charge of:

(i) vetting these bidding documents;

(ii) receiving and publicly opening the bids;

(iii) selecting public and independent evaluators;

(iv) reviewing the recommendations of bid evaluation committees;

(v) approving award of contracts; and

(vi) requiring evaluation committees to make new evaluation or further evaluations on specific grounds.

(f) Bid Evaluation Committees in charge of the examination, evaluation and comparison of bids and determining the lowest evaluated bids.

(g) the Independent Review Panel referred to in Sections 44 and 45 of the Act.

2.2 Sections 43, 44 and 45 of the Act provide for challenge and review mechanism. Unsatisfied bidders shall follow procedures prescribed in Regulations 48, 49 and 50 of the Public Procurement Regulation 2008 to challenge procurement proceeding and award of procurement contracts or to file application for review at the Independent Review Panel.

3. Corrupt Practices

3.1 The Government of the Republic of Mauritius requires that bidders / suppliers/ contractors, participating in procurement in the Republic of Mauritius, observe the highest standard of ethics during the procurement process and execution of contracts.

(h) public body officials and bidders / suppliers / contractors shall conform to the standards of conduct set forth in sections 51 and 52 of t he Public Procurement Act, which provides as follows:

Section 51 Conduct of Public Officials

(1) A public official involved in planning or conducting public procurement proceedings or contract administration shall:

(i) discharge his duties impartially so as to ensure fair competitive access to procurement by suppliers;

(ii) act in the public interest, and in accordance with the objectives and procedures set out in this Act;

(iii) avoid conflicts of interest, and the appearance of conflict of interest, in carrying out his duties and conducting himself;

(iv) not commit or abet any corrupt or fraudulent practice, including solicitation or acceptance of improper inducements;

(v) keep confidential any information that comes into his procession relating to procurement proceedings and to bids, including bidders' proprietary information;

(vi) for a period of 2 years after leaving the public service not accept a position of authority in any private concern with which he had official dealings;

(vii) declare his assets in such a manner as may be prescribed.

(2) Relative

(i) No public official, or his close relative, shall participate as a bidder in procurement proceedings of that Public body and no award of a procurement contract shall be made directly to such official or to any body in which he or his close relative, is employed in a management capacity or has a substantial financial interest.

(ii) in the subsection, "close relative" includes spouse, child, grandchild or parent.

Section 52: Conduct of Bidders and suppliers

(1) A bidder or a supplier shall not engage in or abet any corrupt or fraudulent practice, including the offering or giving, directly or indirectly, of improper inducements, in order to influence an procurement process or the execution of a contract, including interference in the ability of competing bidders to participate in procurement proceedings.

(2) A bidder or a supplier shall not engage in any coercive practice threatening to harm, directly or indirectly, any person or his property to influence his participation in a procurement process, or affect the execution of a contract.

(3) A bidder shall not engage in collusion, before or after a bid submission, designed to allocate procurement contracts among bidders, establish bid prices a artificial non-competitive levels or otherwise deprive a Public Body of the benefit of free and open competition.

(4) A Public Body shall reject a bid if the bidder offers, gives or agrees to give a inducement referred to in subsection (1) and promptly notify the rejection to the bidder concerned and to the Policy Office.

(5) Bidder / Supplier

(i) Subject to paragraph (b), a bidder or supplier who is responsible for preparing the specifications or bidding documents for, or supervising the execution of a procurement contract or a related company of such bidder or supplier, shall not participate in such bidding.

(ii) Paragraph (a) shall not apply to the several bodies (consultants, contractors or suppliers) that together may be performing the suppliers' obligations under a turnkey or design-build contract.

4. Eligible Bidders

4.1 A bidder may be a natural person, private entity, Government-owned entity – subject to ITB 4.6 – or any combination of such entities supported by a letter of intent to enter into an agreement or under an existing agreement in the form of a joint venture or association (JVA). In the case of a joint venture or association:

(i) unless otherwise specified in the BDS, all partners shall be jointly and severally liable, and

(j) the JVA shall nominate a Representative who shall have the authority to conduct all business for and on behalf of any and all the partners of the JVA during the bidding process and, in the event the JVA is awarded the Contract, during contract execution.

4.2 Public bodies may require the submission of singed statements from the bidders, certifying eligibility, in the absence of other documentary evidence establishing eligibility.

Eligibility requirements may concern:

(i) Business registration, for which evidence may include the certificate of company registration;

(ii) Tax status, for which documentation of tax registration and tax clearance are particularly relevant;

(iii) Certifications by the bidder of the absence of a debarment order and absence of conflict of interest; and

(iv) Certification of status regarding conviction for any offence involving fraud, corruption or dishonesty.

4.3 Bidders shall be allowed to participate in procurement proceedings without regard to their nationality, subject to section 17 of the Act.

(k) With a view to facilitating participation by bidders, the Public Body shall accept the submission by bidders of equivalent documentation when particular documents required by the bidding documents are not available or issued, for example, in a foreign bidder's country of origin.

(l) Public bodies may also accept certifications from bidders attesting to compliance with eligibility requirements.

4.4 A Bidder shall not have a conflict of interest. All Bidders found to have a conflict of interest shall b e disqualified. Bidders may be considered to have a conflict of interest with one or more parties in this bidding process, if they are associated, or have been associated in the past, directly or indirectly, with the consultant or any other entity that has prepared the design, specifications, and other documents for the Contract or being proposed as Project Manager for the Contract. A firm that has been engaged by the Public body to provide consulting services for the preparation or supervision of the Works, and any of its affiliates shall not be eligible to bid.

Additionally, Bidders may be considered to have a conflict of interest with one or more parties in this bidding process, if they:

(i) receive or have received any direct or indirect subsidy from any of them; or

(ii) have the same legal representative for purposes of this bid; of

(iii) have a relationship with each other, directly or through common third parties, that puts them in a position to have access to information about or influence on the bid of another Bidder; or

(iv) a Bidder participates in more than one bid in this bidding process. Participation by a Bidder in more than one Bid will result in the disqualification of all Bids in which the party in involved. However, this does not limit the inclusion of the same subcontractor in more than one bid; or

(v) a Bidder participated a s consultant in the preparation of the design or technical specifications of the works that are the subject of the bid.

(vi) Have controlling partners in common.

4.5 While submitting any tender, a foreign individual, firm, company or institution, shall specify whether or not any agent has been appointed in Mauritius, and if so:

(i) the name and address of the agent;

(ii) the figure of the commission amount payable to the agent, type of the currency and made of payment;

(iii) any other condition agreed with the agent; and

(iv) income tax registration certificate of the local agent and acceptance letter of the agent.

(v) if a bid submitted stated that there is no local agent, and if it's proved thereafter that there exists an agent or if a tender has stated an amount for a commission and it's proven that their exists a higher amount for that commission, action shall be taken against him under section 52 of the Act for his suspension and debarment.

4.6 A firm that is under a declaration of ineligibility by the Government of Mauritius in accordance with applicable laws, as well as ITB 3 and ITB 19.8, at the date of the deadline for bid submission or thereafter, shall be disqualified.

4.7 Government body-owned entities in Mauritius shall be eligible only if they can establish that they are legally and financially autonomous and operate under the commercial laws of Mauritius. Also, they shall not be dependent agencies of the Government.

4.8 Bidders shall provide such evidence of their continued eligibility satisfactory to the Public Body, as the Public body shall reasonably requrest.

4.9 This bidding is open only to prequalified Bidders unless otherwise stated in the BDS.

【参考译文】

投标须知

1. 投标范围

1.1 根据招标数据表（DBS）中投标邀请函的规定，公共机构（定义见招标数据表）发布本招标文件，采购第六节《工程要求》所规定的工程。该公开招标项目（OAB）的名称、标识与批次（合同）均列明于招标数据表当中。

1.2 对于大型或复杂合同，未经中央采购委员会（定义见《投标须知》第二节）事先批准，任何公共机构均不能发布、邀请、寻求、呼吁进行投标，或颁布这类合同。除非中央采购委员会已经批准了决标及合同草案，否则任何投标单位均不能与公共机构签订任何大型或复杂合同。

1.3 在招标文件中：

(a) 术语"书面"指的是通过书面方式进行沟通，并且进行签收；

(b) 除非上下文另有规定，否则以单数形式出现的单词也包括其复数形式，以及以复数形式出现的单词也包括其单数形式；

(c) "天"指的是"日历天"。

2. 与招标文件相关、审查及上诉的公共组织

2.1 与招标程序及招标文件相关的公共机构如下：

(d) 采购政策办公室，是独立的采购政策制定与监控机构，负责发布标准招标文件；

(e) 中央采购委员会，具体负责：
（i）审查招标文件；
（ii）接收投标文件，进行公开开标；
（iii）选择公共与独立评估单位；
（iv）审查评标委员会的推荐意见；
（v）审批中标单位；
（vi）要求评标委员会对具体情况进行新评估或深入评估。

(f) 评标委员会负责审查、评估与对比标书，决定最低评估出价。

(g) 独立审查专家小组见《公共采购法》(Public Procurement Act) 第44、45节。

2.2 《公共采购法》第43、44与45条规定了询问与审查制度。不满意的投标单位应按照《公共采购条例》(2008)第48、49与50条规定的程序来询问采购进程及采购合同发包情况，或向独立审查专家小组请求复审。

3. 腐败行为

3.1 毛里求斯共和国政府要求任何参与毛里求斯共和国采购项目的投标单位、供应商、承包商在采购过程中与合约执行过程中均需要遵守最高的道德标准。

(h) 公共机构官员与投标单位/供应商/承包商均需遵守《公共采购法》第51、52条所规定的行为标准，相关内容如下：

第51节：公务员行为标准

（1）参与规划或实施公共采购进程或合同管理的公务员应：
（i）秉公行使职权，确保所有供应商均活动平等的竞争机会；
（ii）维护公共利益，符合《公共采购法》所规定的目标与程序；
（iii）在行使职权过程中，避免利益冲突或出现利益冲突；
（iv）不参与或教唆任何腐败或欺诈行为，包括教唆或接受任何不当得利；
（v）对投标单位专利资料等与采购过程及招投标相关的任何信息均严格保密；
（vi）在离开公务员岗位后两年期间，不能够进入与其存在官方交易的私营部门接受任何职务；
（vii）可能会根据规定公布其财产状况。

（2）亲戚
（i）任何公务员或其近亲均不能作为投标单位参与该公共机构的采购程序，也不能向该公务员或公务员及其近亲从事管理职务或具有实质金融利益的单位直接发包采购合同。
（ii）在本节中，"近亲"包括配偶、孩子、孙子或父母。

第52节：投标单位与供应商的行为

(1) 投标单位或供应商不能参与或教唆任何腐败、欺诈的行为，包括直接或间接提供或给与不当得利来影响采购程序或合约履行，包括影响其它投标单位参与采购程序的能力。

(2) 投标单位或供应商不能参与任何强迫性行为，威胁直接或间接损害人身安全或财产，从而影响他人参与采购程序或干涉合同履行。

(3) 投标单位在提交标书前后均不能参与串通舞弊，从而达到在投标单位之间瓜分采购合同，造成投标价格人为地处于非竞争水平，或反过来剥夺公共机构行使自由、公开竞争权益。

(4) 如果投标单位提供、给与或同意给与在上文（1）条所提到的不当得利，公共机构应该拒绝该投标，并且立即将拒绝相关投标单位的情况通知采购政策办公室。

(5) 投标单位／供应商

(i) 根据上文（b）小节规定，负责编写技术规范或招标文件、或监督采购合同实施的投标单位或供应商，或这些投标单位或供应商的关联公司均不能参与投标。

(ii) 上文（a）段规定不适用于根据总包合同或设计—施工合同规定一起落实供应商义务的多个机构（顾问公司、承包商或供应商）。

4. 合格投标单位

4.1 投标单位可以是自然人、私营企业、国有企业——根据《投标须知》4.6条规定——或是上述机构组成的组合（通过签订意向书来签署协议或以合资公司或联合体方式的现有协议）。如何投标单位为合资公司或联合体：

(i) 除非招标数据表中另作说明，否则所有合作伙伴均负有连带责任；

(j) 合资公司或联合体应任命一名代表来行使管理所有业务，并且在招标过程中（如果合资公司或联合体中标，还包括在合同实施过程中）代表合资公司或联合体中任一个或全部合作伙伴。

4.2 如果投标单位不具备能够证明其资格的其它证明文件，公共机构可以要求投标单位提交一份签字声明，证明其资格。

资格要求包括：

(i) 工商注册，可以提供公司注册证书；

(ii) 纳税情况，税务登记证与纳税清算文件相关；

(iii) 投标单位证明不存在排除订单与利益冲突的文件；

(iv) 关于欺诈、腐败或诈骗等犯罪行为的证明文件。

4.3 根据《公共采购法》第17节规定，投标单位不分国籍，均允许参与采购程序。

(k) 考虑到投标单位的参与积极性，公共机构接受当招标文件要求的某项文件（如在外国投标单位的原产国中）不存在或没有出具时，投标单位可以提交同等文件。

(l) 公共机构还接受投标单位提供的证明其符合资格要求的证明文件。

4.4 投标单位不应存在利益冲突。所有投标单位一旦发现存在利益冲突，立即取消资格。如果投标单位与本招标程序的一方或多方存在关联关系或过去曾经直接或间接地域编写过合同设计、技术规范及其它文件或被合同项目经理提名的顾问公司或任何其它机构存在关联关系，那么投标单位可能会被视为存在利益冲突问题。公共机构曾经聘请提供工程准备或监理咨询服务的公司，以及其关联公司均不符合投标条件。

另外，投标单位如果存在如下情况，也可能被视为与本招标程序一方或多方存在利益冲突：

(i) 从本招标程序的一方或多方收到或已经收到任何直接或间接的补贴；

(ii) 对于本次投标而言，具有相同的法人代表；

(iii) 相互之间直接或通过第三方存在相互关系，能够获得对方的相关信息或对其它投标单位的投标产生影响；

(iv) 在本次招标程序中，一家投标单位参与一个以上的投标。投标单位参加一个以上投标将导致该方所参与的所有投标均不合格。然而，这一规定不限制多个投标方案均采用同一分包商；

(v) 在本次招标工程设计或技术规范编写过程中，投标单位作为咨询顾问参与其中。

(vi) 拥有共同的控股合作伙伴。

4.5 在提交投标文件时，外国个人、单位、公司或机构应明确说明是否在毛里求斯境内制定代理；如果指定了代理，则：

（i）提供代理的名称与地址；

（ii）应向代理支付的佣金金额、货币类型与付款方式；

（iii）与代理协商的其它情况；

（iv）当地代理的所得税登记证与代理承认函。

（v）如果已提交的投标文件声明没有当地代理并且在后来期间被证明存在代理，或如果投标文件中声明有佣金数额并且证明实际支付佣金超过声明数额，将会根据《公共采购法》第52条规定采取行动，暂停合同或进行开除。

4.6 在投标截止日期或以后，如果某一公司被毛里求斯政府根据适用法律、《投标须知》第3节与第19.8条规定宣布不合格，那么将取消该公司的资格。

4.7 毛里求斯国有企业只有确定其在法律上、财务上完全自治、并且根据毛里求斯商业法律开展业务，才能作为合格的投标单位。另外，这些国有企业不能是政府的从属机构。

4.8 根据公共机构合理要求，投标单位应提供延续其资格的相关证明，达到让公共机构满意的程度。

4.9 除非招标数据表中另有说明，否则本招标项目只对通过资格预审的投标单位公开。

◆ 实战七：协议书英译中 ◆

【原文】

MASTER SERVICE AGREEMENT

THIS AGREEMENT (the "AGREEMENT") is entered into by and between A COMPANY CORPORATION, a US corporation, (hereinafter called "A COMPANY") and SHANGHAI B COMPANY, a Chinese corporation, (hereinafter called "B COMPANY") in respect of the basic terms and conditions for certain computer software-related services to be rendered by B COMPANY, as set forth in the following.

Article 1. Application

This AGREEMENT is intended to stipulate the basic terms and conditions of the service transactions between A COMPANY and B COMPANY as generally applicable to individual transactions covered by the AGREEMENT. If any specific agreement for such an individual transaction (hereinafter called an "Individual Agreement") has provisions inconsistent with the provisions of the AGREEMENT, then the provisions of the Individual Agreement shall prevail over the provisions of the AGREEMENT for the purposes of such individual transaction.

Article 2. Services

2.1 A COMPANY hereby requests B COMPANY and B COMPANY hereby agrees to accomplish certain computer software-related services pursuant to the AGREEMENT and the Individual Agreements.

2.2 The services requested by A COMPANY to B COMPANY (hereinafter called the "Services") shall be as set forth in the respective Individual Agreements. Each such Individual Agreement shall come into existence when B COMPANY provides A COMPANY with a written acknowledgement of B COMPANY in response to A COMPANY's order sheet accompanied by any other documents describing the Services requested, items to be delivered, completion date, fees, and other terms and conditions of the Services.

2.3 B COMPANY shall secure competent and experienced expert engineers for implementing the Services, and shall on its own keep in good order all the facilities, equipment, materials, etc. of B COMPANY needed for implementing the Services.

Article 3. Results and Delivery

3.1 B COMPANY shall deliver to A COMPANY the results of the Services specified in an Individual Agreement (hereinafter referred to as the "Results") at the location designated by A COMPANY no later than the date specified in the Individual Agreement.

3.2 Except for cases where the delivery is put off pursuant to the agreement set forth in Paragraph 3.4 below, A COMPANY shall be entitled to damages for the delay as determined by mutual agreement between A COMPANY and B COMPANY if B COMPANY fails to deliver the Results to A COMPANY no later than the date referred to in Paragraph 3.1 above (or, the later date as agreed upon, if applicable).

3.3 The title to, and any and all other rights and interests to or in the Results shall be vested in A COMPANY upon payment of the fees for Services specified in the Individual Agreement.

3.4 The delivery may be put off by mutual agreement between A COMPANY and B COMPANY if B COMPANY requests a postponement on account of occurrence of circumstances that make it impossible for B COMPANY to comply with the delivery date specified in the Individual Agreement, including without limitation, any change in the Services as requested by A COMPANY.

Article 4. Fees for Services

4.1 The fees for achieving the successful results of the Services shall be specified in the Individual Agreements.

4.2 The fee amount may be revised by amending the Individual Agreement by mutual agreement between A COMPANY and B COMPANY, if the Services actually required to be carried out by B COMPANY are substantially different from the Services specified in the Individual Agreement.

Article 5. Payment Terms

The terms of payment for fees for Services shall be specified in the Individual Agreements.

Article 6. No Assignment

B COMPANY shall not assign or transfer or offer as security to third parties any and all rights that B COMPANY may have under or in connection with the AGREEMENT and the Individual Agreements unless a prior written consent is obtained from A COMPANY.

【参考译文】

主服务协议

本协议("协议")由 A 公司,一家美国企业(下称"A 公司")与 B 公司,一家中国企业(下称"B")就 B 公司提供的某些计算机软件相关服务的基本条款而订立。具体内容如下:

第一条　适用

本协议旨在规定 A 公司与 B 公司之间服务交易的基本条款,这些基本条款对本协议所涵盖的个别交易普遍适用。如果针对某个别交易的任何特定协议(下称"个别协议")的条款与本协议所载条款不符,则为该等个别交易的目的,个别协议条款将优先于本协议。

第二条　服务

2.1 A 公司特此要求 B 公司且 B 公司特此同意,根据本协议和个别协议完成某些计算机软件相关的服务。

2.2 A 公司要求 B 公司提供的服务(下称"服务")如相关个别协议中所列。当 B 公司对 XXXX 的订单及其它用来说明所要求的服务、交付项目、完成日期、费用和其它服务条款的随附文件而向 A 公司提交书面确认书时,该个别协议方可成立。

2.3 B 公司须安排称职的、经验丰富的软件工程专家来实施服务,并须自行管理实施服务所需的所有设施、设备和材料等。

第三条　成果和交付

3.1 B 公司须按照个别协议的规定在 A 公司指定的地点不迟于个别协议规定的日期向 A 公司交付服务成果（下称"成果"）。

3.2 除了 3.4 条规定的可推迟交付的情形之外，如果 B 公司未能在不迟于 3.1 条所列日期内向 A 公司交付成果（或双方同意的更晚日期，如有），则 A 公司有权针对其与 B 公司通过相互协商认定的延误要求 B 公司支付赔偿金。

3.3 在 A 公司根据个别协议支付了服务费用之后，成果的所有权以及与成果有关的任何其它权利和利益均将属于 A 公司。

3.4 如果 B 公司因为某些情况的发生（包括但不限于 A 公司提出变更服务的要求）而导致其无法按照个别协议中规定的日期交付产品而要求推迟交付，交付可以在 A 公司和 B 公司相互协商一致后予以推迟。

第四条 服务费用

4.1 成功完成服务的服务费用应在个别协议中明确规定。

4.2 如果 A 公司实际要求 B 公司开发的服务与个别协议中规定的服务有重大不同，则双方可协商一致修改个别协议从而达到变更费用的目的。

第五条 支付条款

支付条款应在个别协议中应明确规定。

第六条 无转让

除非事先从 A 公司获得书面同意，否则 B 公司不得向第三方转让 B 公司拥有的、在本协议和个别协议下的或与本协议和个别协议相关的权利，也不得将该权利用作对第三方的担保。

翻译练习参考译文

翻译练习一

参考译文 1

造物说

沙伦·杜·皮瑞兹（新西兰）

我看到群山峰顶皑皑白雪
落日映红雪峰似火焰炽烈
蝴蝶在花丛间翩翩起舞
身边美景让我目不暇接

我看到郁金香花儿慢慢绽放
为终日忙碌的蜜蜂袒露心底
白云如絮，悠悠浮于漫漫天际
港湾如镜，轻风吹起阵阵涟漪

我看到一匹骏马高大壮硕
在墨绿的旷野上疾驰奔跑
乌云攒动，雷震九天
空气中弥漫了下雨的味道

天地间色彩斑斓，五味俱全
情感丰富，恐惧各异，风情万种，美景连连
有彩虹，也有隆隆的雷声
还有许多东西无人听闻识见

我们敬畏的造物者创造了万物
让我们使用、欣赏与享乐
我的灵魂溢满了爱与敬
——溢满了熊熊的烈火（蒙永业译）

参考译文 2

　　因为翻译是一种通常需要通过大量实践来获得的技巧，所以大多数人认为翻译是可以教会的，在一定程度上讲，这种说法是正确的。然而同样正确的是，真正出类拔萃的译者是天生的，而非后天造就的。打算专门从事翻译的人必须具有创造性地使用语言的高超天赋，否则就不可能在这个行当中高人一筹。也许学习翻译技巧的最大好处就是能发现自身的局限性，这正是翻译斯坦贝克《人与鼠》一书的汉译者应该知道的。这样，他也就不会把英语中的 mule-skinner（赶骡子的人）译成中文的"剥骡皮的人"（a person who skins the hide off mules）。

　　对许多人来说，计算机时代仍然需要人工翻译似乎是不可思议的。既然现代计算机可以存储整本整本的词典和语法书，为什么不让计算机来做这项工作呢？如果能保证充分的译前编辑和译后编辑，计算机是可以完成某些非常简单的语际翻译的。但是无论是广告小册子还是抒情诗歌，都不可能简化到计算机所要求的逻辑程序。如果参与人员已经大体知道文本的内容，那么计算机打印出来的译文通常是可以读懂的。但是机器翻译出来的东西，语言通常很不自然，有时简直荒诞离奇，而且仅靠修改程序或增加规则也不能真正改善译文。人脑不仅具有数字功能和类推功能，它还有一整套与生俱来的价值观念系统，这种价值观念系统使人脑在结构上具有机器所无法比拟的优势。对于任何文体优美、语义深奥而且极富交流价值的文字，人工翻译都是无法被替代的。

然而，最难翻译的并非文学色彩很浓的作品，而是那些言之无物的文字，即政界人物和参加国际论坛会议的代表们所惯用的那种语言。实际上，纽约联合国总部一些专职翻译就曾说过，最难译的就是演讲者或作者根本就不想把实质性的东西讲出来的文字。其次最难翻译的文字就是通篇充满讽刺或嘲弄的那类文字，因为在书面文字中，对词义的副语言暗示手段通常要比口头上讲出来的更难捕捉。也许第三类最难翻译的东西就是论述翻译的书籍或文章，这主要是因为其中的示例大都是牵强附会的缘故。（严久生译）

翻译练习二

参考译文 1

中国经济如何平稳运行，美国没有资格指手划脚

作者：约瑟夫·斯蒂格利茨

第二个认识误区是，中国会从自由浮动汇率中得到好处，应该让市场的力量决定价格。市场经济国家从来没有放弃过对汇率的干预，更确切地说，从来没有放弃过对宏观经济的干预。各国政府经常对金融市场进行干预，比如，它们对利率进行的调整。一些市场原教旨主义者声称，所有这些都不是政府应该做的。然而，今天却没有任何一个国家同意这样的观点，在德高望重的经济学家中，也很少有人持此观点。现在的问题是，什么样的市场干预措施最为有效？汇率波动代价高昂，一些国家为了稳定汇率，在实施干预时理智而谨慎，而另一些国家则不然。从总体上说，那些理智而谨慎的国家工作更有成效。

汇率风险给公司带来巨大的成本压力，它不仅代价高昂，而且常常无法防范，在发展中国家尤为如此。在汇率管理方面，一个更具广泛意义的问题是：国家在管理经济时应该如何发挥作用。几乎所有人今天都承认，正如政府干预过多可使国家遭受损失一样，政府干预过少同样可使国家遭受损失，而中国在这两者之间一直寻求着某种平衡。在过去的20年中，中国的市场变得越来越重要，而政府的作用则越来越小，但政府依然发挥着关键性作用。中国这种将二者相结合的做法独具特色，非常适合中国的国情，这不仅表现在二十多年来中国的年收益一直以9%的惊人速度增长，而且表现在经济增长的累累硕果广泛得到分享。从1981年至2001年，已有4.22亿中国人摆脱了贫穷。

美国经济的增长速度是中国的三分之一。贫穷在美国正不断增加，家庭收入中值呈实际下降趋势。美国的净储蓄总额要远远低于中国。在培养全球经济竞争中不可或缺的工程师和科学家方面，中国培养出的人数要远远多于美国；而美国由于军费开支的增加，正不断减少对基础研究的投入。与此同时，美国的债务继续飙升，而美国的总统却希望为美国的最富有群体实施永久性减税。考虑到所有这些因素，无论在如何管理汇率或经济的问题上，中国的领导人都没有必要听从美国的忠告。

参考译文 2

Nevertheless, the lessons that China has drawn from the crisis may well have implications beyond money. First, China has truly realized that its foreign trade dependency of over 50 percent has affected the real economy, thus reducing its capacity to combat the crisis. Since an excessively high ratio of exports to national economy has been the root cause of the structural imbalance in the Chinese economy, the financial crisis has incidentally provided an enormous opportunity for China's economic restructuring.

Second, the crisis has created an environment conducive to growth in household consumption. As external demand falls, the expansion of domestic demand is highly expected. Some measures taken by the government since the beginning of this year — the improvement of social security system, the implementation of a comprehensive medical reform, transferring part of the state-owned shares to the National Social Security Fund (NSSF), and the proposal for the reform of the income distribution system, etc. —are all aimed at increasing residents' incomes and stimulating public expenditure.

Third, the crisis unveils the vulnerability in China's foreign reserves featuring a rather skewed currency composition, and allows China to see clearly the defects in the international monetary system. It seems inevitable that China will have to accelerate the diversification of its foreign reserve assets, and its proposal for a super-sovereign reserve currency system will also help facilitate the healthy development of the global financial system.

翻译练习三

参考译文 1

英雄的生与死

你最好把怜悯丢在克里斯托弗·里夫通风良好、充满阳光的家门外。他的家掩映在纽约州北部起伏的草地和白色木头畜棚之间。他被推进房间时,首先吸引你的是他那令人肃然起敬的高度。宝座一样的轮椅将他臂膀宽阔的硕大身躯从地面托起。落座之后,你发现,你得仰起头看他。

那场事故对他的影响正在减小,他说,呼吸机吸着气,哐哐作响。万籁俱寂之时,他不会再突然惊醒,又一次面对颈部以下失去知觉的事实。坐车经过饲养"巴克"的牲口棚时,他也不再转过脸避开。"巴克"是一匹纯种马,1995年,他正是从这匹马上摔下来跌断了脖颈。但是,学会在瘫痪状态下生活和听命于瘫痪不是一回事。"我还从来没有梦见过自己已是残疾人,"他说,"从来没有。"他曾经发誓五十岁时重新迈开双腿,尽管这曾引起颇多争议。因为那时,距离最后期限还有三个星期。

里夫坚称,五十岁时再走路只是希望,并非预言。但是,他的死讯之所以让人们如此不知所措,是因为这样一个事实:从某种角度看,我们那么多人都认为,即使比他的"时间表"晚几年,他最终也许真的能迈开双腿走路。当然,在回答人们不可避免提出的关于电影主题的问题时,他总是强调,普通伤残人才是真正的超级英雄。但是,对于我们大家,他个人的故事太具魅力而无法抗拒:回到现实生活中的超人,最终完全依靠意志的力量,又一次赢得胜利。(李尧译)

参考译文 2

梯形台上的中国:徘徊于经济成功与民族渴望之间

中国的时装设计在世界舞台上得到的认可尚不能与其经济成就相媲美,原因之一是,世界时装之都等级森严、恶名远扬、难以颠覆。中国的时装业同时也受到自身问题的困扰,世界舞台上中国民族时装的展示,刻意彰显着高度的民族自我意识,其设计不过是中国文化的复制品。

2002年有人问皮尔·卡丹,谁有可能引领二十一世纪世界时装潮流,他的回答让中国设计师欢欣鼓舞:"我可以肯定中国的时装将会变得非常强大,"他说,"我知道中国有许多人才,有可能成为世界时装最具影响力的国家之一。"最后他谨慎提醒:"时装与民族性无关,而是天才的展示。"

皮尔·卡丹最后的话引发了关于国际时装符号意义,特别是地名强大影响力的争论。那些源自巴黎、纽约、伦敦、米兰和东京的时装设计,以其时尚之都的名义标榜着自身的荣耀;而时尚之都又将自身的文化声望赋予了那些业已成名或初出茅庐的设计师。这一点在巴黎身上体现得淋漓尽致,在与时尚如此紧密的结合中,巴黎已俨然成为了时尚的代名词。西方媒体对中国的时尚报道一贯充满惊奇与发现,好像中国人还在穿着"毛式"服装。早在2003年,《国际先驱论坛报》就宣布"狂热的时尚风潮席卷了新中国",一年后墨尔本的《时代报》也鼓吹"中国卷起了美丽的神话。"虽然改革开放历经25年,但中国的时装设计依然属于"晚辈"。其实,"晚辈"的中国时装起步并不晚。中国的时装业早在20世纪之交就已初露端倪,而上海的时装业也早在上个世纪20年代展现雏形。

翻译练习四

参考译文 1

这一定是世间无数对夫妻的生活写照,这种生活模式给人一种天伦之美。它使人想起一条平静的溪流,蜿蜒畅游过绿茵的草场,浓荫遮蔽,最后注入烟波浩渺的汪洋大海;但是大海太过平静,太过沉默,太过不动声色,你会突然感到莫名的不安。也许这只是我自己的一种怪诞想法,在那样的时代,这想法对我影响很深:我觉得这像大多数人一样的生活,似乎欠缺了一点儿什么。我承认这种生活有社会价值,我也看到了它那井然有序的幸福,但我血液里的冲动却渴望一种更桀骜不驯的旅程,这样的安逸中好像有一种叫我惊惧不安的东西,我的心渴望一种更加惊险的生活。只要生活中还能有变迁——以及不可知的刺激,我愿意踏上怪石嶙峋的山崖,奔赴暗礁满布的海滩。(萨姆塞特·毛姆《月亮与六便士》)(傅惟慈译)

参考译文 2

In recent years, Chinese exporters have seen their efforts increasingly undercut by the impact of the spreading financial crisis in Asia. The lifeless economies of many countries in the region have caused their consumer markets to shrink. Their teetering currency rates have caused their purchasing power to be weakened. In some cases political instability, changing economic circumstances, mounting projectionist barriers or diplomatic rows have make it difficult for us to export to those countries. We must find ways to beat the export slump.

We must press forward with the reform in the management system of foreign trade. Conglomeration-forming allies with farming, manufacturing, or scientific research with foreign trade as the locomotive-points the way ahead to strengthened competitiveness. Outmoded state enterprises, large and medium-sized, should be revamped to become more viable. Those enterprises better positioned should be granted the license to move into exporting field. The orientation of industry towards the export market is a major step in the reform of China's foreign trade regime.

The traditional pattern of export products needs to be optimized. Gone are the days when merchandise geared to price competition on mass market had its way. Now, in the highly competitive world the concepts of "fine quality or else no export" and "good service before and after sales" should be the order of the day. Methods of fine or intricate processing should be used to increase the added value on export commodities. And efforts must be made to turn out premium and novel products or the so-called "hard-punch" items that can edge into foreign markets. With the market changing so quickly, export companies should keep moving up-market — go where others cannot go or do whatever they have a competitive edge over their rivals.

It is important to tap the market potential extensively around the world. And geographical diversification is the key to survive the unsteady world market. It is no good to "put all our eggs in one basket" as the saying goes. The selection of new markets should be done by evaluating both their risks and opportunities simultaneously and quickly.

Monitor all markets constantly so that we can export to the right countries or regions and at the right time. Only a dynamic, forward-looking and viable export company is capable of weathering over the bad times and making a good killing in good times. When some markets slump, there are always other markets remaining buoyant. Therefore, we can gain on the swing what was lost on the roundabout.

Our export products must have first class quality, design, styling and presentation. But effective publicity, advertising and promotion are also essential. Development of expertise in advertising in foreign languages targeted at foreign markets is particularly important. Discovery of profitable outlets and connections is also of great significance. Participation in trade fairs abroad, foreign travels by sales forces and the setting up of production facilities or sales outlets overseas must ensure that they are result-ended. Finally, the injection of new know-how and new capital resulting from the attraction of foreign firms into our economy will help increase the productivity and quality of our export products. It is also important to reduce costs through improved management, and to raise the caliber of personnel through enhanced training. With the series of preferential policies implemented to the letter and with infrastructure services provided satisfactorily, we are surely hopeful of stepping up a new upsurge in attracting foreign direct investment. （丁衡祁译）

翻译练习五

参考译文 1

（1）《中国：泥足巨人》：中国在重塑自身的同时，也在重塑着整个世界。不过，从许多方面来说，中国在全球经济中的影响力，仍远不及其在全球人口中所占20%的比重。鉴于巨大的人口潜力，中国在贸易和产出方面的快速增长，可能还将持续多年。（何黎译）

（2）安格斯·威尔逊是一位讽刺作家，他总是迫不及待地向社会发射出讽刺的子弹。他的小说就是射击场，他所刻画的人物就是靶子，这些人不仅有着各自的缺点，而且在思维和情绪上也存在问题。《盎格鲁撒克逊态度》是威尔逊最长的一部小说，该书以最巧妙、最彻底的文学方式，展示了他那无与伦比的枪法。读完此书后，作者对人性丑陋的辛辣讽刺依然挥之不去。

参考译文 2

1) I lie inside the heart of the truck, remembering that clear, warm afternoon. The sunlight was so pretty. I remember that I was outside enjoying myself in the sunshine for a long time, and when I got home I saw my dad through the window packing a red backpack. I leaned against the window frame and asked, "Dad, are you going on a trip?"

He turned and very gently said, "No, I'm letting you go on a trip."

"Letting me go on a trip?"

"That's right. You're eighteen now, and it's time you saw a little of the outside world."

Later I slipped that pretty red backpack onto my back. Dad patted my head from behind, just like you would pat a horse's rump. Then I happily made for the door, and excitedly galloped out of the house, as happy as a horse. (Translated by Andrew F. Jones)

2) After almost ten years of truly romantic experience, love is no longer an unbreakable vow or the emotional fluctuation of bliss and despair. Love is like a high bourn of life, a gentle breeze and light drizzly rain. Love is the echoes of your footsteps coming up from downstairs, the well-washed and neatly-ironed clothes I leave on the ironing board, and a bunch of wild grass I pick up from outside. After all, love is the days piling up on us with undisturbed regularity.

If we feel a sense of happiness in a simple and peaceful life, if we see a whole world in a grain of sand, and if we develop a taste of calmness in our daily household chores, we must have reached an ideal state of our own being. Isn't it true that we are just pursuing that kind of virtue?

Such an ideal state is all love about and all life about. We often encourage ourselves by quoting a saying: "A genuine vision is derived from simplicity of life, and a real success is conceived in serenity of mind." There is indeed some truth in it.

翻译练习六

参考译文1

在 Neuf Brisach 工厂与 Singen 工厂中,特种薄板公司有两个生产部门,拥有 2100 名工作人员,年总产量约为 60 万吨:

- 铝包装事业部(APA)每年为包装行业生产约 43 万吨:罐头用铝板(罐头盒体与罐头盒底)与密封薄板,以及食品包装与专业热卷材。
- 汽车与定制解决方案事业部(ACS)每年供应量约 17 万吨汽车薄板与表面处理薄板,应用于建筑、照明及太阳能利用等。

ACS 的主要客户是法国与德国的汽车工业,他们需要各种特种薄板与带材,用途多种多样,如车身、底盘和驾驶舱等,还有换热器与高度光泽产品(如前灯反射镜与车身装饰件)。

Neuf Brisach 工厂由 Pechiney 创建于 40 多年前,原名为 Rhenalu 铝片材厂。加铝公司于 2003 年收购了这家工厂。生产量扩大到每年生产约 40 万吨铝带与铝薄板产品。(翻译公司译文)

参考译文2

As pointed out in Profit Computation Rules on Yiqing Highway Project, Yibin City, Sichuan Province, "III. Analysis on Economic Benefit of Yiqing Highway: in the first three years, the fourth and the fifth, the sixth to the eighth year, the average traffic flow volume is 12,000/day, 15,000/day, and 21,000/day respectively. If a single vehicle has a load of 6t, which shall be charged by RMB 60, then, the annual revenue will be RMB 259.2m, 324m and 453.6m respectively. After deducting RMB 148.816m, 207.21m, 199.88m (such expenses including depreciation, highway maintenance cost, management expenses, annual interests, sales tax, income tax; the business income tax levied by the government of Gao County is RMB 50.544m, 31.59m and 0 respectively) from the said revenue, the annual after-tax profit will be RMB 110.384m, 116.790m and 253.72m." The total after-tax gross profit in the first eight years (the first ten years excluding the two-year construction period) shall be RMB 1.331892bn. After deducting RMB 120m for emergency and maintenance from the said figure, the profit will be RMB 1.211892bn.(翻译公司译文)

参考译文3

各郡在州议会上均具有同等席位,这跟各州在美国议会具有同等席位一样。乔治亚州新宪法规定各郡在州众议院的具体席位数量。州参议员任期三年,众议员任期一年。州参议员年龄必须在二十八岁以上,在美国居住年限不少于九年,其中在乔治亚州至少居住三年,在参选所在郡居住年限半年以上。参议员还要求至少拥有二百五十英亩土地或二百五十镑以上其他财产。众议员年龄必须在二十一岁以上,在美国居住年限不少于七年,在乔治亚州至少居住两年,在参选所在郡居住三个月以上。(学生译文)

翻译练习七

参考译文1

新型卷材镀膜作业线的亮点

新作业线生产能力约为 6 万吨/年,对于带材薄薄的厚度而言,这是相当高的数值了。为了加工各种铝卷材,应用于不同合金(1xxx、3xxx、5xxx、与 8xxx 系列)的包装制品及建筑制品,该作业线设计能够处理从 0.15 至 0.8 毫米各种厚度的带材,铝板宽度为 1050~2050 毫米。该作业线速度高达

250米/分钟,使得西半球其他生产罐盖原料的高速镀膜厂只能望其项背。

带材尺寸范围广对工厂灵活性提出了极其苛刻的要求。对于这一点,Samara工厂一大亮点为在罐盖作业线中加入一个旋转裁边剪截机,从而能够在不同卷材切换之间快速改变带材宽度。

为了获得所需的带材扁平度,该作业线配备了新一代Levelflex拉伸-弯曲-矫直机。这一高科技设备确保了带材获得理想的扁平度,无需考虑卷材进料的质量问题。

BWG公司最近开发出的这一带材镀膜设备引起了特别关注。除了镀膜轧辊全自动调整外,还有一个"旋转倒退式轧机",BWG公司为此已经提出了专利申请。旋转倒退式轧机能够朝着滚筒方向、或选择性朝着带材拉伸方向进行镀膜。后者尤其适合于厚度小于0.3毫米的带材;例如,在带材宽度变化或带材不平衡运转时,避免在反面涂上不想要的镀膜。关于水溶性涂料的使用,这一特点一开始就被证明有利于Samara工厂运营。

两种镀膜机的后续硬化工艺均利用了BWG VITS金属处理公司开发的"悬挂烘干"技术,在浮动式熔炉中进行。表面修饰镀膜机熔炉后工艺在轧辊之间的距离为86米——是同类型中最长的距离,实现最大节能效果。在正常运行过程中,Samara工厂每小时使用了1100千克溶剂,这一能量用于"热自动补偿"运行模式。在这一模式下,一旦启动了工序,整个作业线的运行几乎不需要使用一次气体了。溶剂能量足以运行可再生热氧化剂(RTO),将烟囱温度降低至150°C,并且为清洁工序准备热水。

该作业线完全由计算机控制,配备有所有必需工具,为操作人员与周边环境提供安全的操作条件。例如,位于镀膜舱的一个组合式进出风系统完全能够在一小时内完成60次换气。

整套镀膜作业线由BWG公司在德国杜伊斯堡市开发和供货,是同类当中最新的技术。多年来,BWG公司在有色金属与钢铁设备与机械方面拥有其技术诀窍。该公司在2000年开始制定现行标准,但在上世纪80年代就向当时的德国VAW公司(现在的Hydro公司)及美铝英国公司供应高速罐头原料作业线。在将蒂森"EBA2"电解电镀作业线改造为薄膜镀涂厂(用于生产高级汽车铝板)过程中,BWG公司与蒂森克虏伯钢铁集团联合开发了全新的镀膜机理念。利用这一专业技术,BWG公司能够扩大其在铝业的参与度;其成功故事始于获得法国Merxheim市美铝建筑制品公司的合同。该合同设备能够镀膜2米宽铝带,产品主要应用于建筑领域。(翻译公司译文)

翻译练习八

参考译文1

不可抗力

1. 当破坏由不能预见、不能避免并不能克服的客观情况,包括但不限于天灾、骚乱或军事当局/民间暴乱、战争、罢工火灾及其他不能由协议双方所控制的原因引起时,在本协议项下双方可不履行本协议义务。

2. 一方因不可抗力不能履行合同的,应及时通知另一方,以减轻可能给对方造成的损失。如果不可抗力导致连续30天不可履行义务,任何一方都可提出终止本协议,并以书面形式通知另一方后立即生效。

3. 根据不可抗力事件导致的后果,双方应尽力对工作定单做必要修改。(翻译公司译文)

参考译文2

At the end of the 1970s, the CPC, after summarizing historical experiences, and especially learning painful lessons from the "cultural revolution," made an important decision to shift the focus of national work to socialist modernization, and adopted the policies of reform and opening-up. It also made clear the importance of the principle of governing the country by law. To guarantee democracy for the people, it is necessary to strengthen the socialist legal system, institutionalize democracy and make laws to ensure democracy. The goal was to make the system and laws stable, consistent and authoritative — not changing with changes of state leaders or state leaders' opinions or attention — and achieve the goal of having laws to go by, laws that must be observed and strictly enforced, and lawbreakers prosecuted. This was set up as the basic idea for the rule of law in the new era of reform and opening-up. Under the guidance of the basic principle of developing socialist democracy and improving the socialist legal system, China promulgated the present Constitution and basic laws, such as the Criminal Law, Criminal Procedure Law, Civil Procedure Law, General Principles of the Civil Law and Administrative Procedure Law, ushering in a new development stage of the rule of law.

In the 1990s, China started to promote the development of a socialist market economy in an all-round way, further laying the economic foundation and putting forward higher demands for the rule of law. In 1997, the 15th CPC National Congress decided to make "the rule of law" a basic strategy and "building a socialist country under the rule of law" an important goal for socialist modernization, and put forward the significant task of building a socialist legal system with Chinese characteristics. In 1999, "the People's Republic of China exercises the rule of law, building a socialist country governed according to law" was added to the Constitution, ushering in a new chapter in China's efforts to promote the rule of law.

Entering the 21st century, China is continuing this undertaking. In 2002, the 16th CPC National Congress decided to take further improvement of the socialist democracy and socialist legal system, comprehensive implementation of the rule of law as important goals for building a moderately prosperous society in all respects. In 2004, "the state respects and guarantees human rights" was included in the Constitution. In 2007, the 17th CPC National Congress expressly called for comprehensively implementing the fundamental principle of rule of the country by law and speeding up the building of a socialist country under the rule of law, and made arrangements for strengthening the rule of law in an all-round way.（官方译文）

参考译文3

Confidentiality

I agree at all times during the term of my Employment by the Company and from then on to hold in strictest confidence, and not to use, except for the benefit of the Company, or to disclose, transfer or reveal, directly or indirectly to any person or entity any Confidential Information without the prior written authorization of the Company.

Prior Works

In connection with Section 4 above, I understand and agree that all Intellectual Property which I made prior to my association with or Employment by the Company are excluded from the scope of this Agreement. I have attached a complete list of all Prior Works in Exhibit A, including patent numbers and brief descriptions of all Intellectual Property in which I claim an interest.

Third Party Information

I recognize that the Company has received, and in the future will receive confidential or proprietary information from third parties, subject to a duty on the Company's part to maintain the confidentiality of such information and to use it only for certain limited purposes. I agree that I owe the Company and such third parties, during the term of my association and from then on, a duty to hold all such confidential or proprietary information in the strictest of confidence and not to disclose it to any person, firm or corporation (except as necessary in carrying out my work for the Company consistent with the Company's Agreement with such third party) or to use it for the benefit of anyone other than for the Company or such third party (consistent with the Company's Agreement with such third party) without the express written authorization of the Company. Any such information shall be considered Confidential Information for the purposes of this Agreement.

Return of Materials

At the request of the Company or on the termination of association or Employment by the Company, I will immediately deliver to my immediate supervisor at the Company all papers, notes, data, reference materials, sketches, drawings, memoranda, documentation, software, tools, apparatus and any other materials furnished to me by the Company or that were prepared or made, in whole or in part, by me at any time during my association with or employment by the Company, together with the attached Termination Certification, which I agree to sign and deliver.

Trade Secrets of Others

I understand that it is the firm policy of the Company to maintain the rights of any party with whom I have a confidentiality or proprietary rights Agreement. I will not disclose to the Company or induce the Company to use the proprietary information of others. I do not have any existing obligation to others that might be inconsistent with any of the provisions in this Agreement, except for those obligations identified on a separate page and attached to this Agreement as Exhibit B.

At Will Employment, Surviving Terms

My association with or my employment by the Company is "at will" and may be terminated by me or the Company at any time; however, my obligations in this Agreement will survive the termination of my association with or Employment by the Company. I will assist the Company in obtaining and protecting patents and copyrights in Intellectual Property in all countries. Upon rendering assistance to the Company after my association, the Company will pay me a reasonable sum as determined by the Company for my time and expenses.

Notice

I authorize the Company to notify others, including customers of the Company and my future employers, of the terms of this Agreement and my responsibilities.（翻译公司译文）